SPIRAL GUIDE

FLORIDA

AA
Publishing

Contents

the magazine 5

Finding Your Feet 37

Orlando 49

Miami and the South 109

Written by Gary McKechnie
with Nancy Howell
Where to... sections by Mitchell Davis, Jane Miller and Gary McKechnie
Lodging and restaurant selection courtesy of AAA Publishing
Additional research by Debra Wood

Copy edited by Janet Tabinski
Designed by Amanda Chauhan and Mike Preedy
Indexed by Marie Lorimer
Verified by Gary McKechnie

Published by AA Publishing, a trading name of Automobile Association
Developments Limited, whose registered office is Southwood East, Apollo
Rise, Farnborough, Hampshire, GU14 0JW. Registered number 1878835.

ISBN-10: 0-7495-4431-7
ISBN-13: 978-0-7495-4431-7

A CIP catalogue record for this book is available from the British Library.

Cover design and binding style by permission of AA Publishing
Colour separation by Keenes, Andover
Printed and bound in China by Leo Paper Products

Find out more about AA Publishing and the wide range of services the AA
provides by visiting our website at www.theAA.com.

A02141
Maps on pages 180–181 and 220–223 produced from mapping
© Mairs Geographischer Verlag / Falk Verlag, 73751 Ostfildern, Germany

the magazine

THE MAGIC OF

Walt Disney

**In cosmic terms, the arrival of Walt Disney World®
Resort on October 1, 1971, was the Big Bang of Florida's
tourism industry. Today, it is as important to Orlando as the
Kremlin is to Moscow, the Eiffel Tower to Paris, and
Buckingham Palace to London. It may seem like heresy to
elevate a resort to such exalted status, but it's true. Face it,
even with all the other attractions in Orlando, you wouldn't be
coming here if not for Disney.**

It all started in Anaheim, California, where because Walt Disney couldn't afford more property, Disneyland® became surrounded by inexpensive hotels and tourist traps cashing in on his success.

In May 1965, an article appeared in the *Orlando Sentinel* newspaper announcing that two large tracts of land costing $5 million had been sold in Orange and Osceola counties. Over the next month, mysterious companies such as the Latin American Development and Management Corporation and the Reedy Creek Ranch Corporation were listed as the purchasers of several other parcels of flat, pine-covered ranchland and cattle pastures.

Some surmised the buyer was the government. Others suspected aerospace and automotive manufacturers were the mystery industries. By late June, the newspaper calculated that more than 27,000 acres (10,900ha) had been sold – but no one knew who had bought it.

Four long months passed before the story broke: It was Walt Disney. With his identity revealed, Walt, along with his brother Roy, held a press conference with Florida's governor, showing a few films to prepare the local and state

*Above: Walt
Disney is
Hollywood's
Oscar king,
with 64
nominations
and 26 wins!*

*Previous page:
Miami Beach's
distinctive
art deco
architecture*

governments for the assistance and special favors the Disney team would need to achieve their goals.

Why did Walt pick Orlando? It wasn't an automatic decision. He and his team had spent four years combing the country looking for an area that offered what was needed: Access to a major population center; good highways; a steady climate; and, most importantly, inexpensive and abundant land. By a process of elimination, Orlando was it.

Walt envisioned something far superior to a simple park. His resort would include hotels, lakes, horse trails, airports, golf courses, nightclubs, theaters and a residential community for his employees.

More than 27,000 acres (10,900ha) had been sold – but no one knew who had bought it.

Sadly, Walt never saw its completion. A year later, he was diagnosed with cancer and died in December

Next, there were government obstacles. It would be nearly impossible to build Walt Disney World® Resort if he had to fight a bureaucracy. The Florida legislature recognized the economic impact of the project. In 1967, the legislature passed measures that allowed Disney to establish self-governing municipalities on the land. Disney was free to set up zoning restrictions and building codes, then construct its own roads, bridges, hotels and theme parks.

1966. Roy stepped in to oversee construction and, as a tribute to his brother, changed the name from "Disney World" to "Walt Disney World," so visitors would know that his brother was the resort's creator. Roy died shortly after the park opened, a bittersweet end to the story of Walt Disney World® Resort's early days.

Just over a decade after the grand opening, it appeared as if Walt's dream would die as well. By the early 1980s, Disney management was in disarray.

Above: Walt Disney World® before construction began

Construction cost overruns and lower-than-expected attendance at Epcot® had created a drop in profits in 1982 and again in 1983. Start-up costs for The Disney Channel and a poorly performing film division were also taking their toll. On the other hand, the parks were taking in $1 billion a year, and company assets were worth far more than the $2 billion price tag created by market valuation.

Sadly, Walt never saw its completion.

This made it a prime target for a takeover. One of the first to attempt it was Saul Steinberg who, in the summer of 1984, purchased nearly 10 percent of Disney's outstanding shares. Disney paid a premium to buy back Steinberg's shares.

As other bids surfaced there were major changes in the executive suites of The Walt Disney Company. Walt's son-in-law, Ron Miller, was replaced by Michael Eisner and Frank Wells.

Eisner, the former president of Paramount Pictures, became the CEO and chairman. Wells, the past vice-chairman of Warner Brothers, signed on as president and chief financial officer. Their creative spark ignited Disney. The company reestablished itself as the leader in animated features such as "Aladdin," "Beauty and the Beast" and "The Lion King." And in a new approach to marketing, each film was given a boost when the theme parks staged movie-themed parades and stocked park stores with a slew of movie-related merchandise.

Although Wells died in a helicopter accident in 1994, by then Disney had the momentum to grow beyond belief. Today, The Walt Disney Company owns several publishing companies, television broadcasting groups, radio stations, film companies...the list is endless.

The Emperor of Entertainment changed the world – and created new ones

The Growth of Disney

Walt Disney World Resort in 1982 was two theme parks, two hotels and a campground. In 1988, two new resorts opened. Disney-MGM Studios premiered in 1989, as did Typhoon Lagoon and Pleasure Island, and in 1990 there were more resorts (Yacht and Beach Club, Swan and Dolphin hotels), followed in 1991 by Port Orleans and Old Key West resorts and in 1992 by Dixie Landings resort. By 1995, Walt Disney World® Resort boasted a new wedding pavilion, 1996 saw the premiere of the Disney Institute, and 1997 saw the grand opening of Disney's Wide World of Sports™ complex, Downtown Disney® West Side and the Coronado Springs resort. In 1998, the fourth theme park, Disney's Animal Kingdom®, came to life and added the grandiose Animal Kingdom Lodge, while the Disney Cruise Lines took its maiden voyage. Also in the 1990s came Celebration, an artificially perfect community near the Magic Kingdom.

Take some ex-Nazi rocket scientists, a government suspicious of Communist spies, add classified missile testing and highly volatile rocket fuel, and you've got a big problem: Where in the world do you test America's newest rockets?

FLORIDA'S
SPACE PROGRAM

The Early Rockets

In the years following World War II, the military was busy launching missiles from a sandy strip of Florida coastline. This 15,000-acre (6,070-ha) site was scarcely developed, located far from residential areas, and test flights could easily be tracked by stations in the Bahamas.

It was an unobtrusive setting for what would become a major Cold War battleground. Although America's missiles were later converted to rockets designed to explore space, when the Russians launched the Sputnik I satellite in October 1957, the Cold War accelerated. If Russia could launch a satellite that could circle the Earth at 17,400mph (28,000kph), it could also drop missiles on the United States.

The Race for Space

The Space Race was on. America tried to match Russia by launching a satellite in December 1957, but its Vanguard rocket rose only 2 feet (0.6m) before it tumbled to the ground in a huge fireball. The failure led President Eisenhower to give Wernher von Braun, a rocket scientist captured by the Americans during World War II, the full support of the government. Shortly after, Americans witnessed two successful launches, and the

Above: STS-73 rockets into orbit from Cape Canaveral

government's purse strings were opened. Through the National Aeronautics and Space Act of 1958, the National Aeronautics and Space Administration was born on October 1, 1958.

As the 1950s came to a close, Russians and Americans were battling for space firsts. Monkeys were rocketed into space, new discoveries were being made, and men from the armed forces of both nations were being recruited for space service. In April 1959, America announced the selection of the Mercury 7 — seven military pilots who would fly aboard the stronger and more powerful Mercury rockets.

If Sputnik had demoralized Americans, they were in disbelief over Gagarin's feat.

Orlando's own John Young during a 1972 moon walk

Russia's resolve was less publicized, but seemingly more effective. On April 12, 1961, cosmonaut Yuri Gagarin was launched into orbit atop a Vostok rocket and circled the globe five times before returning safely to Earth. If Sputnik had demoralized Americans, they were in disbelief over Gagarin's feat. NASA responded as quickly as it could. On May 5, 1961, a Redstone rocket launched from Cape Canaveral lifted astronaut Alan Shepard 115 miles (185km) up and 302 miles (487km) downrange. It wasn't an orbital flight, but no one seemed to care — there was a bigger picture in mind.

On May 25, President Kennedy announced to Congress a challenge that would surpass anything the Russians could attempt. To regain superiority in the Space Race (as the press called it), America would "land a man on the moon and return him safely to the Earth." And it would do it before the decade was out.

America hadn't even sent a man into orbit and now the Apollo program was gearing up to send three men to the moon. In the meantime, Gus Grissom made a suborbital flight similar to Shepard's, and in February 1962, John Glenn orbited the Earth three times.

Three more of the original Mercury 7 astronauts flew orbital flights over the next year and a half until NASA closed down the Mercury program. The subsequent Gemini missions comprised two-man flights that required astronauts to practice maneuvers essential to a moon mission. They would learn to rendezvous with other craft, dock the ships, take space walks and live in space for weeks at a time. Yet, between Mercury and Gemini, two years passed without an American in space. The Russians took advantage by sending the first woman into space (Valentina Tereshkova), orbiting a three-man Voshkod spacecraft, launching two manned spaceships at the same time, and letting cosmonaut Alexei Leonov leave the Voshkod 2 for man's first walk in space.

Lagging far behind, the Americans countered with Gemini 3, which was a five-hour orbital flight testing the maneuverability of the spacecraft. Over the next 20 months, 10 more teams entered these cramped capsules on successful missions.

The Apollo Missions

With the conclusion of Gemini, Apollo was ready for testing. On January 27, 1967, astronauts Gus Grissom, Ed White and Roger Chaffee entered the rocket to rehearse the following month's launch. At 6:30 pm, the astronauts were in the locked capsule when Chaffee shouted, "We've got a fire in the cockpit!" followed by another astronaut pleading, "Get us out of here!" It was too late. The pure oxygen in the capsule fed the fire and the three men perished quickly.

Even before its first launch, Apollo had to be redesigned, and the setback delayed the program nearly two years. In Russia, just three months after the tragedy of Apollo 1, cosmonaut Vladimir Komarov was killed when the parachutes failed to deploy and his spacecraft slammed back to Earth.

In October 1968, Apollo 7 made an 11-day, manned trip into space. NASA, bolstered by its success, had bigger plans for Apollo 8: Three men would orbit the moon. Until now, NASA's most distant flights had been a few hundred miles from Earth.

Now Americans would try to hit a moving target 250,000 miles (400,000km) away. Against all odds, the mission was successful. The view from the moon was humbling: For the first time in history, man saw Earth not as a vast planet, but as a small and fragile oasis floating in the infinite blackness of space. Seven months later, on July 16, 1969, Apollo 11 rose from Cape Canaveral's Launch Pad 39A and began its three-day trip to the moon.

While Michael Collins circled the moon in the command module, Neil Armstrong and Buzz Aldrin descended to its surface in the Eagle, a flimsy contraption known as the lunar module. When Armstrong saw that their computer-programmed landing site was strewn with boulders, he took over with manual controls as he searched desperately for a level plain to land. From Earth, Mission Control reminded Armstrong he was operating with less than 30 seconds of fuel remaining, when he finally reached a

On board a space shuttle

Gemini 4 astronaut Ed White takes America's first space walk

landing site. Three hours later he and Aldrin exited the Eagle and man was on the moon.

NASA had done it. Despite the deaths, setbacks and disappointments, they had transformed a region of Florida marshland into America's doorway to space and beaten Russia to the moon. Most importantly, they had met President Kennedy's challenge, with five months to spare.

And so to the shuttle...

But the American public was fickle. Following the successful Apollo 12 trip to the moon, few bothered to watch Apollo 13's mission until an oxygen tank exploded, putting the lives of the astronauts at risk. By the time the program came to a close in 1972, NASA needed another project to capture the public's imagination.

On May 14, 1973, the unmanned Skylab space station was launched from the Kennedy Space Center. Its marathon mission did not stir the public's imagination. However, by the time the program closed, the three 28-, 59- and 84-day missions exceeded the combined totals of all of the world's previous space flights. Despite the lack of interest, Skylab had made great strides in demonstrating technical skills for scientific, operational and maintenance functions.

NASA was still anxious to recapture the glory days of the Mercury program. For its next project, it joined forces with the Soviet Union. NASA's scientists rose to the challenge, and when the Apollo and Soyuz spacecraft docked on July 17, 1975, they proved that the two countries could rely on an international docking system and joint flight procedures.

Like most NASA missions, Apollo–Soyuz was a public

everything NASA claimed. The missions were becoming routine. But on January 28, 1986, just seconds after launch, an O-ring that sealed the fuel inside the solid rocket booster gave way. The flame ignited the external tank and the space shuttle Challenger disintegrated, killing all seven astronauts on board.

NASA needed another project to capture the public's imagination.

It would be two more years before another flight was attempted, and 17 years after that before another shuttle encountered a similar fate. On February 1, 2003, the space shuttle Columbia broke apart upon reentering the earth's atmosphere. All seven astronauts aboard perished.

Despite the tragedy, few called for an end to manned spaceflight, and the space shuttle fleet is set to be back in action in May, 2005. Proponents of space travel and NASA's expeditions are closely watching the future.

relations coup with a short shelf life. After watching the orbital handshake and follow-up splashdown, Americans went back to work. NASA, meanwhile, continued another project that had been on the drawing board since 1972: The space shuttle.

Instead of disposable rockets, NASA would launch a reusable spacecraft comprising an orbiter, two solid rocket boosters and an external fuel tank. According to NASA's projections, the shuttle could transport up to eight astronauts and a cargo bay filled with satellites and scientific experiments in a 17,322-mph (27,876-kph) orbit around the Earth. When its mission was complete, the shuttle would glide back to Earth and land on a runway – like an airplane.

For years following its 1981 maiden voyage, the fleet of four space shuttles did

The space shuttle – it's basically a rocket-fueled glider

Life's a Beach and Then You Fry

If you're looking for the perfect place to slather on the lotion and relax by the ocean, you've come to the right state. Whether you head to Miami, Tampa Bay or the Space Coast, or to some of the Panhandle's quartz-sand shorelines, Florida offers hundreds of beaches. There are more than 1,000 miles (1,600km) of coastline in Florida and no part of the state is more than 60 miles (100km) from saltwater. With more top-rated beaches than any other state, no wonder people are drawn to the coast here. And why not? Florida's beaches are blessed with soft sand and warmed by the semitropical sun.

Miami

You can tell from vintage photographs of Miami bathing beauties that the ocean has a special allure for South Floridians. For decades, its barrier islands, quiet inlets, county parks and fabled South Beach have attracted beach bums from around the world. And where are they headed?

Miami Beach, arguably the most famous beach in the world, offers something for everyone. You can find beaches that attract people based on their nationality, age, sexual orientation, desire for privacy, or need to access civilization.

The best-known stretch of South Florida sands runs from 1st to 15th streets at Lummus Park in South Beach. This is the Art Deco District. A curving sidewalk (pavement) is perfect for jogging or inline skating. At Lummus Park there are volleyball courts, palm trees, a playground, restrooms and restaurants immediately to the west. Immediately to the east is the blue Atlantic. Seniors enjoy this in the morning, but as the sun rises they retreat and give the beach over to the toned youth.

The gay community has staked its claim to the portion between 11th and 13th streets, while all along the shore going topless is accepted.

Attracting Europeans and French Canadians is the stretch of beach between 72nd and 96th streets. Even when Miami was down in the dregs, they continued to make this area their winter hideaway. A two-block section, between 73rd and 75th streets, is a little quieter, and shopping is conveniently close on Collins Avenue.

Midway down Key Biscayne, Crandon Park is highlighted by a 2-mile (3-km) lagoon-style beach where the sand is soft and the parking is inexpensive and plentiful. Farther along, at the southern tip of Key Biscayne, the Bill Baggs Cape Florida State Recreation Area has picnic shelters, a café, and walking paths and boardwalks that reveal Miami's striking skyline.

Along with white, sandy beaches are bicycle and skate rentals, a playground, fishing piers, kayak rentals and the 1846 Cape Florida Lighthouse, South Florida's oldest structure. Parking is less expensive than at Crandon.

Tampa Bay
You can spot the difference between Atlantic and Gulf beaches: The Atlantic coast rumbles with crashing waves while the Gulf of Mexico is as smooth as silk.

Tampa Bay beaches can be calm and relaxing. When you need to jazz things up, try swimming, wind surfing, snorkeling, parasailing, jet skiing, cruising, diving and fishing.

Off the tip of the peninsula, at the end of Highway 679, at the mouth of Tampa Bay, Fort DeSoto Park may be one of Florida's best beach and camping bargains (▶ 167).

At the south tip of St. Pete Beach, Pass-a-Grille is a quiet residential community with a secluded beach (the shelly sands can be tough on your feet). Still, it's a place few outsiders know about. There's a concession kiosk, and a few blocks away, at 8th Avenue and Pass-A-Grille Way, you can rent waverunners, schedule a fishing excursion or embark on a sunset cruise from Merry Pier.

Hangin' loose and chillin' out on the beach

Warning Riptides

Riptides – caused by a break in the sandbar – and undertows are so strong that the flow of water could yank you out to sea. If you're caught in an undertow, don't fight it – you won't win. Instead, let the tide carry you as you swim parallel to the shore. Wait until you're out of the strong current before swimming back to land.

One of many popular beach pastimes

(5km) of uncrowded sands grace Caladesi Island. It's not accessible by car, but there is a ferry from the Honeymoon Island State Recreation Area on State Road 586. It departs hourly, beginning at 10 am.

The Space Coast

Some of the Atlantic seaboard's nicest beaches are between Cape Canaveral and Titusville. Unfortunately, gaining access to them is hard unless you're an astronaut, as this is NASA's property. To compensate, the government has left miles of unbroken beachfront for your swimming and diving pleasure, and you'll find some of the best waterfront in the area south of A1A and Highway 520. This easygoing beach hasn't changed much in the last 30 years. Park the car, grab the blanket, the beach chairs and the cooler, and settle down for a day at one of Florida's finest. Although the beach continues south for another 40 miles (64km), the best sands are within 2 miles (3km) of this junction.

Heading north on Highway 699 (also known as Gulf Boulevard), you will reach one of Treasure Island's beach entrances at 112th Avenue. The broad beach includes changing facilities, metered parking, volleyball, cabanas, a gift shop and snack bar. Suspended in the 1960s, this heavily touristed area is wall-to-wall with hotels, miniature golf, and tacky shell and gift shops. But the beach! It's a knockout!

Park the car, grab the blanket, the beach chairs and the cooler...

Continuing north on Highway 699, you will pass beach entrances in quiet communities such as Redington Shores, Indian Rocks Beach and Belleair Shores. All are fine for a day on the sands, but the very best is Clearwater Beach. The powdery sand crunches beneath your feet, hotels, motels and restaurants promise easy access to essentials, and the water is wonderful. At the end of State Road 60, Pier 60 is a popular spot for fishing, dining, shopping and generally hanging out.

If you really want privacy, north of Clearwater Beach, 3 miles

It's hard to be on your own on a beach in South Florida

If you want to experience more touristed waters, the pier just north of Highway 520 is a gathering spot for surfers, barflies and fishermen. Whether you head north or south, most beaches here grant easy access to nearby convenience stores and hotels.

If you prefer to hit the sands sans suit, drive down Highway 402. A half-mile (0.8-km) hike north of the northernmost parking lot is Playalinda, one of the state's rare nude beaches. Despite ordinances that prohibit nudity, naturists here continue to sunbathe in the buff.

Florida's River of Grass

A few generations ago, the Everglades was viewed as a vast, alligator-infested wilderness of swamps and marshes. Ever hungry for development, Floridians naturally thought the water of this region needed to be channeled, diverted and directed to the thirsty people of Miami.

It was an honest mistake. If you had driven through the Everglades in the 1940s on one of the few roads that traversed the southern end of the state, you would have been stung by giant mosquitoes or eaten by alligators. It was (and still is) an inhospitable place for humans to live.

But the Everglades was never designed for humans. Few people realized that this morass of marsh was in reality a fragile ecosystem that masked a nearly 50-mile-wide (80-km) river, less than a foot (0.3m) deep, that began south of Orlando and worked its way slowly to the state's southern tip at Florida Bay.

Although the Everglades was seen as a "useless" region of swamp grass and muck, it was the largest natural filtration system in the country, and the seemingly dead landscape was teeming with wildlife. For centuries, the southern tip of Florida had been subjected to alternating periods of flood and drought, a natural cycle that helped produce thriving shrimp beds as well as mangrove swamps and the formation of coral reefs. Sportsmen found the

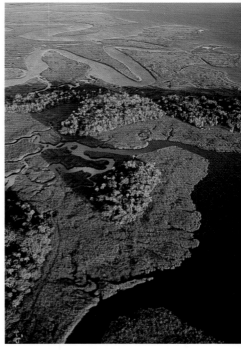

best fishing in Florida in Florida Bay, the terminus of the Everglades, where the brackish water supported an abundance of sea life.

It was a perfect climate to foster the needs of wildlife

Florida's fragile Everglades. Is it beyond salvation?

and other crops could grow almost untended – but not without the water of the Everglades. And finally, there were the environmentalists. They recognized the dangers posed to the state's future if the Everglades was allowed to be claimed for development or drained for farming.

The unofficial spokesperson for the last group was Marjory Stoneman Douglas, a former society columnist for the *Miami Herald* and a native of Miami. She saw that the limited resources of the Everglades could not support the dreams of developers.

In 1947, she published *The Everglades: River of Grass*, a book that correctly defined the Everglades not as an endless source of water to be diverted for farmers or developers, but as a 50-mile-wide (80-km) "river of grass" fed by rivers hundreds of miles to the north, a natural, national treasure that needed to be preserved and protected.

Above: Once endangered, Florida alligators are thriving

Right: Airboats are the best way to see the Everglades

and sportsmen, but it was too good to last. A "flood control" system was begun to divert water to the more populated coasts. The move started a three-ring circus of special-interest groups competing for what they thought was best for Florida.

In one corner were developers who wanted to use the waters of the Everglades to fill the reservoirs of Miami and sustain its growing population. Then there were the farmers. Tomatoes, strawberries, oranges, mangoes, sugarcane

From the early 1920s, local residents recognized the need to preserve the Everglades. In 1929, Congress authorized a feasibility study, and by 1947 the national park became a reality. The park, which covers an area of more than 1.5 million acres (607,000ha), is now America's largest national park east of the Rocky Mountains.

Yet, although the Everglades is protected on paper, special interests and a lack of resolve on the part of the state government continue to erode the natural beauty

Ernest F. Coe Visitor Center

Eleven miles (18km) southwest of Homestead on Route 9336. Take US 1 south out of Miami, turn right at S.W. 344th Street/State Road 9336 and follow signs.

☎ 305/242-7700 ⏱ Daily 8–5 ♿ $

and importance of the region. Canals distribute water to the Miami coast and slowly drain the Everglades. More than 90 percent of the bird life has disappeared since the 1940s, and the Florida panther (which, ironically, is Florida's official animal) is near extinction. Florida Bay is now being infiltrated with saltwater and mercury pollution. Both threaten the delicate ecosystem.

It's a heartbreaking situation, but there is a degree of hope. Legislation against development and pollution has achieved a number of goals, among them the establishment of an Everglades Trust Fund. In 1998 the Clinton administration released a draft $7.8 billion plan, commonly known as the Restudy, to restore the Everglades (filling in back-country canals, leveling water control and restoring natural water flows and reservoirs). Since then, Congress has approved the 30-year re-engineering project, which is now under way. The result will be a rejuvenation of the river of grass.

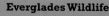

Yet, business interests continue to hanker after what the Everglades has got, and the area is still a battleground of opposing needs. Much-needed government funding has been reduced, and the state's pollution controls have been weakened. Florida governor Jeb Bush, a supporter of Everglades restoration, is facing many challenges as he balances the diverse needs of business and environmental groups. The political situation, for the present anyway, is leaning in favor of business, but opponents continue to point out the detrimental effect of ever-expanding urban sprawl on this unique ecosystem.

> **... a fragile ecosystem that masked a nearly 50-mile-wide (80-km) river, less than a foot (0.3m) deep**

Red mangroves – an unworldly feature of the Everglades landscape

FLORIDA *Characters*

Throughout its history, Florida has had its share of characters whose personalities have run the gamut from extravagant and innovative to dangerous and cruel.

Below: Spanish explorer Juan Ponce de León came in 1513 searching for the Fountain of Youth – or gold

Bottom: Florida's Native Americans meet their Spanish conquerors for the first time

Panfilo de Narvaez

Consider Spanish explorer Panfilo de Narvaez, who arrived in Florida in 1528 accompanied by 400 soldiers and their war dogs. Narvaez claimed the land near Tampa for Spain. In a show of force, the callous conquistador cut off the nose of a Tocabago chief and threw the chief's protesting mother to the dogs.

Determined to discover the New World's non-existent gold, Narvaez sent his ships up the coast, while he and the rest of the soldiers marched north in an unsuccessful search. Fed up with the foreigners, Apalachee warriors attacked, chasing the Spanish to the Gulf, where they were forced to build rafts and set sail for Mexico. Narvaez died at sea.

Julia Tuttle

The quest for land is a constant in Florida's history. Julia Tuttle, daughter of homesteader and state senator E.T. Sturtevant, visited the state during the 1870s. Two decades later she moved south and forever changed the area. Tuttle recognized that South Florida's potential rested on reliable transportation. Railroad titans Henry Plant and Henry Flagler were running railroad lines and building hotels for sunseeking

Ron Rice

In the late 1960s, Ron Rice was a Daytona Beach high school biology teacher who, after school, spent his time mixing natural oils together in a garbage can, which he bottled and sold at pools along the beach. It was an inauspicious beginning, but Rice's Hawaiian Tropic proved to be popular with sun lovers everywhere.

Northerners, but neither had plans for the Biscayne Bay area.

Tuttle purchased property along the Miami River and led a comfortable life. After a major freeze hit the rest of the state, Tuttle had an idea. She plucked a few fresh orange blossoms from a tree and mailed them to Henry Flagler, the railroad pioneer who was building a line down Florida's Atlantic coast.

Flagler, a former grain dealer-turned-cofounder of Standard Oil, was impressed by the proof of Miami's frost-proof climate and agreed to run his trains farther south – provided Julia gave him the land on which he could build one of his opulent hotels. She agreed, and 300 Miami residents cheered the arrival of the first train in 1896.

Hamilton Disston

Other land speculators weren't as lucky. In 1881, Hamilton Disston made a deal with Governor William Bloxham to purchase 4 million acres (1.6 million ha) at 25 cents per acre. Florida needed Disston's $1 million to repay debts, and Disston hoped to become even richer by growing sugarcane. He drained his new property and cultivated the cane plants, laying the foundation for the state's sugar industry which, in the early 20th century, produced one-fifth of the country's sugar. Things didn't work out so well for Disston, though. After losing much of his fortune during a recession, he committed suicide.

Benjamin Green

Benjamin Green, a Miami druggist, began whipping up batches of suntan cream in the 1940s. Experimenting with different concoctions, he tested the solutions on a readily available surface: His bald head. His head was tinted a nice shade of brown by a blend he developed in 1944, and by 1951 Coppertone was being sold nationwide.

Andrew Jackson

During the War of 1812, a young United States was once again battling Britain. Andrew Jackson became an instant hero after trouncing the better-fortified Brits at Pensacola and New Orleans. His timing was a bit off. In those days word traveled slowly – he was unaware that a peace treaty had already been signed in the Belgian city of Ghent, a few weeks earlier. Nonetheless, his victory sparked a popularity that eventually carried Jackson to the White House, where he served as president from 1829 to 1837. Jackson was also in Florida to fight in the First Seminole War in 1818 and serve as military governor in 1821 when Florida became a U.S. possession.

Mary McLeod Bethune

Mary McLeod Bethune, the 15th of 17 children, grew up wanting to learn to read and write. She dedicated her life to education, starting a school in Daytona Beach for the black children of railroad workers.

With $1.50 for supplies, a shack beside a garbage dump for a classroom, and using the juice of squeezed berries for ink, Bethune's girls' school grew from five to 250 students. After merging with Jacksonville's Cookman Institute for Men, it became the Bethune-Cookman College in 1923. The school is still thriving. From such humble beginnings, Bethune was later asked by President Franklin Roosevelt to become the Director of Negro Affairs in the National Youth Administration.

> **Not all Florida entrepreneurs need land to enjoy living. Several have made good use of the state's most abundant commodity: Sunshine.**

Ray Charles

One of America's most celebrated recording artists grew up in Greenville, Florida. When he left the St. Augustine School for the Deaf and Blind, Charles played piano in the dives and gin joints of many Florida towns for a few dollars a night. In 1949, realizing his career was at a dead end, he asked a friend to look at a map and find the largest city that was the farthest distance from Orlando. A few weeks later, he was on his way to a new life and the dawn of stardom in Seattle, Washington.

Edward Leedskalnin

When Leedskalnin, a Latvian immigrant, came to America, he began his 20-year labor of love: A 1,100-ton "coral castle" built using only simple chains, pulleys and recycled auto parts. He worked alone at night to create his home, which includes an 8-foot (2.5-m) high wall made from huge blocks of coral rock, a 2-ton rocking chair so delicately balanced it moves with the touch of a finger, and a 9-ton gate that a

The Two Henrys

In the 1800s, railroad systems built by Henry Plant and Henry Flagler boosted the state's fledgling tourist economy and expedited shipment of citrus to northern markets. The two pioneers also constructed lavish hotels to accommodate sunseeking rail passengers. Many of these properties still stand in testament to this gilded era.

Thomas Edison
Down in Fort Myers, prolific inventor Thomas Alva Edison built a winter retreat, one of Florida's first prefabricated homes. He had sections of his home built in New England and shipped to Fort Myers, where the pieces were patched together. And after a hard day's work, he could splash around in his swimming pool, one of the first modern pools in Florida, built in 1910.

child can push open. How he managed to move coral rocks weighing up to 35 tons without the use of machinery remains a mystery. Coral Castle (28655 S. Dixie Highway, Homestead, Miami, tel: 305/248-6345) is open daily 7 am–9 pm.

Lawton Chiles

Chiles served in the Florida House of Representatives and State Senate before deciding to run for a seat as a U.S. senator. At a time when American politicians were becoming more synthetic, Chiles displayed his Florida roots by pledging to walk from one end of the state to the other to meet and listen to the people. On his 91-day trek, he walked 1,033 miles (1,662km) from Pensacola to Miami, earning the respect of voters who elected "Walkin' Lawton" to three terms as senator between 1971 and 1989, and Florida's two-term governor beginning in 1990. He died in office in 1998.

THE BEST OF OLD FLORIDA

Florida is a large state full of cultural diversions. There's far more to the Sunshine State than you could possibly see in one visit, so just plan another trip or, better yet, extend this one. Once the sand gets into your shoes, you'll want to explore what locals refer to as "Old Florida," the backroad, old-fashioned attractions and historic villages.

St. Augustine

Without a doubt, Florida's most beautiful and historic village is St. Augustine (► 184), 120 miles (193km) northeast of Orlando, on the Atlantic Coast. Although it's a popular part of Florida folklore, Ponce de León never actually landed here in 1513; but he set the path for future explorers, and by 1565, St. Augustine had been established, making it the oldest permanent European settlement in the United States.

Today, the town is a popular getaway for romantics and a vacation destination for families. With its European flair, stylish architecture, artsy alleyways and intimate bed-and-breakfast inns, it's a perfect place for walking or taking a spin in a horse-drawn carriage. Brimming with art and antiques showrooms, gift shops, courtyard cafés, microbrew pubs and ice-cream parlors, it is also home to stunning Flagler College (formerly Henry M. Flagler's grand Ponce de León Hotel), as well as America's oldest school, house and pharmacy.

A wide, white sandy beach is a few miles south of the

treasured Bridge of Lions, which spans Matanzas Bay and overlooks the 17th-century fortress, Castillo de San Marcos. Fortunately this scenic city has not been overrun by development, and a historical tour should not be missed.

Amelia Island
About an hour north of St. Augustine, Amelia Island (► 191) is the only place in America that has been ruled under eight flags. In the early 1900s, the island's colorful cast of characters ranged from bawdy ladies to salty sailors, and a Northern newspaper dubbed the town "a festering fleshpot." Nowadays, you can enjoy oceanfront horseback riding, deep-sea fishing and the downtown shopping district of Fernandina Beach. On Centre Street there's a trendy collection of antiques and art shops, specialty stores, candy counters and casual cafés.

The wonderful Palace Saloon is believed to be Florida's oldest bar and is definitely haunted, say employees. This charming town is a neighborhood of vintage homes and small inns. For a larger-than-life piece of history, Fort Clinch hosts tours featuring character guides who adopt the persona of Union soldiers from 1864.

Mount Dora
The picturesque hillside town of Mount Dora (► 94, 30 miles/48km northwest of Orlando) is the home of the historic 1883 Lakeside Inn, a relaxing retreat on the shores of Lake Dora. Strolling along Donnelly Street, you'll easily sense an atmosphere akin to a bustling New England village. There are antiques and gift galleries, fashion boutiques, bookstores, jewelers, florists and candle-makers. There are also ice-cream and coffee bars,

outdoor cafés and cantinas, and cozy bed-and-breakfast inns. Stay awhile and smell the orange blossoms, catch a concert or festival at Donnelly Park, play shuffleboard or a game of tennis, or enjoy a nature walk on Palm Island.

Micanopy
A tiny town (pop. 700) tucked away between I-75 and US 441 just south of Gainesville (about two hours north of Orlando), Micanopy has received an unusual amount of attention. The frontier feel of Florida's second oldest town was captured in the Michael J. Fox film "Doc Hollywood." With its dirt roads, ancient oak trees, and Spanish moss, it continues to welcome droves of curious tourists every weekend. They're here to roam around the antiques shops, bookstores and craft stores that surround the town

Top left: Donnelly House, in picturesque Mount Dora

Bottom left: Practicing an ancient art in America's oldest community, St. Augustine

St. George Street, St. Augustine

State Capitol –
Tallahassee

square. A well-preserved slice of Old Florida, you can stay here for an afternoon (or evening at the local bed-and-breakfast) and get back to doing what sometimes needs to be done: Absolutely nothing (tel: 352/466-3121 for information).

Tallahassee

As the only Southern capital spared in the Civil War, Tallahassee (▶ 186) is the perfect – albeit out of the way – place to see Florida's Southern charm. The Old Capitol has several rooms open for museum displays, and the new State Capitol has a great observation tower on the 22nd floor, with an outstanding view of Leon County. Look for Florida State University, City Hall, Leon County Courthouse and other landmarks listed on the observation charts. On a clear day, you may be able to see Georgia, about 15 miles (24km) to the north, or the Gulf of Mexico, 30 miles (48km) to the south. A few blocks from the Capitol is the Museum of Florida History. Covering 12,000 years, the displays highlight the unique geological and historical events that have shaped the state. Exhibits include a mammoth armadillo grazing in a savannah and the remains of a giant mastodon found in nearby Wakulla Springs.

Perhaps the best parts of Tallahassee are to be found on the outskirts, where canopy roads lead to an old-fashioned environment of general stores and fishing holes. No other Florida city rivals Tallahassee for its ability to let time pass by.

St. Augustine Visitors Information
✉ 10 Castillo Drive, St. Augustine 32084
☎ 904/825-1000; www.oldcity.com

Amelia Island Tourist Development Council
✉ 961687 Gateway Boulevard, Suite 101 G, Fernandina Beach 32034 ☎ 904/261-3248 or 800/226-3542; www.islandchamber.com

Mount Dora Chamber of Commerce
✉ 341 Alexander Street, Mount Dora 32757
☎ 352/383-2165; www.mountdora.com

Tallahassee Convention Visitors Bureau
✉ 106 E. Jefferson Street, Tallahassee 32301
☎ 850/413-9200; www.seetallahassee.com

THE CONCH REPUBLIC

I f you weren't watching the news in April 1982, you probably missed the world's shortest revolution. That month, the United States Border Patrol established a blockade in Florida City outside a watering hole called Skeeter's Last Chance Saloon as they searched for smuggled drugs and illegal immigrants. It may have gone unnoticed elsewhere, but the road was US 1 – the only route to and from the Keys. The effect was that residents of the Keys had to prove their citizenship before they could enter the American mainland. To Keys residents, this was a diplomatic slap in the face.

Key West mayor Dennis Wardlow, along with fellow citizens from the islands, traveled to Miami's Federal Courthouse to request an injunction to stop the blockade. His pleas were in vain. Following the proceedings, Wardlow stepped outside and, before a phalanx of television cameras and microphones, made an announcement unheard since the start of the Civil War. "Tomorrow at noon," said Wardlow, "the Florida Keys will secede from the Union!"

At noon on April 23, 1982, the citizens of Key West met at Mallory Square. Tension and patriotism filled the air as the mayor read the proclamation of secession and announced the formation of the "Conch (it rhymes with honk) Republic."

The Conch Republic has its own legal documents

The Great Battle for the Conch Republic, 1982

You say you want a revolution? Well...

Right: Revolutionaries re-create the infamous battle

Although not as historically significant as firing on Fort Sumter, which sparked the Civil War, Wardlow's rebellion did have its moments. To symbolize the civil rebellion, Wardlow took a loaf of stale Cuban bread and broke it over the head of a man dressed in a U.S. Navy uniform.

Below: Entrant in Ripley's Believe It Or Not! Conch Republic Drag Race

They were free. They had thrown down the gauntlet of rebellion at the feet of the American government and were at war. Against all odds, the fledgling Conch Republic managed to withstand the pressures of the siege for 15...30...45...and then 60 long seconds, until a full minute had passed. Wardlow, now the Prime Minister of the Conch

Republic, suddenly realized the full impact of his actions. Facing vastly superior forces, he surrendered his nation to a United States admiral.

The revolution wasn't in vain. As with other nations defeated by the might of the American military, Conch Republic citizens felt they were owed war reparations. Prime Minister Wardlow asked for $1 billion in foreign aid to help rebuild his shattered nation.

In the upcoming years the Conch Republic took on a life of its own. The publicity stunt was ignored by the United States government. Since it didn't respond to the "secession," it unwittingly helped establish sovereignty for the Conch Republic under international law governing "adverse possession between

The Conch Republic's Foreign Policy

The Conch Republic has its own, very brief, foreign policy: "The mitigation of world tension through the exercise of humor." *(Used with permission, Office of the Secretary General)*

sovereign nations." In an unparalleled move, on April 20, 1994, the Monroe County Commission met and, before the statute of limitations expired, actually voted on Resolution No. 124–1994. In the formal language of an official document, the county commission described the events leading up to the secession from the blockade by the U.S. Border Patrol in April 1982, to the suffering inflicted on the individuals and businesses in the Keys, and the federal courts' refusal to grant meaningful relief. The document also notes Wardlow's stirring proclamation and the fact that he spoke for all residents of the Keys.

It was an incredible moment. By unanimous vote, the resolution recognized Wardlow's actions by, of and for the people of the Florida Keys. Residents of the Florida Keys now hold dual citizenship of the United States as well as the Conch Republic – an area stretching from the doors of Skeeter's to the southernmost tip of Key West.

Each April the Conchs celebrate their independence in Key West (their capital) during a weeklong festival held in a "public and notorious manner."

Among the more notable events, the Conchs raise their flag over Fort Taylor to start the proceedings and later reenact the famous "Great Battle for the Conch Republic" which, of course, is followed by a victory party over the evil forces of the United States Border Patrol.

Part Utopia, part Woodstock, the world's first – and only – "Fifth World" country exists as a "State of Mind" and aspires only to bring more warmth, humor and respect to a planet the Conchs feel is in need of all three. When you think about it, the Conch Republic has seceded where others have failed.

For more information on the creation of the Conch Republic – and how you can get a Conch citizen (or diplomat) passport – check out: www.conchrepublic.com.

When in the Conch Republic, do as the Conchs do...

- Drink a beer at Sloppy Joe's.
- Catch the street performers during the Sunset Celebration at Mallory Square. Bring some change – but watch your wallet.
- Have a slice of Key lime pie.
- Buy a coconut – eat the flesh and drink the milk.

Life as a Florida Retiree

So you come to the end of your trip, go home and call your friends over to see slides of your Florida vacation. By 4 am, they've made excuses and fled, but you're still chattering away about the Sunshine State until you start thinking... Maybe we should just retire to Florida!

About 100,000 retirees move to Florida each year

Retirees have been coming here since the 1940s, buying houses or renting apartments as they spend their days enjoying the good life. But in the last decade, the stakes have been raised. Massive retirement communities have appeared on the landscape, luring pension-rich retirees into relocating to a seniors' Valhalla. And this new breed of retiree is quick to snap at the bait.

Florida retirement – time to relax and enjoy life

Thanks to new senior communities, the influx of older residents has made the state one of the four fastest-growing in America. For senior citizens, there are several compelling reasons to call Florida home. First, they no longer have to struggle through brutally cold winters up north. In Florida they can relax from November through March and never even think of shoveling snow or buying heating oil.

Next, they have company. Approximately 20 percent of the state's population is older than 65 – and in some counties, that figure is as high as 35 percent. Recreation is another huge factor. There are more than 1,000 golf courses in the state (more than anywhere else in America), as well as fishing, bicycling trails, tennis, bowling and a wealth of planned activities at retirement communities. An interested

retiree can always find someone to join them in an exciting game of shuffleboard or bingo.

Perhaps the major consideration for retirees is cash, and this is where Florida hits the jackpot. Unlike most American states, Florida has no state income tax since tourist dollars make up for that missing revenue stream. With that advantage, a senior's pension fund, monthly Social Security check, investments and bank account interest can keep them relatively solvent. Some can even afford to live as "snowbirds," wintering in Florida and returning to their summer home up north to enjoy a perfect balance of weather.

Naturally, the financial road goes both ways. While the state saves them some money, seniors give Florida far more in return. So when it comes to seniors, Florida's learned that old news is good news.

A retiree hangin' out on the beach near his new Florida home

Facts and Figures

- Seniors donate 7.5 million volunteer days.
- They pay more than $1 billion in local school taxes.
- Seniors provide $3.5 billion in charitable contributions.
- They command $135 billion in spending power.
- They account for 50 percent of new home building.

FUN FACTS & TRIVIA

Armed with the following information, you can pass yourself off as a native Floridian, able to share with friends little-known facts regarding the state's history, geography and folklore. What, for example, is the Miami Circle? Which river runs the wrong way? And why can Malaysian monitor lizards be found living in Central Florida?

Deborah Harry

Who's on First?
In 1565, the Spanish founded St. Augustine, making it the oldest permanent settlement in the United States. This was 42 years before the English arrived in Jamestown and 55 years before the Pilgrims arrived at Plymouth Rock.

Keeping Cool
In 1845, while trying to create a device to lower the body temperature of people with yellow fever, Apalachicola doctor John Gorrie accidentally invented the first ice machine. He received a patent on the device in 1851.

It's Juan for the Money...
The Spanish Governor of Florida awarded Key West to Juan Pablo Salas. He sold it in 1822 for $2,000 to John W. Simonton.

The World's Largest Gulf Course
About 4 miles (6km) off Florida's East Coast, the Gulf Stream is an ocean river that runs from the Gulf of Mexico to Europe.

I Can't Get No Room Service
The Rolling Stones' hit "(I Can't Get No) Satisfaction" was written in a Clearwater hotel room.

You're Going the Wrong Way!
Not only is the St. John's River the largest river in the state, it's one of the rare rivers in this hemisphere that run south to north.

Florida Celebrities

- Blondie's Deborah Harry is from Miami.
- Crooner Pat Boone is from Jacksonville.
- Novelist Zora Neale Hurston was born in Eatonville.
- Pee Wee Herman's real name is Paul Rubenfeld. He graduated from Sarasota High School in 1970.
- The Doors' Jim Morrison is from Melbourne.
- Actress Faye Dunaway is from Bascom.

You're in for a Surprise

Stephen Foster's "Old Folks at Home" was originally called "Way Down Upon the PeeDee River."

Giving Birth to Cyberbaby

The first live Internet broadcast of a woman giving birth took place from an Orlando hospital on June 16, 1998. More than a million people the world over watched the event.

Amphibian-licious!

If you're tempted to try frog legs, you'll find they taste like chicken.

Think Pink

Pink flamingos are not native to Florida – they're not even naturally pink. They get their pink hue from eating shrimp and other pink crustaceans.

A Capital Idea

In 1845, Tallahassee was chosen as the capital since it was midway between the state's two provincial capitals under Spain – St. Augustine and Pensacola.

Tricky Dicky Does Disney

Richard Nixon's famous "I am not a crook" speech was given at Walt Disney World's Contemporary Hotel at a convention of newspaper editors in 1973.

Uncovered Treasure

In 1999, construction workers uncovered a 38-foot-wide (11.6-m) Native American stone carving on the shore of the Miami River in the middle of urban activity. Historians believe the Miami Circle could be an ancient celestial calendar or the remnants of a Tequesta Indian village.

Latin Life

Cuban-born Gloria Estefan and the Miami Sound Machine introduced Latin American music to mainstream audiences in the mid-1980s, and the vocalist's popularity soared. While at Walt Disney World Resort, visit Bongos Cuban Café, the nightclub and restaurant created by Estefan and her husband, Emilio, who still live in South Florida.

A Perfect Record

The Miami Dolphins played the National Football League's only perfect season in 1972 (17–0). Although many teams have come close, the record still stands.

The Wright Stuff

Lakeland boasts the largest collection of Frank Lloyd Wright architecture in the world. Wright designed Florida

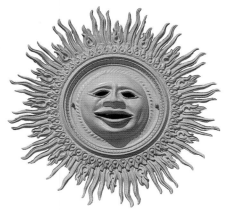

During his 10 years there, he was perhaps best known for frequenting Sloppy Joe's Bar, now the location of Capt. Tony's Saloon. He also wrote some books.

Jaws Galore

More than a million alligators and between 500 and 700 crocodiles live in Florida, making it the only state harboring both reptiles.

A Sweet State

Florida produces more than half the sugar consumed in the United States and is the second-largest honey producer.

Gator Aid

Alligators have approximately 80 teeth which, when you think about it, are not very practical since gators don't chew their food, they just use their teeth to grasp the food and then let their stomach acids do the rest. Like sharks, when they lose a tooth, a new one grows in. Alligators have been around longer than you might think – about 180 million years.

Leaping Lizards

Malaysian monitor lizards, normally found in Africa, Asia, Australia and South America, have been found living in Central Florida. Officials suspect the reptiles outgrew their welcome as pets, so owners released the fierce, fast lizards into Florida lakes.

Above: Ernest Hemingway Southern College between 1937 and 1955, during his "organic" period.

The Old Man and the Sea

Below: The endangered Florida panther Ernest Miller "Papa" Hemingway was one of Key West's most famous citizens.

State Stuff

- The state shell is the horse conch.
- The state tree is the sabal palm.
- The state flower is the orange blossom.
- The state beverage is orange juice.
- The state gem is the moonstone.
- The state bird is the mockingbird.
- The state marine mammal is the manatee.
- The state saltwater mammal is the dolphin.
- The state animal is the Florida panther – of which there are about 30 left.

Hooray for Hollywood East

Florida could have been a contender. Had a few film producers headed south instead of west, you'd be tuning into Oscar night from beautiful downtown Orlando. But it wasn't to be.

The Hollywood the world knows is in California, not the one in Florida (Hollywood happens to be one of the state's favorite southern cities). Although Florida is photogenic, it is stuck with Tarzan swinging through Silver Springs, Esther Williams splashing around Cypress Gardens and Elvis following his dream near Ocala.

However, all is not lost. Back in 1989, director Ron Howard chose Orlando for the Steve Martin movie "Parenthood." Then in 1997, Tom Hanks filmed the award-winning $68 million series "From the Earth to the Moon" at the Disney-MGM Studios.

Between those productions, other directors and stars have come to Orlando and surrounding cities filming "Rosewood," "My Girl," "Passenger 57" and "Matinee." Before he got involved with the blockbuster "Titanic," James Cameron was in Miami directing Arnold Schwarzenegger and Jamie Lee Curtis in "True Lies." Over on Ocean Drive, Robin Williams and Nathan Lane were starring in "The Birdcage," and in 1998 Cameron Diaz, Matt Dillon and Ben Stiller filmed "There's Something About Mary."

Preceding Miami's run of blockbusters, Chevy Chase and Bill Murray shot "Caddyshack" in Broward County, and William Hurt and Kathleen Turner steamed up some scenes in "Body Heat" in Lake Worth. In 2004, another Florida film made a worldwide impression when "Monster" helped actress Charlize Theron win an Academy Award for her portrayal of one of America's first female serial killers, Floridian Aileen Wournos.

Check the archives and you'll find that Oliver Hardy made films in Jacksonville

Shot in Florida:

Top: Arnold Schwarzenegger and Jamie Lee Curtis in "True Lies"

Below left: Bill Murray in "Caddyshack"

Below: Jim Carrey in "Ace Ventura: Pet Detective"

"Key Largo."
Great name.
Great script.
Great setting.
Shot in
California!

Hollywood is so wrapped up in itself that it's a miracle any producer ever leaves the state. They have beautiful homes (and earthquakes) and there's an established infrastructure (and mudslides) and soundstages that can change appearance faster than a patient with multiple personalities.

The reason they come here is cash. Florida is a right-to-work state, so producers don't need employees with union cards to make a movie. It's sometimes easier to fly to Florida where the crews are cheaper, the land every bit as

beautiful as California and the actors just as talented. At least Floridians know that there's a lot of gold in the silver screen.

Rumors

Have you heard the rumor that Jim Carrey gets $20 million a movie? Well, that's no rumor and it never would have happened if it hadn't been for Miami. The city was the backdrop for Carrey's breakthrough "Ace Ventura: Pet Detective."

Finding Your Feet

First Two Hours

Jacksonville International Airport

Landing in Jacksonville (tel: 904/741-2000; www.jaxairports.org) puts you midway between Daytona Beach and Savannah, Georgia – and right on the Atlantic Ocean. JAX is about 14 miles (22.5km) north of downtown Jacksonville. Car-rental services and ground transportation are located at the terminal.

- State route **Route 102/Airport Road** connects the terminal area with **I-95** at Exit 363. I-95 runs north to Georgia, and south through downtown Jacksonville to St. Augustine, Daytona Beach, Melbourne and other points to Miami.
- From I-95, take **Highway A1A/FL 200** eastbound at Exit 373 to Fernandina Beach and Amelia Island.
- **I-295** (a ring road) connects with I-95 at Exit 362 to bypass Jacksonville to the west. I-295 connects with I-10, which runs west from Jacksonville to Lake City and Tallahassee and the Florida Panhandle.

Tallahassee Regional Airport

Tallahassee is a small town, and the airport (tel: 850/891-7802) is easy to navigate. TLH is about 5 miles (3km) southwest of downtown. Car-rental services and ground transportation can be located at the terminal.

- Leaving the airport, **I-10** and **US 90** are to the north of the airport terminal. Turn left onto **Capital Circle/FL 263** and drive north to **Route 20, US 90** and **I-10** at Exit 28 (to be renumbered Exit 196). I-10 runs east to Lake City and Jacksonville and west to Marianna and Pensacola.
- From the airport turn right onto Capital Circle. Turn left on Springhill Road for downtown, Florida A&M University and Florida State University.

Pensacola Regional Airport

The airport (PNS, tel: 850/436-5000; www.flypensacola.com) is located less than 6 miles (10km) northeast of downtown Pensacola near the west shore of Escambia Bay, and just minutes from the Alabama border. Rental cars and ground transportation can be arranged at the main terminal.

- **I-10**, which leads to Tallahassee and Jacksonville (as well as Mobile, Alabama and San Diego, California), is a short distance north of the airport. **US 98**, which skirts the Gulf of Mexico, is to the south.

Orlando International Airport

If your destination is Walt Disney World® Resort in Florida, here's a relatively simple way to get from plane to luggage to transportation at Orlando International Airport (OIA), tel: 407/825-2001; www.orlandoairports.net.

- Domestic flights arrive at all gates from **1–99**, except gates **30–89,** which are usually but not always reserved for international flights.
- All halls lead to a **free electric shuttle** that takes you to the third level of the main terminal. Straight ahead is a fountain, and beyond the fountain to the left is an information booth.
- Take the escalator down one flight to **claim your bags**.
- There are **five currency exchange counters** – one in the center of the airport by the information booth, one each by baggage claim on sides A and B, and one each airside where you get on or off the shuttles.
- Take another escalator down another flight to find the **rental car counters, taxis and buses**. Some rental cars are parked at OIA.
- If your rental car is at the airport, descend yet another level to reach a tunnel that leads to the multilevel parking garages. Otherwise, just outside are buses and taxis to hotels, and shuttle buses and vans to rental car centers.

- Orlando's own buses, the **Lynx** system (tel: 407/841-8240), depart from the A side of the terminal on Level One, but they have no provisions for luggage.
- As you leave, look for **Route 528** (the Beeline Expressway, toll), following the signs to Walt Disney World® and the attractions. Route 528 heads west to **I-4**, access point to International Drive, Universal Orlando and Walt Disney World®.

Orlando Sanford International Airport

Orlando Sanford airport (tel: 407/585-4000; www.orlandosanfordairport.com) is about 30 miles (48km) northeast of OIA, is popular with smaller charter airlines, and is halfway between the ocean and Orlando.

- **American Coaching** (tel: 407/826-9999), across from the terminal, dispatches vans to pick up and deliver passengers wherever they are staying.
- If driving from Sanford, **Route 417** (the GreeneWay) is best. It's a toll highway (you'll need some quarters). Alternatively, **I-4** is about 8 miles (13km) away.

Miami International Airport

Miami's airport (MIA) (tel: 305/876-7000; www.miami-airport.com) seems more crowded and confusing than OIA, but is in fact fairly easy to navigate. (MIA is completing a $5.4 billion expansion of terminals and concourse.)

- The first level is arrivals, the second level is departures, and the third level features a **long moving walkway** that wraps nearly all the way around the horseshoe-shaped terminal with exits at Concourses B–H.
- Use the walkway on Level Three to save your feet; go to Level Two if you need a shuttle bus or the **Main Tourist Information Center** at Concourse E; and go to Level One to retrieve your bags, rent a car or hail a taxi.
- When you leave MIA, the most direct route to South Beach is **Route 836** (also called the Dolphin Expressway), which heads east to the MacArthur Causeway and directly to the southern end of the Art Deco District.
- If your destination is north of South Beach, **Route 112** (Airport Expressway) is a straight shot to the Julia Tuttle Causeway and mid-Miami Beach.
- When you rent a car, ask the clerk to give you a map and mark your route for you. The city has a **"Follow The Sun" system**, which marks the safer routes to popular destinations with huge sunburst logos on directional signs.
- Cab fares from the airport to South Beach, the Art Deco District and destinations as far north as 63rd Street are reasonable. **Yellow Cab** is a safe bet.
- **SuperShuttle vans** (tel: 305/871-2000) run 24 hours a day. They pick up at the ground level of each concourse.
- The last option is an inexpensive Miami-Dade Transit Agency **Metrobus** (tel: 305/770-3131), which picks up on the lower level of MIA.

Tampa International Airport

Tampa International Airport (TIA) (tel: 813/870-8700; www.tampaairport.com) is smaller and is easy to handle. All flights deposit passengers on the third level.

- Although the airport is divided into two sides **(red and blue)**, everyone descends to the first floor to retrieve their bags.
- Here, you'll find rental cars, taxis, buses and courtesy vans (clearly marked) to hotels. **Yellow Cab** charges a reasonable fare to take three people downtown, about 15 minutes away. You can get details of shared-ride services at the first-floor information counter.
- The corners of the airport are numbered 1 and 2 on both the red and blue sides, and is where shuttle buses and limos pick up, but the city bus system, **HARTLine** (tel: 813/254-4278), picks up from Red 1. Look for Route 30.
- Again, rent a car. When you leave TIA, look for **I-275 north** to reach Tampa or **I-275 south** to reach St. Petersburg.

Getting Around

Orlando

If your entire vacation is on Walt Disney World® property, you could just use their transportation (➤ 55). If driving yourself, you may find the road layout difficult to follow. For the most part, you'll need to be concerned only with **I-4**.

- **I-4** is an east–west highway that actually takes a diagonal northeast–southwest route through Orlando. It's densely trafficked during **weekday rush hours (7–10 am and 4–6 pm)**, but it's the main artery from Walt Disney World® Resort in Florida to SeaWorld, Universal Orlando, International Drive and downtown Orlando.
- The distance from **Disney to downtown** is only about 12 miles (19km).
- **Route 528** (the Beeline Expressway), which skirts past the airport, and **Route 408**, which edges through downtown, are Orlando's two major east–west roads.
- Tolls on each range from 25¢ to $1, and the **Beeline Expressway** is best to reach Port Canaveral, the Kennedy Space Center and Cocoa Beach.
- **Route 408** delivers you to **Highway 50**, which leads to Titusville and Cape Canaveral – but only after dealing with city and suburban traffic.

Miami

The fastest way to get to the far north and south of Miami is via **I-95**. **I-75** leads into the city from the northwest, and Route 836 (Dolphin Expressway) connects the airport to downtown, lower Miami Beach and the Art Deco District. A map is necessary (obtainable from airport bookstores), but when in Miami you can take advantage of four sources of inexpensive transportation.

- **Metrobus** rides around the city are inexpensive.
- **Metrorail** is also inexpensive and runs from downtown Miami north to Hialeah and south along US 1 to the Dadeland Mall.
- **Metromover** is an elevated electric tram that runs through downtown Miami.
- The **ELECTROWAVE** (tel: 305/843-9283) is a fleet of electric trolleys that cruise through South Beach. The fee is a nominal 25 cents (Mon–Sat 8 am–1 am, Sun and holidays 10 am–1 am).

Tampa

It's almost too easy to get around Tampa: Most of the city is on a peninsula and the layout is like a grid. When you need to reach St. Petersburg, Clearwater or any of the beaches, it's easy.

- To get to St. Petersburg from south Tampa, take **Highway 92** across the Gandy Bridge or, from north Tampa, via **I-275** and the Howard Frankland Bridge.
- Once you're in St. Petersburg, the beaches are easily reached by taking **Central Avenue** due west to Treasure Island. From here, **Highway 699** goes south and north along the coast.
- You can use **HARTLine** buses in Tampa (➤ 39).

The Panhandle

Florida's Panhandle, which stretches 360 miles (580km) between Jacksonville on the Atlantic Coast and Pensacola on the state's western border, is fairly easy to navigate since there are only a few major highways to deal with and each has its own merits.

- **I-10** is the fastest route between the two cities, and is intersected at Lake City by **I-75**, which leads south to the Florida Turnpike and eventually Miami.

- **US 90** was the original east–west highway and is still a charming back road that runs through several rural counties and into county seats along the way.
- **US 98** is the road along the Gulf that is the best route for reaching coastal cities such as Panama City and Apalachicola.
- **Route 399** between Pensacola Beach and Navarre Beach takes you down Santa Rosa Island, a popular swimming and sunbathing beach.
- Along the way, a few north–south highways intersect the Panhandle between St. Marks and Tallahassee (Route 363), between Panama City and Marianna (US 231), and Route 85, which connects Fort Walton Beach to Crestview.

Rental Cars

Second-rate rental car companies near the airports may be cheap, but beware of additional service charges. The more established agencies have reasonable prices as well, and you can prebook through a travel agent to find the best deals.

- If you live outside the United States, you will need a **valid driver's license** (written in English), you must be at least 25 and carry a major credit card. Before you go, check if your own insurance will cover your rental.
- All passengers have to **wear seatbelts**; headlights need to be used when it's raining; and you have to drive on the right side – no exceptions.
- If you have kids age three and under, they need to sit in a **child's safety seat**, which can be rented from $5–8 a day.
- Be sure to ask the mileage allowance. Some rental fees are based on keeping the car in Florida, or they'll add extra fees if you exceed your limit. You're probably getting a good deal when you get a car with unlimited mileage.

Buses

- **Greyhound Lines** (tel: 800/231-2222; www.greyhound.com) serves major cities.

Tourist Information Centers

Visit Florida ✉ 661 E. Jefferson Street, Suite 300, Tallahassee 32301 ☎ 888/7FLA-USA; www.flausa.com
Orlando Official Visitor Center ✉ 8723 International Drive ☎ 407/363-5872; www.go2orlando.com
Kissimmee/St. Cloud Convention & Visitors Bureau ✉ 1925 E. Irlo Bronson Memorial Highway, Kissimmee 34744 ☎ 407/847-5000 or 800/327-9159 for a vacation guide; www.floridakiss.com
Greater Miami Convention & Visitors Bureau ✉ 701 Brickell Avenue, Suite 2700, Miami 33131 ☎ 305/539-3000;

www.miamiandbeaches.com
Key West Visitors Bureau ✉ 402 Wall Street, Key West 33040 ☎ 800/648-6269; www.keywestchamber.org
Tampa/Hillsborough Convention & Visitors Association ✉ 400 N. Tampa Street, Suite 1010, Tampa 33606 ☎ 813/223-2752 or 800/224-1733; www.gotampa.com
St. Petersburg/Clearwater Area Convention & Visitors Bureau ✉ 14450 46th Street N, Suite 108, Clearwater 33762 ☎ 727/464-7200 or 800/FLBEACH; www.FloridasBeach.com

Discount Passes

At shopping plazas surrounding Disney, and along International Drive, you will see ticket kiosks where you can buy discounted tickets to theme parks and attractions. The catch is you will have to agree to visit a timeshare resort.

Admission Charges

Admission for places of interest is indicated by the following categories:
Inexpensive up to $15 **Moderate** $16–30
Expensive $31–50 **Very expensive** over $50

Accommodations

Hotels and Resorts

Although almost every property in Florida has some sort of pool, hotels and resorts differ from other accommodations by the scope of amenities they offer and their size. In general, resorts offer the most, the idea being that you need never leave the property. Golf and tennis are common resort themes, but Disney has broken the mold by introducing themes such as Polynesia, pop culture, Atlantic City, old Florida New Orleans, the Caribbean and more.

- **Access to a beach** is always a plus, but don't take it for granted. Check if the hotel is right on the water, or whether you need to travel. Keep in mind that waterview is not waterfront. Neither is waterfront – sometimes it's a street.
- Generally, **rooms are large**, and two double beds are standard. Suites, with two or three separate rooms, are increasingly common and offer an affordable alternative for families traveling together.
- The more services the property offers, the more opportunity there is to add hidden charges onto your bill, especially the use of telephones. **If you're on a budget**, make use of pay phones in the lobby, even when making local calls.
- Parking, in-room movies, laundry, room service and other amenities may also **come with exorbitant prices**. Look for a menu of services in the room or quiz the front desk before making arrangements.

Disney

Disney hotels offer the assurance of a clean room, good service, abundant amenities, easy access to the park and numerous guest benefits.

- With your guest ID, **perks include** free parking at theme parks, package delivery, early admission to parks, planned activities and free transportation.
- Even with approximately 25,000 rooms at nearly 20 on-property locations, **lodgings can still be hard to find**. Book as far in advance as possible.
- Staying at one of the "deluxe" resorts such as Disney's Grand Floridian Resort® Spa, Disney's Polynesian and Disney's BoardWalk Inn will cost around $500 a night. However, Disney also offers "value" resorts where rates range from $77 to $124 per night plus tax. Mid-range accommodations are priced between $133 and $219 per night plus tax.
- Every resort has a pool, food service and free transportation, and there are **more services at the higher-end resorts**.
- **For reservations** at any Walt Disney World® hotel, tel: 407/934-7639 or the Walt Disney Travel Company on 800/828-0228; www.disneyworld.com.

Motels and Motor Inns

Motels and motor inns are distinguished from hotels and resorts by having a small or nonexistent lobby and direct access to your room without having to use a central elevator. You also have the advantage of being able to park your car close to your room. The only drawback is security – because the door to your room opens to the outside world, there is less of a buffer between you and unsavory types who target visitors.

Bed-and-breakfasts

In some historic or rural areas of the state, there is the option of staying in a bed-and-breakfast. B&Bs and small inns offer a more authentic sense of local life and the opportunity to meet and interact with people.

■ During the season, many properties insist on a **minimum length of stay** and require advance payment.

Apartment Rentals

An excellent and often economical option is to rent an apartment. Because so many people from the north own vacation condominiums in Florida, there are a lot of vacant apartments available for rent outside the high season (January–March). Since apartments have full kitchens, you can prepare your own meals. Many also have swimming pools and other facilities.

Suites

Self-catering is a popular option. Rooms with cooking facilities, "efficiencies," can be found in most budget and moderate hotels and motels.

Camping

With Florida's good weather, camping can be an economical and fun option. Some campgrounds offer amenities, such as swimming pools and shops, typical of small hotels. Others simply allocate a plot of land to pitch your tent on.

■ **Renting an RV** (recreational vehicle) also gives you some increased freedom and the opportunity to see parts of the state you might not otherwise visit. A popular nationwide service is at www.cruiseamerica.com.

■ For information about where you can **camp or park your RV**, contact Florida's Department of Environmental Protection, Parks and Recreation (tel: 850/488-9872) or the National Park Service (www.nps.gov/parks.html). Reserve America (tel: 877/444-6777; www.reserveusa.com), a nationwide central reservations system, covers 13,000 campsites at 2,000 national forest campgrounds, including a few in Florida. For Florida state parks with campgrounds check www.myflorida.com or www.floridastateparks.org.

Youth Hostels

There are adequate youth hostels available in just about every major destination (and a few out-of-the-way places) in Florida. For information about where the hostels are located, contact the Florida Council Hosteling International (tel: 888/520-0568 or 301/495-1240; www.hiflorida.org).

Tipping

The amount you tip depends on where you are staying. In the finest hotels, doormen, bellmen, room-service staff, concierges, housekeepers and anyone else who performs a service for you should be tipped between $1 and $5, depending on the service, and usually $1 per bag. A few hotels include a daily service charge to cover tipping; ask at reception before you hand out tips.

Diamond Ratings

AAA field inspectors evaluate and rate lodging establishments based on the overall quality and services. AAA's diamond rating criteria reflect the design and service standards set by the lodging industry, combined with the expectations of our members.

The one (♦) or two (♦♦) diamond rating represents a clean and well-maintained property offering comfortable rooms, with the two diamond property showing enhancements in decor and furnishings. A three (♦♦♦) diamond property shows marked upgrades in physical attributes, services and comfort and may offer additional amenities. A four (♦♦♦♦) diamond rating signifies a property offering a high level of service and hospitality and a wide variety of amenities and upscale facilities. A five (♦♦♦♦♦) diamond rating represents a world-class facility, offering the highest level of luxurious accommodations and personalized guest services.

Food and Drink

Climate, immigration and tourism drive Florida's vast, colorful and tasty food scene. On the one hand, the state serves as the test market for nearly every fast-food or theme-restaurant concept. On the other, a cadre of award-winning chefs oversees nationally acclaimed restaurants. In between, you can get good food at good value.

- Restaurants throughout Florida **are more casual** than in other East Coast cities such as New York. Although the fancier places require jackets, most other places will let you eat in T-shirts and sometimes even shorts.
- Service is **almost always welcoming and friendly**, even in South Beach's trendiest places. Waiters are used to helping people from other places navigate their way through the menus and pricing systems. Don't forget to tip.
- Florida is a place for cars, and consequently all restaurants **have ample parking**. The more chic eateries offer valet service.

Orlando
Orlando is overrun with dining spectacles where food is an afterthought – medieval jousting, car racing and mystery are among the main attractions. But that doesn't mean there are no quality options.
- Perhaps the **biggest gastronomic strides** in the area have been made by Walt Disney World® Resort in Florida, which has upgraded its dining facilities. Every October, Epcot® hosts a month-long international food and wine festival that brings chefs, restaurateurs and vintners from around the world to taste each other's fare.
- Because the restaurants in and around Orlando cater primarily to a captive tourist audience, the **prices are generally high**. Perhaps more concerned with quantity than quality, people generally eat early and fast. But if you stray off the beaten path, you can find a more authentic local experience.

Miami
The restaurants of Miami run the full gamut. There are great gastronomic temples and hole-in-the-wall dives. A number of chefs creating what's known alternately as Floribbean (for Florida and Caribbean) or New World cuisine mix tropical ingredients and classic techniques to produce an exciting style of fusion cooking characterized by bold flavors and striking presentations.
- The **trendy crowds of South Beach** have sparked a restaurant boom. (Several New York eateries have even opened outposts there.) Although the attitude is sometimes as important as the cooking, the results are nevertheless impressive. Sushi restaurants are becoming popular.
- The **streets of Little Havana** are lined with authentic Cuban restaurants, where you can have a delicious and satisfying home-cooked meal for very little money. And Miami still has its early-bird eaters, most of them elderly, who dine from 4:30–6 pm to take advantage of bargain-priced dinners. Late-night diners will find plenty of places that stay open late.

Tampa
Route US 19 in Pinellas County, outside Tampa, is home to one of the densest restaurant populations in the country. Marketers believe that if a concept can make it there, among so much competition, it can make it anywhere. As a result, there are some great dining experiences in Tampa. Steak and Italian are among the best options, and there's certainly great wine.

Tipping
Bars (standing up) $1–2 per drink; (sitting down) 10–15 percent.
Restaurants 15–20 percent. Valet parking attendant $1–2.

Citrus Capital
Florida is the citrus capital of the world. Although most of the oranges are turned into juice, truck stops (laybys), fruit stands in season and souvenir shops often have bags of them for sale. The best grapefruits come from Indian River County. Be careful not to buy juice oranges, which are difficult to peel and slightly bitter. On your travels, why not try Key limes or kumquats. You can also ship cases of citrus home.

Specialties
Fish and seafood are another specialty of the region. Though overfished and polluted in parts, the Gulf of Mexico still yields some delicious specimens. With their sweet, white, flaky flesh, red snapper and pompano are perhaps the most common. Escolar is more difficult to find, but the search is worth it. The succulent, firm white flesh is so rich it has been likened to foie gras. Often served chilled with a tangy mustard sauce, large stone crab claws are worth seeking out. Only one claw is harvested, and within two years the crab generates a new one.

Vegetarian Food in Florida
Although Florida is more often associated with fruits than vegetables, vegetarians will have an easy time finding suitable dishes. Restaurants always have at least one vegetarian appetizer and entrée, and many of the better establishments offer complete vegetarian *dégustation* menus.

Glossary of Select Florida Food
Café con leche – strong, rich Cuban coffee mixed with hot milk.
Cherimoya – also known as custard apple, this tropical fruit has very sweet, creamy white flesh and black seeds.
Cuban sandwich – a hot, pressed sandwich of roast pork, ham, cheese and pickles.
Dolphin – be assured it's the fish, not the mammal.
Early-bird specials – special bargain-priced dinners available in the late afternoon and early evening.
Key limes – juicier and sweeter than their more common cousins, these yellow-green limes (named for the Florida Keys) provide the juice that makes the state's favorite dessert, Key lime pie.
Mangoes – the sweet, fleshy fruit is a south Florida specialty.
Stone crabs – only the large meaty claws of these crabs are eaten.

Pan Asian Cuisine
Many Florida chefs cook in a Pan Asian style, blending the ingredients and techniques of Asian countries to create a vibrant cuisine that sounds and tastes Asian, but is uniquely American. Results are sometimes more interesting than they are delicious.

Diamond Ratings
As with the hotel ratings (➤ 43), AAA field inspectors evaluate restaurants on the overall quality of food, service, decor and ambiance – with extra emphasis given to food and service. Ratings range from one diamond (💎) indicating a simple, family-oriented establishment to five diamonds (💎💎💎💎💎) indicating an establishment offering superb culinary skills and ultimate adult dining experience.

Shopping

Like just about anywhere in the United States, shopping is a major cultural pastime in Florida. High-school students meet in shopping malls after class, elderly people walk along pedestrian promenades to catch some sun, and tourists hunt for mementos and souvenirs to take back with them.

Malls
The principal venue for shopping is the mall, with its large "anchor" department stores (such as Saks Fifth Avenue, Neiman Marcus, JC Penney and Sears), smaller chain stores (such as the Gap, Pottery Barn, Crate & Barrel, Victoria's Secret and Barnes & Noble Booksellers) and sometimes a few locally owned independent boutiques with eclectic collections of goods for sale. Because of Florida's warm weather, there are also pleasant outdoor malls that offer a range of stores and restaurants.

Factory Outlets
Shopping at factory outlets is now a major part of the picture. These stores are often owned by the manufacturers themselves and can offer discounted prices on merchandise (some of it last season's styles, some are seconds or flawed items). It is not unusual to see merchandise being sold simultaneously at a retail mall and an outlet store with as much as a 50 percent difference in price. Outlet stores are often located alongside major highways and thoroughfares.

Superstores
Superstores, too, have made their presence felt in Florida. These giant stores (such as Home Depot, Borders Books & Music, Bed Bath & Beyond) specialize in one type of merchandise (hardware, books, bathroom and kitchen accessories, respectively) and offer reasonable prices along with an impressive inventory.

Food
If you shop for food, the best option is the large grocery store often attached to a strip mall. You can also buy food at the local bakery, delicatessen or butcher shop, though it may cost more than the supermarket. Grocery stores often carry other items (such as film and pharmaceuticals) and many open 24 hours a day.

Specialty Shopping
Because of its cosmopolitan nature and large residential population, Miami is often the place to find unique things to buy. South Beach is filled with urban and avant-garde boutiques offering everything from fashion to eyewear to crafts. The most exclusive stores are also aplenty in the affluent neighborhoods of the city – international brands such as Cartier, Prada and others are all represented. You are less likely to find specialty items outside Miami.
- Orlando is one of the most tourist-laden cities in the United States, so **souvenirs are available all over**, especially at Walt Disney World® Resort's huge range of shopping opportunities (➤ 104).
- In Tampa **look for cigars**, which are often rolled before your eyes, and **sporting goods**.

Opening Times
In residential areas, stores are generally open from 9 or 10 am until between 6 and 9 pm. On Thursdays and Fridays many stay open later. In tourist areas, stores often have extended hours to accommodate busy sightseeing schedules.

Entertainment

Florida has always been one of America's premier tourist destinations, long before the opening of Walt Disney World® in 1971, and there is truly something for everyone to do, from the good clean family fun of Disney theme parks to Miami's steamy club scene.

A high demand among Floridians for cultural events means there are many high-quality venues for everything from opera to foreign film. In addition, the influx of large numbers of Northerners to the state has resulted in a greater demand for sporting events not readily associated with Florida: Hockey and basketball have become extremely popular.

Following is a partial calendar of the more unusual and interesting annual festivals, parades, parties and other goings-on around the major Florida cities. This is by no means a complete listing of all there is to do around Florida. To obtain complete information contact the visitor center or tourism bureau for the specific city with dates of your stay. October through March is high tourist season in Florida, so many events that cater to visitors happen during this time.

January

Orange Bowl: Usually held on January 1, the Orange Bowl is one of the premier bowl games in college football. Miami's Pro Player Stadium is the stage for two of the best teams to go head to head. Following a long-standing tradition, the King Orange Jamboree Parade kicks-off the festivities the day before. Pro Player Stadium is 15 miles (24km) north of downtown Miami, which is the parade's location. For tickets, tel: 305/371-4600; www.orangebowl.com.

Florida Citrus Bowl: Another exciting college bowl game, this one is held in Orlando's Florida Citrus Bowl, complete with a colorful parade and a lavish New Year's Eve celebration. For information, tel: 407/423-2476; www.fcsports.com.

Outback Bowl: A week's worth of parties, parades, breakfasts and firework displays heralds in Tampa's own bowl game, the Outback Bowl. See two tough college teams battle it out at Tampa's Raymond James Stadium. For tickets and complete event information, tel: 813/874-2695; www.outbackbowl.com.

February

Silver Spurs Rodeo: Since 1944 the Silver Spurs Rodeo, held on weekends in late February and October in Kissimmee, has provided rodeo fans with a chance to see bronco riding, bull riding, roping and more. Spectators can attend one day, or see and participate in a whole weekend's worth of events. For more information, tel: 407/67-RODEO; www.silverspursrodeo.com.

Gasparilla Festival: The name of this annual Tampa event originates from the infamous pirate José Gaspar, who terrorized the Tampa area 200 years ago. Since 1904 Ye Mystic Krewe of Gasparilla has staged a mock attack on the city, and in recent years the event has evolved into a month-long series of attractions including parades, races, firework displays, art shows and more. The highlight is the pirate attack, usually in February. For information call Ye Mystic Krewe of Gasparilla on 813/251-4500; www.gasparillapiratefest.com.

Miami Film Festival: The premier film festival in Florida since its inception in 1984, the Miami Film Festival is particularly noted for introducing many Spanish and Latino filmmakers to America. In addition to the 10 days of screenings, there is a host of parties and seminars where attendees can rub shoulders with actors and filmmakers. For information call the Film Society of Miami on 305/237-3456; www.miamifilmfestival.com.

March

Bay Hill Invitational: This PGA-sanctioned tournament at the Bay Hill Club (9000 Bay Hill Boulevard, Orlando) is hosted by Arnold Palmer. Spectators at the week-long event will have the chance to see many of the country's top golfers in action. For more information and tickets, tel: 407/876-2888; www.bayhill.com.

May

Fringe Festival: Held at a wide range of indoor and outdoor venues around Orlando, the Fringe Festival is a diverse assortment of performances that lasts for 10 days starting in late April. During the festival you can see everything from Shakespeare to circus acts. Prices vary. For information, tel: 407/648-0077; www.orlandofringe.com.

June

Coconut Grove Goombay Festival: Celebrate Florida's Caribbean heritage at this day-long party in Miami's Coconut Grove. The event is free and thousands of people show up to sample ethnic food and hear live music.

July

Hemingway Days Festival, Key West: Celebrating the Key West days of novelist Ernest Hemingway, this multi-day event features a Hemingway look-alike contest, as well as arm-wrestling contests and celebrations of his literary works. (Note that his relatives are making it harder for this event to continue.)

October

Fantasy Fest: The wildest event of the year takes place in Key West, Florida's wildest town. The Mardi Gras-style celebration features drag queens, naked parties, public drunkenness, Caribbean balls and tattoo shows. For information, tel: 305/296-1817; www.fantasyfest.net.

Halloween Horror Nights: During weekends and the last two weeks of October, Universal Orlando is transformed into a ghoulish party designed to shock and scare attendees. There are monsters, gremlins and walking dead all over the park, as well as haunted houses and live concerts. Not recommended for young children. For tickets, tel: 407/363-8000; www.universalorlando.com.

St. John's Pass Grouper Festival, Madeira Beach: One of Florida's largest seafood festivals attracts more than 100,000 people annually to taste savory shrimp, fish, crabs and other specialties of the sea. For information, tel: 727/391-7373.

November

International Film Festival: Independently produced films premiere at this annual film festival in Fort Lauderdale. For information, tel: 954/760-9898; www.fliff.com.

December

Mickey's Very Merry Christmas Party: One of the highlights of Disney's Christmas festivities is the annual Christmas Party held in the Magic Kingdom. December in Walt Disney World® is full of other holiday events including concerts, firework displays and storytelling. For more information, tel: 407/824-4321; www.waltdisneyworld.com.

There are thousands more festivals across the state every year. For more information check out www.flausa.com, www.myflorida.com or the local convention and visitors bureaus. For information on other entertainment in Orlando, Miami, Tampa, St. Petersburg and the Panhandle, see the individual chapters.

Orlando

Getting Your Bearings

Until October 1, 1971, Orlando was a sleepy town surrounded by orange groves, cattle ranches and a few military bases. Then Walt Disney ushered in a whole new world. Orange groves were frozen out in the 1980s, and tourism took root. In their place evolved a universe of new worlds: Flea World, Hub Cap World, Liquor World, Lobster World, Speed World… Orlando is World Headquarters.

Drop by a theme park and you have instant access to Alaska, the South Pacific, the Canadian wilderness, the streets of New York, the hills of San Francisco, London, Paris, Morocco, China and all points east.

Not only does the diversity of the theme parks make Orlando the world's favorite tourist destination, the city's cleanliness, friendliness and climate make it a perfect getaway for families, honeymooners, seniors and solo travelers. Another draw is the city's strategic location: Rockets blast off less than an hour away; Atlantic Ocean beaches are 50 miles (80km) east; the Gulf of Mexico is just 60 miles (96km) west; there are small villages filled with antiques; suburban enclaves where hip college students watch art films; and freshwater springs that are perfect for picnics, snorkeling and canoe trips into a forgotten Florida.

Despite appearances to the contrary, Orlando and its surrounding towns do have a history. If you take time to look, you will find historic museums, older neighborhoods displaying wonderful architecture, and pockets of Greater Orlando that survive without dependence on theme parks and the tourist dollar.

Previous page:
SeaWorld Orlando

⭐ **Don't Miss**

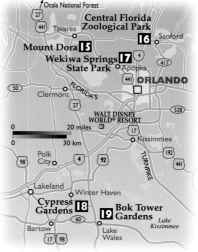

Assuming you'll spend at least a full day at each of Disney's major theme parks, here's one way to enjoy a powerful week.

Orlando in Seven Days

© Disney

Day One

Visit the **❶ Magic Kingdom® Park** first (► 56–61), whether or not you have children (right, Cinderella Castle). This was the first park to open at Walt Disney World® Resort and it's sure to get you in the fantasy spirit. If there are fireworks, stick around. If not, have a late dinner at Downtown Disney.

Day Two

Early morning Rise and shine for an early half day at **❶ Disney's Animal Kingdom® Theme Park** (► 71–75), since the wildlife retreats to cooler habitats by noon.

Mid-afternoon Spend a lazy afternoon at one of **❶ Walt Disney World® Resort's** water parks (► 76).

Evening Return to Disney's Animal Kingdom® or, if you have a park-hopper pass, to **❶ Epcot®** (► 62–65) for dinner at one of the World Showcase restaurants. France and Italy are the most popular, but all offer something special. Stick around until closing – there'll be fireworks.

Day Three

Take a break down the road at **❷ SeaWorld Orlando** (left, ► 86–88). This whale of a theme park is more casual and easier to tackle than the sensory overload of Disney. The park's Makahiki Luau is a fun dinner show and a nice way to wrap up the day.

Day Four

Make this a **1 Disney-MGM Studios** day (➤ 66–70). Stay for an early evening parade followed by dinner at the Hollywood Brown Derby (➤ 70). After a quick rest at your hotel, head to Pleasure Island (➤ 106–107) for an evening of club-hopping.

Day Five

3 Universal Orlando (➤ 77–85) is home to Universal Studios (a movie theme park, right) and Islands of Adventure (an amalgam of themed islands). Both are tremendous fun, and each will take a full day. Try dinner at the world's largest Hard Rock Café and, if you have the stamina, party till the wee hours at the nightclub-rich CityWalk (➤ 108).

Day Six

With your energy dwindling, this may be the best day to see **1 Epcot®** (➤ 62–65) since there are fewer "must-see" attractions.

Day Seven

Use today to revisit your favorite Disney attractions, the Universal park you missed, or get away from the theme parks for a canoe trip down the **17 Wekiwa River** (➤ 95), a visit to the **20 Kennedy Space Center** (left, ➤ 96–97), or a day at an **Atlantic** or **Gulf Coast beach** (➤ 14–16).

Wrap up the night at Downtown Disney – and make it count.

Finding Your Feet at Walt Disney World® Resort in Florida

Walt Disney World® Resort is not an amusement park, it is a 47-sq-mile (120sq km) fiefdom with all the features of a major city. It is large, sprawling, exciting, crowded, peaceful, noisy, tranquil, confusing and obvious. If you ignore the plentiful extraneous offerings of Walt Disney World® Resort, you'll have a better chance of seeing what's important.

First Two Hours

Once you've settled into your hotel, return to the lobby to get some insider information from Guest Services. Now is the best time to buy tickets, since buying at the gate is crowded and confusing; or you can purchase tickets in advance by phone (tel: 407/824-4321), on-line (www.disneyworld.com) or by mail (Walt Disney World, attn: Ticket Mail Order, Box 10140, Lake Buena Vista, FL 32830-0030), although each method adds a surcharge and takes a few weeks to deliver. You can purchase up to nine tickets online and save between $7 and $12 each.

There are more than a dozen types of ticket, and selecting just one can be daunting. Make your choice based on your length of stay, how many parks you will hit in a day (be realistic), and which parks you want to see. Below is a small selection of options available. Keep in mind tickets don't need to be used on consecutive days and unused tickets will never expire. Remember also that prices and ticket details can change so check ahead (tel: 407/824-4321 or 407/939-6244).

Which Ticket?
- A **One-Day Ticket** is valid for only one park (i.e. Magic Kingdom® Park, Epcot®, Disney-MGM Studios or Disney's Animal Kingdom® Theme Park) for one day. Approximately $55 adults, $44 children 3–9. Not a good idea if you'll be here more than a day. Otherwise...
- A **Hopper Pass** is good for any park at any time of day. Some include options such as a visit to a water park, Pleasure Island, or an event at Wild World of Sports. Children's prices are for ages 3–9. Over 9, they pay the adult price.
- You can choose a **Four-Day Hopper Pass** (approximately $219 adults, $176 children), a **Five-Day Hopper Pass** with two options (approximately $249 adults, $200 children), a **Six-Day Hopper Pass** with three options (approximately $312 adults, $250 children), a **Seven-Day Hopper Pass** with four options (approximately $342 adults, $274 children).
- For Disney Resort guests only there is **The Ultimate Park Hopper** (also known as Unlimited Magic) with unlimited admission to theme parks, water parks, nature parks, the sports complex and Pleasure Island (two days and one night approximately $129 adults, $104 children; 10 days and nine nights approximately $446 adults, $357 children; with the 10 nights, add a visit to DisneyQuest).

Getting Around

For resort guests it's far easier to park your car and take advantage of Walt Disney World® Resort's Transportation System.

- The most common mode of transportation is **buses**, which run about every 15 minutes from roughly an hour before park openings to a half hour after they close. Buses go to each resort area, picking up from each hotel. It can take between 10 and 30 minutes depending on how many stops are involved.
- It's great to be chauffeured, but take your car if you're in a hurry since buses can take a circuitous route to your destination.
- If you drive your own car or are entering from off-property, ask for directions before leaving your hotel. Highly traveled routes are well marked with bright signage, and some street lines are color-coded to lead you to your destination. **Parking** is easy and attendants will direct you to the massive parking lot outside each park. Walt Disney World® Resort guests do not pay for parking.
- For practical or pleasurable reasons, you can **board a monorail** at the Transportation and Ticket Center (TTC), located across the Seven Seas Lagoon from the Magic Kingdom. It has two loops: one leaves TTC and goes to the Polynesian Resort, Grand Floridian, Magic Kingdom and Contemporary Resort; the other goes to Epcot and back.
- **Hot tip:** On one monorail journey, ask to sit up front with the driver. It's worth waiting for the next one.

Top Tips

- **Guest Relations** is your best bet for a full range of assistance. Located near the entrance of every theme park, this is where you can leave messages, pick up foreign-language guide maps, exchange foreign currency, make reservations for hotels and priority seating for dining, and get information on behind-the-scenes tours.
- Check out **FASTPASS**, the ingenious virtual line system that "stands" in line for you.
- It's hot in spring, and very hot in summer with temperatures into the 90s. **Bring sun hats, sunglasses and sunscreen**. A water bottle is also a good idea.
- Some thrill rides have **height and health requirements**.
- If you are traveling with kids, you can attend a **character breakfast** at the theme parks and resorts. For information, tel: 407/939-3463.
- From any park, you will need a **handstamp and ticket** for reentry.
- Resort designers have sprinkled the parks with abstractions and symbolic representations of Mickey Mouse's head. Finding these **Hidden Mickeys** has become an obsession for some Disney aficionados, an amusement to others. Look up, down and around. Clues to finding them are located near the Disney descriptions on the pages that follow. For the most extensive list of Hidden Mickeys, check www.hiddenmickeys.org.

Opening Times

Opening times vary depending on season, but in general **Magic Kingdom** is open 9–7; **Epcot** 9–9 (Future World at 9 and World Showcase at 11), **Disney-MGM Studios** 9 am to about an hour after dark, and **Disney's Animal Kingdom** 7 or 8 am to an hour after dusk.

For information on all parks ☎ 407/824-4321 or 407/824-4500; www.disneyworld.com.

Magic Kingdom®
Park

By now you've read about the arrival of The Walt Disney
World® Resort and how to find your way around this
sprawling community. There's no better place to start
than with the cornerstone of it all…the Magic Kingdom.

This is the most inviting, most fun and most picturesque of all of Walt Disney World® Resort's theme
parks. If you don't have time to visit Epcot, Disney-MGM
Studios or Disney's Animal Kingdom® Theme Park, you
can find traces of all three right here.

HIDDEN MICKEYS
The shadow of the lamps on Main Street, U.S.A., make Hidden Mickeys.

© Disney

There's no "right way" to hit the Magic Kingdom, although there are several ways you can take advantage of what others don't know. Keep in mind that this approach targets the must-see attractions adults prefer. If you have children, tack on Fantasyland and Mickey's Toontown Fair (➤ 61).

First, the Magic Kingdom is a masterpiece of design. From the plaza (or "hub") in front of Cinderella Castle, seven "lands" branch off like spokes on a wheel (left to right, Adventureland, Frontierland, Liberty Square, Fantasyland, Mickey's Toontown Fair, Tomorrowland and Main Street, U.S.A.). It's easy to navigate and much easier if you arrive early, since lines will be significantly longer by mid-morning.

Morning

After exiting the monorail, ferryboat or bus, you'll pass through the turnstiles, and to your right are stroller (pushchair) and wheelchair rentals. Before you are the archways of the Main Street Train Station. Expensive lockers are inside and require a refundable key deposit (inexpensive). Get a key at the kiosk in the center of the station. Remember this location: You might want to return here to watch the fireworks.

Now the fun begins. As you step into **Town Square**, you will instantly experience everything you hoped for. The street reflects an America that never was but will always be cherished. The fragrance of fresh popcorn is in the air, flowers burst from planters, marching bands parade on the street, and horse-drawn streetcars await passengers.

No need to rush. Step to the center of the square, take a break and get your bearings. To your left is City Hall (dinner reservations, information, schedules and tours), an ATM (cash-point), lavatories and a fire station/gift store. For a real treat make a dinner reservation for Cinderella's Royal Table now, and indulge in a royal feast at the end of your day. Across Town Square is an Italian restaurant and Camera Center. From the center of Town Square, look to the end of the avenue and get ready to be dazzled.

Rising into the sky at the end of Main Street, U.S.A., is **Cinderella Castle**. No matter how many times you see it, you'll never forget its beauty. It will draw you down the road, past confectioneries and bakeries and a host of new stores that, sadly, have turned Main Street into a mall. **Main Street, U.S.A.** is active and interesting but better seen at night when there are fewer people and brighter lights. As you walk down it, you may be asked to pose for a photograph by a Disney photographer. You can check out your photograph later at the Camera Center at Town Square. If you like it, you can buy it.

Coming up on your left, the Main Street Gazette is an information board listing show times, ride wait times and park hours. A cast member is usually there to answer any questions. Now it's decision time. Some guests go through the castle straight to **Fantasyland**, but most go left and follow a clockwise circle of the park. The best approach is to avoid the rush by turning right into **Tomorrowland** so you can hit two hot attractions before the seats are warm.

First on your left will be **Stitch's Great Escape** (which replaces the ExtraTERRORestrial Alien Encounter). Based on

Cinderella Castle – focal point of Magic Kingdom Park

© Disney

the hugely popular animated feature about the misadventures of a wild (but lovable) alien, this features cutting-edge audio-animatronic technology and high-energy escapades in which you'll be recruited to provide additional security when the Galactic Federation learns of Stitch's whereabouts.

From the exit, **Buzz Lightyear's Space Ranger Spin** can be a quick stop if you have kids, and the **Astro Orbiters** are fun if there's no wait – but there usually is. You will be better off

**Hold on tight!
Big Thunder
Mountain
Railroad**

heading straight to **Space Mountain**. No aliens here, just a screaming fast roller-coaster ride in the dark. Nearly three minutes long and up to 28mph (45kph), it's one of Disney's best and the reason you hit Tomorrowland first. If there's no line when you're done, do it again.

You can skip Tomorrowland Speedway, and plan on missing most of **Mickey's Toontown Fair** and **Fantasyland** (unless you have kids). You may like whirling, swirling and spinning inside huge tea cups at **Mad Tea Party** if you are strong-stomached. Next is **Mickey's Philharmagic**. Rated by guests as one of their favorite attractions in all of Disney's four theme parks, the 3-D film is shown on a 150-foot-wide (46-m) screen as Donald Duck attempts to use Mickey's baton to conduct an out-of-control orchestra that takes him – and you – through scenes with Aladdin, Ariel ("The Little Mermaid") and Simba ("The Lion King"). In addition to 3-D effects, 4-D sensations include splashes of water, gusts of wind and pleasing scents.

TAKING A BREAK

It's approaching lunchtime and you have reached the halfway point. At the entrance to Liberty Square grab a quick lunch at the somewhat classy **Columbia Harbour House** restaurant or continue hitting the rides until 2 pm (while everyone else is eating). For quick fuel, there are dozens of food kiosks and snack stands in each land, that serve the standard fare. Lines are shorter than at most of the sit-down restaurants.

Midday

If you can hold out, rush over to the wonderful **Haunted Mansion**. After being greeted by a cadaverous host, you'll be ushered into the portrait gallery (look up when the lights go out), and then board a "Doom Buggy" to travel through darkened hallways, past the ghostly ballroom, into the attic and through a graveyard. It will remain one of your favorite haunts.

After the ride, the **Hall of Presidents** can be skipped. Following a patriotic film, each president is introduced, and then Abraham Lincoln makes a speech. Although they're Audio-Animatronics characters, it's interesting to watch them fidget and whisper during the presentation. Save for later, or when you want to escape the heat.

It's probably approaching 1:30 pm, and you'll be in the thick of other park guests. With two lands to go, slow it down at three popular attractions – Country Bear Jamboree, Splash Mountain and Big Thunder Mountain Railroad.

The **Country Bear Jamboree** stars a group of hillbilly bears; all gifted musicians, they will entertain you with their virtuosity on the jug, banjo, guitar and washboard bass. The concept is weird, but it's a fun, frivolous, cool escape from the ordinary.

Head toward the sound of screaming guests and you will be at **Splash Mountain**. Don't worry about following the storyline (Disney's film "Song of the South"), just be ready for the log you are riding in to take some fast drops and big splashdowns.

Close by, **Big Thunder Mountain Railroad** whips through tight turns, high hills, past possums, goats and a cowboy in a bathtub. Not nearly as fun as Splash Mountain, but it's worth a ride if the line is short.

Mid-afternoon

Every afternoon at 3 pm Disney's Share a Dream Come True Parade starts at Main Street, U.S.A. Every character you know will be featured, and you may even be asked to become part of the parade. Following the 15-minute blowout, there'll be a minor exodus as many resort hotel guests leave to rest up for the remainder of the day. You can try this, or continue your tour in **Adventureland** at **Pirates of the Caribbean**, perfect on a hot day. After entering a darkened cave, you will board a boat and follow the adventures of pirates who are gleefully ransacking a village, auctioning women, swilling rum and killing each other. The cannon shells, burning villages and repetitive theme song ("Yo Ho, A Pirate's Life for Me") make this 10-minute tour one of the Magic Kingdom's better attractions.

A popular attraction is next door at the **Jungle Cruise**. The 10-minute tour down the mysterious rivers of the world is narrated by a comedian/skipper who keeps the one-liners going. The ride ranges from thrilling (hippos attack your boat) to cute (the sacred bathing pool of the Indian elephants), but most of all, it is funny. If you do nothing else in the Magic Kingdom, do this ride.

It could be around dusk now. You have hit the park's major attractions and will likely have a few more hours to pick up ones you have missed, return to your favorites, have an enjoyable meal at Cinderella's Royal Table (reservations made earlier), or take an hour or so shopping along Main Street, U.S.A. The largest gift shop inside the Magic Kingdom is the **Emporium** on the corner of Town Square and Main Street, U.S.A., with every Disney item you can imagine and many you can't. And yes, they sell mouse ears in all sizes.

HIDDEN MICKEYS
A stack of cannon balls on the deck of the *Jolly Roger* in Peter Pan's Flight throw a shadow that makes a perfect Mickey symbol.

Battling it out in Pirates of the Caribbean

© Disney

SNAP HAPPY
It is estimated that vacation snapshots taken at Walt Disney World® Resort or Disneyland account for 4 percent of all amateur photographs taken in the United States.

Kid-Friendly Attractions

In **Fantasyland**, **Peter Pan's Flight** takes an aerial tour above nighttime London and past Captain Hook's ship. **Dumbo the Flying Elephant** is a smaller version of Astro Orbiters and can entertain kids for hours. Across the way, **Ariel's Grotto** is backed up with parents waiting patiently so their kids can be photographed with the mermaid. **Snow White's Adventures** is a trip through the movie into the mines and features a surprise visit from the Evil Queen (unsettling for some kids). One ride you may enjoy is **Cinderella's Golden Carrousel**, a beautifully restored 1917 edition which plays bouncy Disney songs.

Responding to the popularity of Pooh, Mr. Toad's Wild Ride was replaced with **The Many Adventures of Winnie the Pooh**. Here you ride through scenes featuring Pooh, Tigger, Eeyore, Kanga and Roo. Be prepared for a long wait as parents and kids crowd in for a glimpse of fantastic animation and an overdose of cuteness. Don't miss **Mickey's Philharmagic** (➤ 59), and then head over to **it's a small world**, a boat ride past dolls from different nations with a theme song you'll never forget. Hot tip: Hit these rides later in the afternoon or evening and the lines will be much shorter.

Connected to Fantasyland is **Mickey's Toontown Fair**, a small area filled with whimsical architecture, a kid-size roller-coaster (**The Barnstormer**) and the chance to meet Mickey. You can walk through Donald Duck's boat, Minnie's Country House and Mickey's Country House. To meet Mickey, walk through his house, out the back door and into the Judge's Tent.

➕ 229 A3 ☎ 407/824-4321 🕐 Daily 9–7, varies according to season

---

MAGIC KINGDOM: INSIDE INFO

Top tips If you are a Walt Disney Resort® guest **save the Magic Kingdom for Sunday or Thursday** when you can enter an hour earlier than everyone else.
• The best spot for a photograph of you and Cinderella Castle is from **the sidewalk near the Tomorrowland entrance**.
• Depending on the season, **SpectroMagic** lights up the Magic Kingdom once or twice an evening. The parade features 600,000 miniature lights, 72,000 watts of sound, holographic effects, electro-luminescent technologies, light-spreading plastics, smoke, liquid nitrogen and traditional lights.
• Replacing **Fantasy in the Sky** is the super-spectacular **Wishes**, which blows any other fireworks out of the sky. It's best seen from Main Street, U.S.A., with Cinderella Castle as the backdrop. During the 12-minute show, Jiminy Cricket launches more than 650 fireworks, each timed to explode in sync with a glorious music track. For the best view, get to the second floor of the train station.
• You can visit the mythical **"underground" and "backstage" areas** of the Magic Kingdom for $58. A host or hostess will take you on a 4.5-hour behind-the-scenes "Keys to the Kingdom" tour (tel: 407/939-8687 for this and other tours). Avoid it if you want to keep the illusion alive.

One to miss Unless you are returning for a second day, you can forget the *Liberty Belle* riverboat around the Rivers of America and the **raft ride to Tom Sawyer Island**. The time you will spend on these is greater than the fun returned.

☉ Epcot®

Epcot, not the Magic Kingdom®, was Walt Disney's greatest dream. In his mind, Epcot® (an acronym for Experimental Prototype Community of Tomorrow) would be a utopian community where citizens would develop solutions to the world's ills. It didn't quite work out the way Walt pictured it.

The concept is simple: You enter Future World and visit pavilions where mega-corporations present their latest products. Next comes World Showcase, where 11 nations display their country through detailed architecture, gift shops and restaurants – with perhaps a ride or a movie. This park is twice the size of the Magic Kingdom and there's a lot of walking. Be prepared. Although Epcot is adding a few more exciting rides, it's a mixture of science fair, video arcade and travelog. Here's the best way to see it.

Future World

HIDDEN MICKEYS
At the entrance of Spaceship Earth, a mural shows cloud formations on the left side. They form the head and ears of a Hidden Mickey

© Disney

As always, get an early start. You will arrive by car, bus or monorail and be channeled to the Entrance Plaza. Lavatories and a currency exchange are on your right, just before the turnstiles. You are in **Future World** now and approaching its focal point, **Spaceship Earth** (it looks like a big golf ball). There's a ride inside, but you can skip it for now. And forever.

Since it usually doesn't open until 11 am, don't race toward World Showcase. Instead, walk past Spaceship Earth and the two semicircular buildings to your left and right (**Innoventions East** and **Innoventions West**) and turn left for **Test Track**.

After seeing how new cars are tested on banked curves, high-speed curves, with special brakes, without special brakes, over bumpy roads and in crash tests, you board a six-passenger vehicle (minus a steering wheel and brakes) and experience what you just saw. There are 65-mph (105-kph) straightaways, hairpin turns and near-collisions. You will exit into a make-believe assembly line, a showroom for GM cars and then a gift shop. Next head for **Honey, I Shrunk the Audience**. Located inside **Journey into Imagination**, this is a 25-minute presentation that begins with a brief preshow before you step inside to watch Professor Wayne Szalinski, star of "Honey, I Shrunk the Kids," demonstrate his latest inventions. The 3-D special effects include mice invading the theater, a cat clawing at you, and then, after you are shrunk to the size of an insect, a giant kid picking you up.

Sensing that the attractions of Epcot® bordered on boring, Disney has been adding rides that inject a burst of adrenaline. One that's due to open in 2005 is **Soarin'**, borrowed from Disney's California Adventure™ Park. Here you'll sit under the wings of a hang glider, be hoisted 40 feet (12m) high inside a giant projection screen dome, and then glide around California, all the while smelling pine forest, orange blossoms, and the ocean.

The giant golf ball: Spaceship Earth and monorail

➕ 229 B2 ☎ 407/824-4321 ⏰ Daily 9–9 (Future World opens at 9, World Showcase at 11), but varies according to season

© Disney

Mission: Space is a high-tech, high-thrill attraction. Created in conjunction with former NASA advisors, astronauts and scientists, the simulated space adventure will launch you from a pulse-racing lift-off to a rendezvous with weightlessness. Exercise caution, as it's very easy to get nauseous.

Test Track – a combination of rollercoaster and simulator

The remaining attractions in Future World don't offer that much. The only borderline attraction is **The Living Seas**, which begins with a short film and then takes a brief tram ride past an artificial reef and into Sea Base Alpha. The two-level aquarium is filled with moray eels, barracuda and bonnethead sharks.

World Showcase opens at 11 am, but if you want to beat the lunch crowds, walk next door to **The Land**. This pavilion features **Living With the Land**, a boat ride that drifts past experimental gardens. Focus on the food court. Several counter-service stands sell soups, fruit salads, sandwiches...the usual fare.

World Showcase

After lunch, walk to the **World Showcase Lagoon,** the start and end of a 1.2-mile (2-km) circular walk. This half of the park is far more inviting, with native flowers and trees, entertainers, craftspeople and gourmet restaurants at nearly every pavilion. There is no right way to go, just visit those that interest you most. If you start counterclockwise, the first pavilion is **Canada**, highlighted by a reproduction of Ottawa's Chateau Laurier. The attraction here is "O Canada!," an 18-minute Circle-Vision 360 movie which puts you in the middle of Canadian prairies, cities, rivers and wilderness. Next, **United Kingdom**, with no movies or rides, presents street performances by an improv comedy troupe and a Beatles sound-alike band. Most guests here prefer a pint and a meal at the Rose and Crown pub.

Just past the International Gateway is **France**, which has the most beautiful movie ("Impressions de France"), the most delectable pastries (Boulangerie Patisserie) and the finest gourmet dining (Chefs de France) at Epcot.

Morocco is next and, without a movie and ride, makes do with craftspeople, street performers, a restaurant and several stores. Next door, **Japan** follows the route of Morocco and adds koi ponds, rock gardens, a pagoda, a small cultural gallery and a very large department store with Japanese gifts.

The American Adventure is the halfway point and features perhaps the best show in the World Showcase. An audio-animatronic Mark Twain and Ben Franklin introduce America's historical highlights in an inspiring, patriotic show.

There is a busy counter-service restaurant next door, but unless you are starving it's best just to grab a snack from one of the many food stands.

You will come to **Italy** next. No rides or movies, just more stores, street musicians and a restaurant. **Germany** is the same, but its Biergarten features lively entertainment – oompah bands, yodelers and dancers who perform as you eat.

Although **Africa** doesn't have a complete pavilion, it's represented by street performers and a store. **China** is recognizable by the towering Temple of Heaven, which houses a Circle-Vision 360 theater showing a movie shot by the first Western crew granted access to previously off-limit sites. There is also a store and a restaurant. **Norway** has a 14th-century castle, Akershus; a gift shop filled with trolls; a restaurant; and the Maelstrom, an occasionally scary boat ride through a troll-filled forest, and the raging North Sea. The last pavilion, **Mexico**, has stores, two restaurants, and a boat ride – El Rio del Tiempo – similar to Norway's Maelstrom though not necessarily as exciting.

If it's nearing closing time, stick around. The park's grand finale is the fantastic, surreal **Illuminations: Reflections of Earth**, a 13-minute synchronized symphony of fireworks and lasers. The big show kicks off at closing time and can be seen from anywhere in the World Showcase, so be sure to get close to the shoreline at least a half hour early.

There you have it. You have circled the world and seen the future.

EPCOT: INSIDE INFO

Top tips If you are a guest at Walt Disney World® Resort, **save Epcot® for Wednesday** when you can enter an hour earlier than everyone else and see selected Future World attractions.

• Can't wait to see your snapshots? The **Camera Center** near the Entrance Plaza and World Travel in the International Gateway has two-hour developing.

• A **Guest Relations counter** is next to Spaceship Earth. Stop here first if you want to make reservations for dinner. Dinner reservations can also be made by calling 407/939-3463.

◨ Disney-MGM Studios

At Disney-MGM Studios, Disney has managed to capture the spirit of Hollywood's Golden Age, the mythical era of the 1930s and 1940s when the title "movie star" actually meant something. Through art deco architecture, bright and bouncy Disney movie scores, and re-creations of legendary Hollywood hot spots, for a day at least, you will be able to relive those halcyon times.

Here's how to get the most out of your Disney movie day.

As if you haven't heard this enough already: GET HERE EARLY. Hours vary seasonally, so call ahead. Guests who arrive late will spend half their time waiting in line and the other half waiting to get in line.

Whether you arrive by car, bus or boat, you will be directed to the entrance, which opens onto Hollywood Boulevard. Before the turnstiles, note that Guest Relations and lavatories are down the sidewalk (pavement) to your left.

Beyond the turnstiles, lockers are to your right as well as strollers (pushchairs) and wheelchairs housed within Oscar's Super Service, a pseudo gas station.

Cast members are there to provide you with a park guide that includes a map and show times. If not, ask a guide at the booth in front of you for information. Hit the highlights first and make a second sweep to see remaining attractions when lines are not so long.

HIDDEN MICKEYS
At Star Tours, in the boarding video, passengers are shown boarding the Star Speeder. Three Ewoks climb in – the second is carrying a Mickey Mouse toy.

Morning

Start out on **Hollywood Boulevard**. Walk past the palm trees, camera shops, souvenir stores and snack stands, and at the first street on your right, Sunset Boulevard, turn right. There's a chart here listing wait times, show schedules and park hours. Just walk past the stores and the plaza where they sell frozen lemonade, turkey legs, hot pretzels, ice cream, cold fruit and hot dogs. At the end of the street there are restrooms. If you don't use them now, you may need to use them during the next ride. It's that scary.

It is attractions such as **The Twilight Zone™ Tower of Terror** that make Disney worth visiting. After you snake through the entrance and lobby of the abandoned hotel, you will be ushered into a library where you will get the story line:

Catastrophe Canyon, the highlight of the Backlot Tour

© Disney

This grand hotel was struck by lightning in 1939, and an entire wing – as well as five hotel guests trapped in an elevator – vanished. A secret door opens, you enter the boiler room and snake through another line until you are seated in an elevator. It's worth the wait. You will be hoisted to a hallway where the doomed guests appear, your car drifts through a mysterious dimension, a door opens and you see the park 150 feet (46m) below. Then the doors close. What happens next is worth every cent you spent to get here. The cable breaks, your car plunges straight down – stops – rises again – and takes yet another dive down the elevator shaft, then again and again for good measure. It's scary to say the least, and you will want to do it again. Remember seeing a bright flash when you fell? At the exit, you can buy a picture of yourself screaming like a baby.

✚ 229 A2 ☎ 407/824-4321 ⏱ Daily 9–about an hour after dark, but varies according to season

Located on Sunset Boulevard, near The Twilight Zone™ Tower of Terror, is Disney's state-of-the-art **Rock 'n' Roller Coaster Starring Aerosmith**, featuring the music of the Grammy-winning rock band. Here, guests board a Limotrain and, after an Aerosmith recording session, are launched from 0–60mph (96kph) in 2.8 seconds (as fast as an F-14 Tomcat) and reach forces of 5 Gs as they speed through twists, turns, loops, corkscrews, hills and dips. A special Aerosmith soundtrack is pumped through a total of 900 speakers with more than 32,000 watts of power. To reach the next must-see attraction, return to Hollywood Plaza, which is highlighted by the iconic **Sorceror Mickey hat**. Standing 122 feet (37m) tall, it is coated with enough fabric to cover 500 Cadillacs.

Behind the hat is **Mann's Chinese Theatre**, which houses **The Great Movie Ride**, a guided tour where you board a large vehicle and enter scenes of famous films ("Singin' in the Rain," "Casablanca," "Mary Poppins"). In a few moments you will be accosted by gangsters, watch desperadoes blow up a safe, enter an alien-infiltrated spaceship, travel to Munchkinland and witness the frightening arrival of the Wicked Witch of the West. Scary for kids, but satisfying for adults who love the movies.

Must-see number four is **Star Tours**, which you reach by crossing the plaza and heading toward a small boat/expensive ice cream stand at tiny Echo Lake. The venue **Sounds Dangerous Starring Drew Carey** (a sound effects-based attraction) is on your right, but pass this by and head straight to Star Tours.

With the return of George Lucas's "Star Wars" prequels, the ride has been upgraded to include effects from the film. You will recognize droids R2D2 and C-3PO, who are working on a spacecraft. Then you will climb aboard your own star speeder for a voyage to the Moon of Endor. Strapped and locked inside the craft (a motion simulator) you start your trip smoothly but it soon goes wrong – of course. This is not for sissies. The ride pitches, rolls, banks and dodges giant ice crystals and lasers fired by enemy fighters. You will need stamina, a strong back, a healthy heart and an iron stomach for this one.

Dude, where's my car? In front of Rock 'n' Roller Coaster Starring Aerosmith

TAKING A BREAK

It's now shortly past 11 am; you have made it to the Big Four and can start to slow your pace. The next big attraction will be the **Indiana Jones™ Epic Stunt Spectacular**. Check the schedule for the next performance. You may want to take in an early lunch nearby at **Soundstage**, where Disney movie characters congregate during the day. Another early lunch option is the 1950s **Prime Time Café** just past the stunt stadium, which serves "comfort foods" such as meat loaf, fried chicken and pot roast. If you want to save the big meal for later, just order some fries and a Coke or milk shake.

And so on to the Indiana Jones™ Epic Stunt Spectacular. This is easily the most exciting live performance in the park. Why go to California for earthquakes, explosions, rock slides and fights when you can see the highlights of "Raiders of the Lost Ark" performed right here? It is edge-of-your-seat entertainment made even more fun when they reveal a few tricks of the trade.

ROOM TO SPARE You would need a spare 61 years if you wanted to spend one night in every guest room currently available throughout all Walt Disney World® property.

© Disney

Afternoon

Now the rest of the park is up to you. Early-afternoon lines should be nominally shorter, as other guests go to lunch. From here it's easy to follow a clockwise route around the park.

Jim Henson's **Muppet*Vision 3-D** stars nearly every Muppet you remember in an all-star, sensory-overload performance that kids (and adults) will enjoy – especially since it ends with a bang.

Now you are on the streets of New York and have the option of visiting the oversized world of **"Honey, I Shrunk the Kids" Movie Set Adventure**. Leaving New York, you enter Mickey Avenue and arrive at the **Studios Backlot Tour**. This takes you through an actual working studio, past the wardrobe department and prop shop, and then into **Catastrophe Canyon** for a display of special effects. It's startlingly real – especially when the ground buckles beneath the tram.

There are two types of attractions left: Those revealing how movies are created and those that capitalize on Disney movie hits. When you leave the tour you will be on Mickey Avenue and where **Who Wants To Be A Millionaire – Play It!** brings you an exact replica of the game show set, showing how the game is played and produced. The next venue is **Walt Disney–One Man's Dream**, an overview of the man's life, with stories from his childhood and intriguing items such as his original animation camera. Before you reach the final section, **Animation Courtyard**, you may be lucky and catch a presentation on Disney's latest movie release or hit TV show.

Voyage of the Little Mermaid is a kid-friendly stage show featuring songs and stars from the animated movie. Sit farther back and kids can see the stage better.

On **The Magic of Disney Animation** tour you can watch local artists creating upcoming animated films. This is a great way to see how the cartoons are developed, and an animator also answers guest questions. The Robin Williams/Walter Cronkite preshow is as good as any attraction here.

It's probably approaching 6 pm. From the Animation Courtyard you are in the perfect position to enjoy a leisurely dinner at the **Hollywood Brown Derby** (having arranged priority seating earlier). This California icon was re-created here, complete with celebrity caricatures, private booths and the "Cobb Salad" (created by original owner Bob Cobb), as well as featured meat and fish dishes.

Finish your meal in time to wrap up the evening with two more shows. **"Beauty and the Beast" – Live on Stage** is a 20-minute performance that captures the essence of the animated movie. It's a terrific stage show that stars singing silverware, a beautiful Belle and a thrilling finale; fun for young and old.

The grandest grand finale is next door at **Fantasmic!**, which is based on the wild dreams of Mickey Mouse. Like most Disney extravaganzas, this is filled with lasers, lights, fireworks and characters. Seating begins an hour before show time. The amphitheater seats 6,900 guests and 3,000 standing, so you don't have to rush it. Just sit near the back so you have a great overall view of Mickey battling the forces of evil.

HIDDEN MICKEYS
There are lots of Mickey heads on the fence at the gates to Disney-MGM Studios

---

DISNEY-MGM STUDIOS: INSIDE INFO

Top tips If you are a Walt Disney World® Resort guest, **save this park for Tuesday or Saturday** when you can enter the Disney-MGM Studios an hour before opening time and see selected major attractions.

• Here, as in any Disney park, if it's too crowded in the afternoon return to your hotel and cool off with a swim. In peak season, **the parks are open later**, and you can always come back. Have your hand stamped and keep your ticket for readmission.

• The **Hollywood Boulevard parade** is usually themed to Disney's latest movie release ("Aladdin," "Mulan," "Pocahontas," etc.) and takes place at 3 pm. Stake your claim on the sidewalk (pavement) at least a half hour earlier.

• If you decide to put off the highlights for later, you can usually hit all the major attractions, **often without waiting**, in the 90 minutes before closing.

⬛ Disney's Animal Kingdom® Theme Park

Animal Kingdom® was the fourth Walt Disney World® Resort theme park to be built, but in terms of enjoyment it outperforms earlier arrivals Epcot® and Disney-MGM Studios.

Despite the themed architecture, shows, storylines and thrill rides, this is really a safari park at heart. You will have to see it at the animals' pace, so adjust your schedule accordingly. The biggest mistake is arriving late and rushing to the premier attraction, Kilimanjaro Safaris. After mid-morning, lines are ridiculously long and animals are taking cover to escape the heat.

Since Disney's Animal Kingdom® opens before the other parks (sometimes at 7 am or earlier), plan to safari early

Meeting the animals on safari is a highlight of the park

© Disney

✚ 229 A2 ☎ 407/824-4321 🕐 Daily 9–about an hour after dusk, but varies according to season (or much later) in the day and fill in the middle hours with shows, rides and indoor attractions. Don't think you are missing everything as you scurry from place to place. As in other parks, you will retrace your steps after hitting the highlights.

To simplify things, the park is divided into two major sections: Asia to your right and Africa to your left (other "lands" include **The Oasis**, **Safari Village**, **DinoLand U.S.A.** and **Camp Minnie-Mickey**).

From the bus stop or parking lot you will arrive at the ticket booths of the Entrance Plaza, which you can bypass if you bought tickets earlier. Lavatories, lockers and a mail drop are on your far left, with phones, lavatories, an ATM (cashpoint) and pet boarding facility on your right.

Morning

After the turnstiles, it's easy to get confused. You are in **The Oasis**, an area of trees and waterfalls that interferes with your natural desire to race to the first attractions. This is Disney's way of telling you to slow down. You will hear flutes, steel drums and waterfalls, and see banana trees, exotic birds, rare plants, orchids, hidden tunnels and small animals. All of this is meant to relax you. Let it.

After navigating The Oasis, you will cross a bridge to **Safari Village**. On your right is the premier store of the park, **Disney Outfitters**, a good stop when you leave the park, not now. Ahead is the park's focal point, the **Tree of Life**, a towering baobab tree with more than 325 animal images carved into the trunk. One of the greatest shows on earth is inside this tree, **"It's Tough To Be a Bug!,"** but save it for later. If you need park information, look to your right and there is an information board and a Disney host handing out maps and show schedules.

If the weather is cool to pleasantly warm, walk to the left of the tree and head to **Africa**. Just over the bridge you arrive in **Harambe Village**. It's too early to get a full meal at Tusker House Restaurant, so grab a pastry or a snack at the fruit-and-drink stand in the plaza.

You are heading for the **Kilimanjaro Safaris**, Africa's top attraction. The line should be relatively short (i.e. not out to the sidewalk), and while waiting to board your safari vehicle, you will see a video about threatened animals. The journey follows this storyline as you drive through a well-stocked reserve looking out for poachers as you try to photograph the black rhinos, lions, wildebeests, giraffes, crocodiles, hippos and other animals. You need a sharp eye: The driver can't stop for your pictures. Regardless, it's a fun – sometimes scary – trip.

Next, to hit **Asia's** top attraction you will need to retrace your path to the edge of Africa and turn left before crossing the bridge. If you pass soaking-wet people along the way, you are on the right track to the **Kali River Rapids**. Although most people save this for the hottest part of the day, they invariably get burned by a line more than 30 minutes long. If you're on schedule, it's only mid-morning and you should be able to board fairly quickly.

There are no lockers here, so stow your valuables inside a not-so-waterproof area in the middle of the circular raft. There's

HIDDEN MICKEYS

In Harambe Village there is a sack of grapefruit hanging from a window above the bathrooms. Three of the fruit facing the street are arranged into a perfect Mickey.

no way out as you float to the top of a hill and then set off on a bouncy, splashing, very moist whitewater tour through a rain forest and slash-and-burn logging camp. If you are not wet after some great falls, guests squirting you from a bridge will make sure you are.

A close encounter with a critter at DINOSAUR!

One more great ride and it's lunchtime. Leaving Asia, walk to your left and follow the signs to **DinoLand U.S.A**. The most exciting ride is **DINOSAUR!**, which is far less nauseating than simple motion simulators. Here you actually board a Jeep-like vehicle to travel back in time to retrieve a dinosaur for a scientist. Problems arise when you are transported back to three minutes before the dinosaurs are doomed by a meteor shower. Dodging projectiles and a very angry dinosaur makes this combination roller coaster/motion simulator a real scream.

Well, you've now hit the best attractions in Africa, Asia and DinoLand U.S.A. There's much more to see, but it's a good time to take a prerush lunch break.

TAKING A BREAK

On your right, outside DinoLand U.S.A, the gorgeous **Indonesian Flame Tree Barbecue** has one of the loveliest settings of any Walt Disney World® Resort restaurant. The garden-like atmosphere overlooks a lake, and colorful lanterns make a soothing backdrop for a leisurely lunch of salad, smoked chicken, ribs, pork and beef.

Afternoon

Following lunch, return to the Tree of Life (straight ahead) and follow it to your left again – not to Africa but a sharp left into **Camp Minnie-Mickey**. It's primarily for kids, but **Festival of the Lion King** appeals to everyone. This is easily the liveliest and most colorful stage show in the park. Inside the huge open-air theater is a multicultural carnival of music and motion as acrobats, singers, dancers, fire jugglers, stiltwalkers – and a few audience members – get in on the act.

After the show, you will find lavatories and phones to your left and character-greeting areas straight ahead. For the park's last highlight, return once again to the left side of the Tree of Life and look for the long and winding entrance to **"It's Tough To Be a Bug!"** This very funny 3-D movie adds sensory effects so you will receive the full impact of an acid-spraying termite, cockroaches, a wasp, tarantula, bug spray and, as if that wasn't enough, the fragrant gloom of a stinkbug. You could see this dozens of times and still not get enough, it's that much fun. Hint: Sit near the back and get the full effect.

It's around mid-afternoon now. You have circled the park, had lunch and seen the highlights. Check your schedule for show and parade times. Otherwise, from the movie's exit you will be at the entrance to DinoLand U.S.A., where you can begin a counterclockwise sweep of the park and drop in on other rides if the lines are short.

In **DinoLand U.S.A.**, a huge tent hides **Dinosaur Jubilee**, a collection of real dinosaur skeletons, including a huge prehistoric turtle and a Tyrannosaurus rex. **The Boneyard** is a kids' playground where they can dig up fossils and climb around until they're exhausted. Great if you want a break.

In **Asia**, the **Maharajah Jungle Trek** is hidden within the ruins of an ancient shrine. Inside is a beautiful (and sometimes crowded) walk-through attraction that does a terrific job of showcasing giant bats, tigers, deer, tapirs, komodo dragons and exotic birds. Guides from India are here to explain what you're looking at.

Back in **Africa**, the counterpart to the Jungle Trek is the **Pangani Forest Exploration Trail**. Here, the stars are naked mole rats (kinda creepy), birds and gorillas. Another follow-up, **Conservation Station**, is reached via the Eastern Star Railway Wildlife Express. This is where you can see – and possibly touch – more animals, many of which are being cared for by vets and researchers.

You may have time for another safari, an attack by a tarantula, a look at the tigers or any other attraction you have missed or loved. On your way out, stay to your right and treat yourself to dinner at the **Rainforest Café** (arrange priority seating earlier from Guest Relations). Kids love the audio-

HIDDEN MICKEYS

Inside a fenced storage area at Mammoth Dig, in The Boneyard, a fan and two hardhats create a Hidden Mickey.

"It's Tough To Be a Bug!"

animatronic elephants, gorillas and tigers stationed around the dining room, and adults like dishes that add a creative spin to ethnic cuisine. No one really likes the prices – which can border just above reasonable – but the food and the cool rain-forest setting are a nice way to wrap up a wild day.

DISNEY'S ANIMAL KINGDOM: INSIDE INFO

Top tips Walt Disney World® Resort guests can enter Animal Kingdom an hour earlier than other guests on a Monday or Friday.
• As you explore the park, look for the **subtle touches Disney is famous for**: leaf imprints in cement; details hidden within the Tree of Life; silks and brass bells hanging in the prayer trees of Asia; and literally thousands of artistic secrets.

© Disney

❶ Water Parks in Walt Disney World® Resort

With the Atlantic Ocean on Florida's east coast and the Gulf of Mexico to the west, why would you go to a Walt Disney World® Resort water park?

There are two good reasons: They are closer and cooler, and on a hot day they can be terrific fun. You may not have time to devote a full day to diving and splashing around, and if it's wintertime even the bright Florida sun won't warm up the waters much, but the water parks are a fun place to spend a few hours relaxing.

At their core, Typhoon Lagoon and Blizzard Beach are roughly the same. Each is themed and has water slides, lockers, a beach, a central lagoon, kiddie pools, snack bars and other concessions.

Taking the plunge at Blizzard Beach's Summit Plummet

© Disney

Bear in mind that a lot of swimming, diving and running are going to wear down the kids – although they won't necessarily show it until you leave the park. Try to schedule in a few hours to recuperate after you're done with your day in the water. For your day at the waterpark, you may also want to pack a few essentials such as toys, bottled drinks, towels, sunscreen lotion and snacks.

Typhoon Lagoon

The 56-acre (23-ha) Typhoon Lagoon is centered on the Surf Pool, which re-creates the appeal of the ocean by adding a sandy white beach and some pretty big waves that crash across the lagoon every few minutes. Less intense is Castaway Creek, where the most relaxing 45 minutes of your life begins when you hop into an inner tube and drift on a lazy river beneath a misty rain forest and through caves and grottoes. The most harrowing few seconds of your life may be on the Humunga Kowabunga, where you will reach speeds of up to 30mph (48kph) as you take a sheer drop on this very long water slide inside Mount Mayday.
✚ 229 B2 ☎ 407/560-4141

Blizzard Beach

Blizzard Beach follows the same formula by featuring a large wave pool, a slow river ride and areas for kids. The highlight here is Summit Plummet, a high-speed, 60-mph (96-kph) water slide. Teamboat Springs is fun in a different, less invasive way, since you get to sit inside a five-person raft as you speed down a 1,200-foot (365-m) series of waterfalls.
✚ 229 A1 ☎ 407/560-3400

③ Universal Orlando

Universal Orlando is an all-encompassing resort destination that includes the original movie theme park, Universal Studios; the fantasy theme park, Islands of Adventure; and the nightclub/restaurant district of CityWalk. Three luxury hotels – Portofino Bay, Royal Pacific and the Hard Rock Hotel – have generated an increase in quantity and quality that makes it hard to justify spending all your vacation time down the street at Disney.

Still in a quandary where to go? If time limits you to visiting one movie theme park (Universal Studios or the Disney-MGM Studios), pick Universal Studios – it's more energetic, more creative and more fun overall. Although it had a rocky start, the bumps have long been smoothed out and the rides are in equal parts exciting, terrifying, exhilarating, sickening and fun. Here's one way to approach it.

You never know who you'll meet at Universal Studios

Universal Studios

There are no trams here, just two massive multilevel parking lots (write down your space number) and a moving walkway to take you to CityWalk. From here you can walk straight ahead to reach Islands of Adventure (► 82) or to your right to reach the ticket kiosks of Universal Studios. Follow the lane to your right, over a bridge, under an arch and, after buying your tickets, through the turnstiles and you're in.

You may now feel crowded by other guests, but the lavatories and lockers to your left give you an excuse to duck out for a moment. Guest Services is to the right and can help make dining reservations, provide foreign-language maps, hold items for lost and found, and care for lost children. You may be tempted to visit **Nickelodeon Studios**, but considering that they no longer tape shows here (they only re-create them for tourists), you can probably find better things to do.

A small plaza on your right gives you room to concentrate, so take a moment here and review your map and show schedule. Unlike other theme parks, sections here are loosely defined and may be difficult to distinguish. Your best bet is to just ignore the section names and blitz the park, hitting the popular attractions as quickly as possible. This will mean circling the park twice, visiting premier attractions on your first trip and picking up the strays and revisiting your favorites on the second loop.

Early Start

If you arrived early, you will notice other guests are heading left toward Twister…Ride It Out. Resist temptation, walk to the next corner, turn right and go to **Terminator 2: 3-D Battle**

Terminator 2: 3-D condenses two hours of thrills into 12 minutes

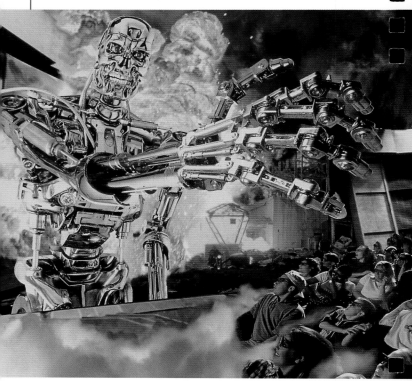

Across Time. This attraction, based on the films starring Arnold Schwarzenegger, will jump-start your day. A demonstration of law-enforcing robots goes awry and triggers a high-energy, 100-mph (160-kph), 12-minute series of 3-D special effects, filmed scenes and live action that ends in a very loud and chilly grand finale. Better than a night at the movies, this attraction promises to have you buzzing all day.

If you are hungry, when you exit turn left and grab a quick pastry at the Beverly Hills Boulangerie, or turn right and pick up a snack (ice cream, soft drink or sandwich) at Schwab's Pharmacy. You may not want to wait, though, since you can hightail it to the far end of the park to **Back to the Future: The Ride** – in just a few hours the line will be as long as the Great

Wall of China. With virtual reality rides cropping up everywhere, you may feel this is more of the same. It's lots of fun, however, if you don't mind being pitched, rolled and slammed back and forth as you travel via an eight-passenger DeLorean to the past, present and future. The 70-foot (21.5-m) screen removes all sense of space, so, depending on the strength of your stomach, the ride is proportionally more thrilling or more nauseating.

One more must-see is **Men in Black: Alien Attack**, an interactive ride through dark city streets where you fire a laser gun at aliens who pop up from unexpected places. The only way you know if you've zapped an alien, however, is a readout on your "training vehicle" console.

Midmorning

It should only be around 10:30 am now, and with another must-see attraction you have hit nearly half the park. Based on the film, **Jaws** starts as a gentle boat ride on the waters of Amityville...at least until a shark (surprise!) breaks the surface. Even though you know the fish is fake and the explosions are rigged, several surprise attacks by this monster will scare you silly. Adding to the effect, the heat of exploding fuel tanks and crackling electrical lines mean things can become uncomfortably warm.

At the ride's exit, turn right and bypass the midway games that suck kids in like a whirlpool. Your goal should be **Earthquake – The Big One**, a seriously scary experience just a few feet down the street. An audience participation preshow demonstrates how special effects were created for the film, after which you enter a subway train that rolls into a darkened station. It's no surprise when things start to shake, rattle and roll, but wait for the adrena-

Visitors can follow the fortunes of Shrek and Princess Fiona in Shrek 4-D

line rush when the attraction starts falling to pieces above, below and all around you. A definite stop worth waiting for even if there is a line.

A few blocks ahead, is **Revenge of the Mummy**. Entering an Egyptian tomb, you'll walk past hieroglyphics and artifacts and then step into a roller coaster that takes you deeper into the realm of the dead. What follows is a jolting, twisting, turning, wrenching, back-and-forth ride in the dark where you're subjected to an infestation of beetles, flames, smoke, and fog. Caution: Leave all loose items behind; they'll all be thrown overboard.

Keep going. You'll have fun at **Twister...Ride It Out** – the attraction that everyone else raced for earlier in the morning. After the preshow, you will be ushered before a bucolic country scene. It all goes crazy when an ominous funnel cloud appears on the horizon. The tornado takes center stage and kicks off a catastrophic cacophony of flying cows, lightning strikes and wails from kids who find the action too real.

TAKING A BREAK

Congratulations. It's probably around noon now and you've circled the entire park (and missed only a few major rides), and you may want to break for lunch. Across from Twister, the **Classic Monster Café** serves pizza, pasta and salads. A more pleasing option is rewarding yourself with lunch at a table-service restaurant.

Backtrack two blocks, turn left at Delancey Street and drop in at **Finnegan's Bar & Grill**. Irish stew, bangers and mash or shepherd's pie will set you back about $10, and there is a neat little pub in the back. Across from Earthquake, **Lombard's Landing** serves steak, seafood, pasta and sandwiches. If you dine here, take a table outside if the weather is right. If you don't have time for CityWalk later, skip these two and eat at the **Hard Rock Café**. You will have to exit the Studios (be sure to get your hand stamped for reentry) and turn right. The line moves quickly, the service is good, the dishes are original, and the prices are fair. The crowning glory is the rock memorabilia, which ranges from a stained-glass trinity of Elvis, Chuck Berry and Jerry Lee Lewis to the second-floor Beatles room, which includes cut-outs from Sgt. Pepper's album cover, Paul McCartney's hand-written lyrics to "Let It Be" and John Lennon's "New York City" T-shirt.

Midafternoon

The park is now as crowded as it's going to get. Slow your pace as you pick up the remaining attractions and return to your favorites.

Straight down the street from the entrance, are two new rides. The first is **Jimmy Neutron's Nicktoon Blast**, a virtual reality ride where the boy genius is joined by a large collection of Nickelodeon characters including SpongeBob SquarePants and the Rugrats. The ride features computer graphics and high-tech motion-based seats to give you the sensation of zipping through a cartoon universe with a large assortment of characters. On the right, **Shrek 4-D** is an animated saga starring the cartoon characters and their vocal counterparts Mike Myers, Eddie Murphy, Cameron Diaz and John Lithgow. When Shrek and Princess Fiona leave for a honeymoon, the ghost of Lord Farquaad interrupts their plans. This puts you in the middle of an aerial dogfight between fire-breathing dragons and includes a plunge down a 1,000-foot (305-m) waterfall.

The Revenge of the Mummy is the park's latest thrilling ride

Left: Join Jimmy Neutron in saving the world

Warning: Avoid these (and other motion simulators) if you have a weak stomach.

At the exit, head past **Twister** and **The Boneyard** (a collection of old props from forgettable movies) to reach the many refreshment kiosks and concession stands along the way. Also, check the show schedule inside your park map, and you may arrive in time for several shows presented on this side of the park. The Blues Brothers (two actors who look like them) perform outside Finnegan's. In an amphitheater off the streets of New York, **Beetlejuice's Graveyard Review** is a popular, though offbeat, show that features classic monsters singing Motown songs.

On nearly the opposite side of the park, just beyond Back to the Future, **Animal Planet Live!** is based on the popular network's programming. The stars here are incredibly smart animals that push the limits on the cute-o-meter.

When you leave Animal Planet Live!, you will notice kids are lured to the left by **E.T. Adventure, Fievel's Playland, A Day in the Park with Barney** and **Curious George Goes to Town**. If you don't have kids, there is no reason to be here. If you do, you have no choice. E.T. is the most popular ride here, a fantasy trip to the alien's home planet that concludes with a personal greeting. Barney's is a sing-along show, where you will be impressed by preschoolers' knowledge of the purple multi-billionaire's song catalog. If it's a hot day, don't miss Curious George, a super, soaking, splashing water attraction. Fievel's is a colorful

Combined Passes

- **Four-park Orlando Flex-ticket** – up to 14 consecutive days of unlimited admission to SeaWorld Orlando, Universal Studios Florida, Universal Studios Islands of Adventure and Wet 'n Wild water park. Tickets are non-transferable. Adult: $179.95, child (age 3–9): $145.95
- **Five-park Orlando flex ticket** – same as above, but includes admission to Busch Gardens. Adult: $214.95, child (age 3–9): $179.95
- **Orlando value ticket** – includes one-day each at Busch Gardens Tampa Bay and SeaWorld Orlando. Adult: $85.95, child (age 3–9): $72.95

playground where kids can enjoy things to climb up, slide down and crawl through. Not only does it give you a chance to rest, it helps train them for a prospective military career.

Dusk
With darkness falling, it's a good time to drop in at the last attraction, **The Universal Horror Make-Up Show**. If you are a fan of horror movies, this will be like visiting the Smithsonian. If not, you will still get a kick out of the blending of comedy and creepy special effects.

The Incredible
Hulk Coaster

You've done it all now – and hopefully had the sense to go off schedule and wander into the numerous gift shops, snack stands, unscheduled shows and back alleys. After a few miles of walking, resting by the lagoon with an ice cream may be more fun than being attacked by a shark.

Islands of Adventure
Maybe it helped that creative consultant Steven Spielberg offered his advice, because Islands of Adventure's rides, creativity and presentation give Disney a run for its money.

The five separate "islands" comprising Universal Orlando's second theme park are geared toward different areas of interest, so your agenda will vary according to the age level of your group.

Unlike at Universal Studios, the layout here makes it extremely easy to get your bearings and navigate the park.

The entrance is the most colorful and exotic of any theme park – a montage of architecture, landscaping and music from Asia, Africa, India and Europe that takes you out of Florida and into the heart of an adventure. In the plaza, as in every single square inch of the park, there is a contrived storyline: You are an explorer who can buy provisions before embarking on your journey. Just know that you can find film, strollers (pushchairs) and wheelchairs as well as snacks to get started.

After passing the plaza, kids will exert more force than the pull of the sun if they catch an eyeful of Seuss Landing (► 85). The very cool tribute to the good doctor is a masterpiece of design, but try to leave it until the end. Instead turn left and into **Marvel Super Hero Island**, where bold primary colors put you right in the thick of a comic book.

You are walking beneath an extension of the **Incredible Hulk Coaster**, which, unlike slowly accelerating roller-coasters, has a 150-foot-long (45.5-m) glow-in-the-dark tube that catapults you from 0 to 40mph (65kph) in less than two seconds. After being shot out of the barrel, the coaster skims over the water and twists through five inversions before the two-minute ride leaves you frazzled.

Buildings in this surreal land are affixed with comic-book labels. Look to your left for **Doctor Doom's Fearfall** that rapidly hoists you 200 feet (61m) into the air and drops you down again. As you continue, you will find that each ride tries to out-excite the others. You will probably never find a ride as exciting or as fun as The **Amazing Adventures of Spider-Man**. Even when the rest of the park is quiet, the line here is usually long – and for good reason. There is nothing like it anywhere else in the world. Somehow, it combines the technology of Terminator, Back to the Future and pyrotechnics to fool your senses and put you in the middle of a search for the Statue of Liberty. A strange storyline and a very long wait, but it's worth it just to experience the grand finale – a 400-foot (122-m) sensory drop. There's far more than this going on during the few minutes you are inside, but you have to see it to believe it.

Ahead, a bridge leads to **Toon Lagoon**, inspired by the Sunday comics. **Popeye and Bluto's Bilge-Rat Barges** is a whitewater rafting excursion that contends with obstacles, including octopuses, and kids firing water guns at passengers

from Popeye's boat. Ahead on the left, **Dudley Do-Right's Ripsaw Falls** is a water-flume ride that drops 75 feet (23m) below the surface of the water and into the TNT shack as the Canadian Mountie tries to save his beloved Nell.

Camp Jurassic is the next island and the park's halfway point. Overhead, **Pteranodon Flyers** is a ski-lift-like aerial ride – except that passengers overlook Camp Jurassic from beneath the 10-foot (3-m) wingspan. At this island's premier attraction, the **Jurassic Park River Adventure**, you drift past docile dinosaurs before taking a wrong turn and encountering aggressive "spitters" and a *Tyrannosaurus rex* – and now your only escape is via a very steep 85-foot (26-m) drop. Around the corner at **Jurassic Park Discovery Center**, an interactive area helps kids extract the last scintilla of information about dinosaurs.

From here, the bridge crosses to **The Lost Continent**, which is an intriguing blend of myths and legends. Music of old England, Arabic tents and the Alchemy Bar set the stage, and the hypercool Enchanted Oak Tavern (inside a massive oak tree) is like dining inside Sherwood Forest (although the quality of the food can be suspect).

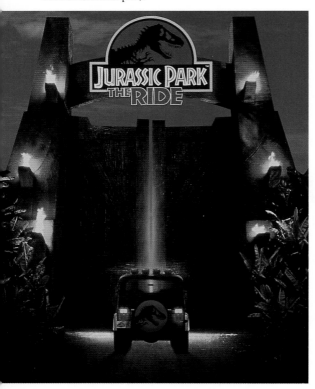

Movies turned rides: Islands of Adventure's winning formula

Two attractions here are worth seeing: **Dueling Dragons** is a twin roller-coaster featuring Fire Dragon (red) and Ice Dragon (blue), whose fight for power finds the intertwining coasters racing by each other at 60mph (96kph), passing within a foot of the other passengers. To make these close calls even closer, a computer weighs the cars to ensure near misses. At **The Eighth Voyage**

of Sindbad, the fabled sailor embarks on a stunt show that includes water explosions, fire dives, shipwrecks and pyrotechnical effects, all staged in a shaded 1,700-seat theater. Before leaving The Lost Continent, look for the feet of the Colossus of Rhodes and you are at **Poseidon's Fury**, a show that starts with a water vortex and concludes with a battle between Zeus and Poseidon.

The final island, **Seuss Landing**, is by far the most visually appealing. Nothing is linear and every image you've seen in the books is presented here in marvelous 3-D to put you inside some of the best children's books ever written. From the Hop on Pop Ice Cream Shop to the Green Eggs and Ham Café to the Caro-Seuss-el, the presentation is a perfect tribute.

One Fish Two Fish Red Fish Blue Fish lets kids guide their Seuss-style fish up or down – depending on the instructional rhyme they follow (if they don't get it right, they get squirted by a flying fish). **A Hat-Full of Fun** is a trip through the classic "The Cat in the Hat" with 130 ride effects and 30 animated characters including, naturally, the Cat in the Hat, Thing 1 and Thing 2.

UNIVERSAL ORLANDO: INSIDE INFO

Top tips The **"Orlando Magicard"** is free and will save you money on hotels, lodgings, car rentals and so on. You can get your free card at the Orlando Visitors Center, 8723 International Drive (Gala Shopping Center). The Orlando tourism office can also mail you a card in advance if you call 407/363-5872 or 800/897-5439. The center is open daily 8–7; ticket sales close at 6.

• If you can swing it, stay at one of Universal Orlando's resort hotels (Portofino Bay and Hard Rock Hotel). You'll save hours with **special privileges** such as early admission to the parks, VIP access to the front of some lines, character dining, priority seating at restaurants and the option of an unlimited-access ticket.

• Use the **Universal Express system**: pick up a free pass at any kiosk and you can reserve a place in line which allows you to see other attractions, have a meal or take a break. Now you just have to return in time to claim priority admission to the ride – a major time-saver.

• **For a great shortcut**, follow signs to "valet" and for around $12 (double regular parking), you can park next to the main ticket booth. Not only is your car safer, it's much closer if you need anything from it during the day.

• Many of the motion rides have **height requirements of 40 inches (1m)**. If you are an expectant mother, have a weak heart or a back condition, don't plan on riding any of the motion simulators or rollercoasters.

• All rides have a **"baby exchange area"** where, after standing in line, one parent can ride and then take over parenting duties so the other can ride without having to wait in line again.

Getting to Universal Orlando

To reach Universal Orlando from Disney, head east on I–4 about a mile (1.6km) past the International Drive exit. Take Exit 75A on the right, and at the light turn left. From Orlando, head west on I–4 and take Exit 74B to the right. Follow signs.
➕ 228 C4 ☎ 407/363-8000; www.usf.com or www.universalorlando.com ⊙ Daily: Universal Studios 9–8; Islands of Adventure 9 am–10 pm, with extended summer, holiday and weekend hours 💲 Expensive; parking moderate

② SeaWorld Orlando

The third installment of Orlando's theme-park trilogy is based on the sea and its inhabitants, and man's relationship with them. Though there's no flash and thunder in the manner of Disney and Universal, this oceanic theme park is worth at least the better part of a day and probably longer. You'll find yourself getting an education even if you aren't aware of it.

After winding your way to the toll plaza ($6), you will park and then be taken by tram to a seaside village where you can purchase tickets at one of three kiosks. Once inside, go straight ahead to the information desk for a park map and schedule of the day's shows. Take a moment to review show times and plan your day. Keep in mind that (A) SeaWorld's design involves backtracking; and (B) the major attractions are not rides but shows. Most shows' finishing times conveniently allow you about 10–15 minutes to reach the next performance venue.

The best bet is a clockwise sweep of the park. Begin by passing through the park's version of Key West, where street performers are the featured attraction, and areas where you can feed and touch a stingray or a dolphin.

Manatees: The Last Generation? is a rather sedate presentation, worth it if only to see a sea cow, a distant aquatic relative of the elephant. More impressive is the 30-minute show at the **Key West Dolphin Stadium**. The theme changes periodically, but the tricks (jumping, diving, splashing, etc.) remain the same.

Journey to Atlantis is a water-coaster based on a battle between Hermes and Allura. It's great if you don't have to wait long, otherwise you may be disappointed by the lack of steep drops. Warning: You will get soaked either by the ride or by guests who fire water cannons at you when you float by.

SeaWorld's second coaster, **Kraken,** is named for an underwater beast kept caged by the Greek god Poseidon. This is the fastest (65mph/105kph), tallest (151 feet/46m) and longest (4,177 feet/1,273m) rollercoaster in Orlando. You go through seven inversions – including a Cobra roll, zero-gravity roll and numerous vertical loops and flat spins.

TAKING A BREAK

Although they are not the park's best restaurants (the full-service Bimini Bay near the park entrance is), both the **Buccaneer Smokehouse** and **Mama Stella's Italian Kitchen** are nearby and serve typical park food. You may want to stop for a bite at **The Waterfront**. A collection of shops, kiosks and cafés, this lakeside setting is a good place to dine on a gourmet pizza alfresco while being entertained by street performers.

Continuing on, just bypass **Penguin Encounter** and **Pacific Point Preserve** (unless you like penguins and seals). The show at the **Sea Lion and Otter Stadium** is fun, and you should arrive early to catch the excellent preshow performance by the mime.

By now you should have covered nearly half the park. If time is tight, forget **Terrors of the Deep** but consider dining on Floribbean and Caribbean cuisine at **Sharks Underwater Grill**. The cavernous restaurant, with its underwater grotto, is reminiscent of the lair of a James Bond villain. Three tiers of

Ticket options
Adults (10 and over) $53.95 plus tax, children (3–9) $44.95 plus tax. Validate your ticket before leaving the park and you can return for a **second day free**. A **FlexTicket** will be your best bet to see parks outside Walt Disney World® Resort. See Universal Orlando (► 81) for details of four- and five-park tickets.

Above: Aquatic shows, not rides, are the foundation of SeaWorld

Right: Dolphins are always looking for a handout

booths and tables front five bay windows that expose a 660,000-gal (2.5 million-L) aquarium filled with multiple species of sharks. Quite memorable (and fairly expensive).

You can sample a free beer or two at the Anheuser-Busch Hospitality Center and see the famed Clydesdale horses in the adjoining stables, and then move on to the **Arcade** (midway games), **Shamu's Splash Attack** (a water-splash area) and **Shamu's Happy Harbor**. If you have kids, you will have to stop at this maze of nets and tunnels and ropes. Next, head to **Shamu Stadium** and try to catch the final show, **"Shamu Rocks America,"** a loud, high-energy grand finale to the day. The first 14 rows are a "splash zone." With his massive fluke, Shamu drenches guests with tons of his bath water.

One of the park's killer whales thrills the audience

SEAWORLD ORLANDO: INSIDE INFO

Top tips Perhaps the best way to wrap up the day is a night of entertainment at **Makahiki Luau** (tel: 800/327-2420). The evening begins with a welcome drink, a quick hula lesson, and the arrival of the Grand Kahuna. The family-friendly stage show includes sing-alongs and spectacular displays of fire torch twirling.
• **Discovery Cove**, next to SeaWorld Orlando, is a man-made creation of colorful coral reefs teeming with thousands of tropical fish, underwater ruins, tropical rivers and gleaming white sands. The big draw is the chance to swim and play with Atlantic bottle-nosed dolphins. Tel: 877/434-7268 for advance reservations; www.discoverycove.com
• If you are traveling with kids, you may want to **bring along bathing suits and towels** for the inevitable visit to Splash Attack.
• Don't wear heels or sandals – you might get your feet wet on the water rides. **Sneakers are the best bet** for comfort and safety.

Getting to SeaWorld Orlando

From Walt Disney World®, travel 10 minutes east on I–4, take Exit 71 and follow the signs. From downtown, head 15 minutes west on I–4 to the Beeline Expressway (Exit 72), take the first exit on the right and follow the signs.

✚ 229 C3 ☎ 407/351-3600 or 800/423-3688; www.seaworld.com
🕐 Daily 9–7; extended hours summer, holiday and weekend

At Your Leisure

4 Loch Haven Cultural Center

A few blocks east of Antique Row is a museum and science center that, depending on your interest, can keep you entertained for a few hours or longer.

Orlando Museum of Art

The 20,000-sq-foot (1,860sq-m) Orlando Museum of Art displays the works of nationally and world-renowned artists and frequently presents exhibitions, tours and classes.

On permanent display is an intriguing collection of primarily American work – 19th- and early 20th-century American Impressionists; a gallery showcasing three centuries of American portraits and landscapes from the Colonial era to the early 20th century; the popular Art of the Ancient Americas; and contemporary art.

Occasionally this museum gets a major traveling exhibition. Guests, such as photographer Ansel Adams and lifestyle guru Martha Stewart, have dropped by to display their talents.

➕ 228 D5 ✉ 2416 N. Mills Avenue, I-4 to Exit 85, head east ☎ 407/896-4231; www.omart.org 🕐 Tue–Sat 10–5, Sun noon–5; closed Mon and major holidays 💰 Inexpensive. Parking free

Orlando Science Center

Shows are particularly educational and entertaining, and appeal to curious children and intrigued adults. The highlight of the plentiful hands-on exhibits and experiments may be a pulley-system display that allows a kid to hoist a Volkswagen single-handed. A tour of the human body will have you entering **BodyZone**SM through a giant mouth – you'll have to go there to find out where the exit is. **TechWorks** offers a chance to create imaginary landscapes using models, simulation and computers, while **ShowBiz Science** puts you in the middle of movies so you can hang off the side of a building, set the mood

Hands-on experiments attract kids to the Orlando Science Center

with lighting and learn the secrets of special make-up effects. If you're under 4 feet (1.2m) tall, you will enjoy **KidsTown**SM, a giant science-related playground. The **Crosby Observatory** has Florida's largest publicly accessible refractor telescope. For an additional fee, you can take in IMAX films on coral reefs, space and the Lewis and Clark expedition.

➕ 228 D5 ✉ 777 E. Princeton Street, I-4 to Exit 85, head east ☎ 407/514-2000 or 888/OSC-4FUN; www.osc.org 🕐 Mon–Thu 9–5, Fri–Sat 9–9, Sun noon–5; closed Mon during school year 💰 Inexpensive; parking inexpensive

5 Antique Row Shopping

The North Orange Avenue Antique District boasts an eclectic array of antique and collectible shops, vintage clothing boutiques, art galleries, outdoor cafés and blue-collar bars. For several blocks south of Princeton Avenue, the shops display a wide variety of goods. If you are a collector, it's worth a few hours.

A must-see is Rock 'n' Roll Heaven (1814 N. Orange Avenue, tel: 407/896-1952), an awesome record shop with venerable vinyl disks and an assortment of collectible toys.

➕ 228 D5 ✉ Orange Avenue (between Princeton and Magnolia streets), I-4 to Exit 85, east one block to Orange Avenue, right ⏰ Daily. Many shops closed Sun

6 Harry P. Leu Gardens

If it's a peaceful afternoon and photo opportunities you're after, this is as good as it gets in the city. This 50-acre (20-ha) garden oasis in the heart of Orlando features the Harry P. Leu homestead, oak-shaded scenic walkways, an orchid conservatory, the largest camellia collection in eastern North America and the largest formal rose garden in Florida. The Garden House, near the shores of Lake Rowena, re-creates a Southern manor home and offers a quiet place to relax and enjoy a romantic view.

Leu Gardens is designed for peaceful reflection

Along the pathways you'll find a huge variety of plants, including beautyberries, bottle brushes, bromeliads, firecracker plants, crinums, dogwoods, flame vines, impatiens, sweet alyssum and violas. Throughout the year, they host special events including the Friends of Florida Folk Concerts and seasonal displays that highlight winter-blooming annuals.

➕ 228 E5 ✉ 1920 North Forest Avenue, I-4 to Exit 85, head east to 17/92, right to Virginia Drive, left about 2.5 miles (4km) ☎ 407/246-2620; www.leugardens.org ⏰ Daily 9–5, longer hours in summer 💲 Inexpensive

7 Orange Avenue

Downtown stores and nightspots pop up and turn over faster than hot pastries. The trendy restaurants and fine clothiers of the late 1980s have been replaced by fast-food restaurants, tattoo parlors and nightclubs that cater to post-teens. Most bars are large and dark and serve beer, but may be worth visiting if you want to see how the locals socialize.

➕ 228 D5 ✉ I-4 to Exit 83, east three blocks

8 Orange County Regional History Center

If you want to know what Orlando looked like before the Mouse, check out the local archives, which contain a large selection of historic Central Florida photographs, souvenirs and relics rescued when the original City Beautiful was dismantled in favor of what you see today.

In 2000, the old county courthouse was renovated to become home to this collection, which includes exhibits telling the story of the area's natural environment, Seminole Indian population, early settlers, the cattle and citrus industries, the advent of tourism, Florida's Space Age and the arrival of Disney.

➕ 228 D5 ✉ Downtown at Heritage Square Park (Central Boulevard and Magnolia Avenue) ☎ 407/836-8500; www.thehistorycenter.org ⏰ Mon–Sat 10–5, Sun noon–5 💲 Inexpensive

9 Lake Eola Park

Lake Eola Park is the beauty mark of downtown Orlando. In vintage postcards you'll see families and lovers walking hand-in-hand around Lake Eola or sitting beneath the stars enjoying a band concert. Decades later, not much has changed. It takes about 30 minutes to circle the park, but slow your pace and soak up the

scenery or pick up your pace and pedal one of the charming swan boats out to the fountain. This watery work of art lights up at night and changes color schemes, making a dramatic backdrop for the amphitheater where you can see Shakespeare in the Park, comedy shows or orchestral performances.

At the south end of the park there are plentiful oak trees where families and lovers relax, and to the southeast there's a playground. Across the street to the northeast is the trendy Eo Inn, which features the equally trendy sidewalk café of the Panera Bread shop. To the west, convenient concession stands are open year round from 10:30–6.

🚩 228 D5 ✉ Downtown, Rosalind Avenue and Central Boulevard I-4 to Exit 83 ☎ 407/246-2827 💵 Inexpensive

⑩ Thornton Park

A few blocks east of Lake Eola, Thornton Park is a small business/residential district of 1920s homes, sidewalk cafés and casual restaurants, where Orlando's young professionals are creating a quasi-Coconut Grove. It's a great place to take a walk, relax with a drink, enjoy an evening meal and see classic Arts and Crafts homes and beautiful Eola Park.

🚩 228 D5 ✉ Washington and Summerlin avenues

The dramatic white amphitheater at downtown Orlando's Lake Eola Park

⑪ Hard Rock Vault

If you're interested in rock memorabilia, then this is the place for you. After decades spent acquiring "the world's largest and most renowned rock 'n' roll memorabilia collection," the Hard Rock has found a place for its abundant stash of stuff: Orlando. At this 17,000-square-foot (1,580sq-m) museum you can view hundreds of items, including a costume worn by Gene Simmons of Kiss, a dress from Stevie Nicks of Fleetwood Mac, Michael Jackson's red "Beat It" jacket and Jim Morrison's leather pants. A few of the more unusual items include a faux electric chair used by the metal band Disturbed, and a quilt made of underwear thrown on stage at Frank Zappa concerts. Add to this a large collection of guitars donated by stars such as Bo Diddley, John Lennon and Elvis Presley. Stick around and record a karaoke-style CD in a replica of the legendary Sun Studios.

🚩 229 C3 ✉ 8437 International Drive ☎ 407/599-7625; www.hardrock.com/vault 🕐 Daily 9 am–midnight 💵 Adults: moderate; children ages 5–12: inexpensive

ⓑ International Drive

When Disney arrived, this was just a lonely little road with one hotel. Today the billboard boulevard is a mecca for tourists searching for outlet bargains, fast-food restaurants, hotel chains, entertainment and family attractions to complement their sunny vacations.

Wet 'n Wild

This theme park is a maze of water slides designed for the thrill of slipping and sliding. Shallow areas have been set aside for kids, but bigger kids looking for adrenaline-pumping action will want to hit **Bomb Bay**, **Der Stuka** or **Hydra Fighter**, a thrill ride that combines the exhilaration of a bungee jump with the power of a water cannon. Changing facilities and snack bars are plentiful, but you can also bring a picnic.

🔲 229 C3 ✉ 6200 International Drive, I-4 to Exit 75A ☎ 407/351-1800; www.wetnwild.com 🕐 Hours vary seasonally 💷 Moderate (half price after 3). Parking and lockers inexpensive. See SeaWorld Orlando, page 87, for additional ticket options

Ripley's Believe It or Not!

It's hard to miss Ripley's Believe It or Not! Just look for the bizarre lopsided building dropping into the ground. The "odd-itorium" is filled with camp, kitsch, gross and bizarre novelties collected from around the world by Robert Ripley – all strangely entertaining.

🔲 229 C3 ✉ 8201 International Drive, Exit 74A ☎ 407/363-4418 or 800/998-4418; www.ripleys.com 🕐 Daily 9 am–1 am 💷 Inexpensive

Belz Factory Outlet World

The idea is that you can buy brand-name merchandise at discount prices because manufacturers are selling items in a low-overhead store. If you believe you can find a deal, check out the two malls, four annexes and more than 170 stores of this enormous complex. It is possible to get discounts of 30 to 60 percent off regular prices. Although this is just shopping, it has become a tourist attraction in itself.

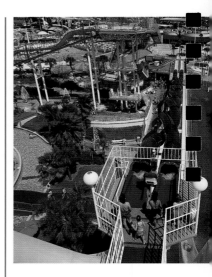

Hot summers are the time to make a splash at Wet 'n Wild

🔲 228 C4 ✉ 5401 W. Oak Ridge Road (northern end of International Drive), Exit 75A (eastbound) ☎ 407/354-0126; www.belz.com 🕐 Mon–Sat 10–9, Sun 11–6

WonderWorks

Going one better than Ripley's, this unusual building is completely upside down. Inside, interactive games geared toward kids (but equally appealing to adults) let you experience the winds of a hurricane or sit in a diner as a 5.3 Richter scale earthquake hits. Virtual-reality games and hands-on science exhibits round out this educational/entertainment experience. One price is good for all exhibits, all day, with an additional fee if you want to play **LazerWorks**, a laser tag game.

➕ 229 C3 ✉ 9067 International Drive,
Pointe*Orlando, Exit 74A ☎ 407/352-
0411; www.wonderworksonline.com
🕐 Daily 9 am–midnight
💲 Inexpensive

🔢 Gatorland

Gatorland bills itself as the
Alligator Capital of the World.
It has earned the right,
considering it is also one
of Florida's oldest
attractions. Here
since 1949, it is
now a breeding
farm. About
1,000 alligators
crawl around
these wetlands
alongside croc-
odiles, reptiles
and snakes,
showing their
strength in
shows such as Gator
Wrestlin' and Gator Jumparoo.

For a native delicacy, go
to Pearl's Smokehouse and
try gator ribs or gator
nuggets, then duck into the
gift shop for a sampling of old-
fashioned Florida souvenirs.
➕ 229 D2 ✉ 14501 S. Orange Blossom Trail
(Kissimmee), US 441 north
☎ 407/855-5496 or 800/393-JAWS;
www.gatorland.com 🕐 Daily 9–dusk
💲 Adults: moderate; children 3–12:
inexpensive

**A Van Gogh created
from a wall of
postcards at Ripley's**

**Left: A recycled
robot. Believe It
or Not!**

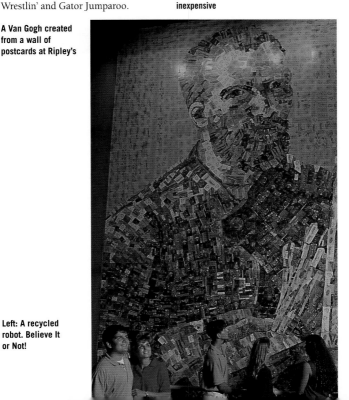

Classic aircraft, restored and ready to fly at Kissimmee's Flying Tigers

The Donelly House in charming Mount Dora

🔟 Flying Tigers Warbird Restoration Museum

If you have a passion for vintage airplanes, drive about 10 miles (16km) south to Kissimmee, where you will find World War II aircraft that have been – or are being – lovingly restored. After restoration, some planes leave for other destinations, but there are always dozens on display. If you have time, enrol in their restoration school.

Next door at **Warbird Adventures**, you can even fly in the front cockpit of a World War II T-6 trainer (a Harvard).

🔢 229 C1 ✉ 231 N. Hoagland Road (Kissimmee Airport) ☎ 407/933-1942; www.warbirdmuseum.com
🕐 Daily 9–5:30 💲 Inexpensive

Farther Afield

🔟 Mount Dora

About 30 miles (48km) northwest of Orlando is the charming New England-style village of Mount Dora. The town was founded by Northern settlers in the 1870s on a low rise overlooking the waterfront. Thanks to a local resident who knew the governor, a new highway was routed around the small town in the late 1950s. Although it delayed downtown

commercial growth for three decades, it preserved the village and eventually outsiders rediscovered the untarnished town. Resting on the shores of a 4,500-acre (1,800-ha) lake, the soft hills, quiet neighborhoods and thriving shopping village perfectly capture a slice of small-town America.

Chamber of Commerce
🔢 224 C4 ✉ 341 Alexander Street, Mount Dora ☎ 352/383-2165; www.mountdora.com 🕐 Mon–Fri 9–5, Sat 10–4

🔟 Gatorland

OSCEOLA PARKWAY

IRLO BRONSON MEMORIAL HIGHWAY

Kissimmee

Flying Tigers Warbird Restoration Museum 🔟

16 Central Florida Zoological Park

If you would like to see a collection of native Florida creatures such as alligators and black bears, along with an arkful of zoo regulars, drive about 20 miles

(32km) north of Orlando to Sanford and spend a couple of hours strolling the boardwalk through different types of Florida habitats to see 400 varieties of native and exotic animals.

➕ 225 D4 ✉ 3755 US 17/92, Sanford, I-4 west from Orlando, Exit 104, follow signs 200 yards (180m) east ☎ 407/323-4450; www.centralfloridazoo.org
🕐 Daily 9–5 💲 Inexpensive

17 Wekiwa Springs State Park

Few places in Orlando rival this park's natural beauty. It's full of places to hike, picnic, fish, camp and swim. The spring-fed water stays a frigid 72–74°F (22–23°C) year round, but diving 15 feet (4.5m) down to peer into the gushing mouth of the spring is worth the goose bumps. Canoeing is a must and rentals are available just beyond the bridge (tel: 407/880-4110, inexpensive first two hours).

➕ 224 C4 ✉ 1800 Wekiwa Circle, Apopka, I-4 east to Exit 94, left to Wekiwa Springs Road, turn right, drive 4 miles (6km) to park entrance on right ☎ 407/884-2008 🕐 Daily 8–sunset
💲 Per car: inexpensive

18 Cypress Gardens Adventure Park

Pastoral Cypress Gardens in Winter Haven was considered to be Florida's first theme park. When it closed in 2003, it was missed so much that, word went out and an entrepreneur

stepped in. Now the botanical park has reopened with the unusual addition of thrill rides, resulting in a mix of peaceful garden paths and screaming fast coasters. For peace and quiet, step into the butterfly arboretum and the colorful gardens. For high-energy excitement, check out nearly 40 rides that include four new rollercoasters and the world's tallest spinning rapids ride.

➕ 224 C2 ✉ Cypress Gardens Boulevard, Winter Haven ☎ 863/324-2111; www.cypressgardens.com
🕐 Daily 9:30–5 💲 Moderate

19 Bok Tower Gardens

For a half day of sightseeing, pack up a picnic and travel 50 miles (80km) southwest of Orlando to Bok Tower, set right in the middle of one of Florida's true treasures, the citrus groves. The spiritual beauty of this sanctuary, a National Historic Landmark garden, has been welcoming visitors since 1929. The centerpiece of the gardens is one of the world's greatest carillon towers. Housed inside the pink and gray Georgia marble and Florida coquina of this 205-foot (62-m) bell tower, the bells will soothe your soul as you lie upon the lawn or stroll the garden paths. The park hosts special events and has a gift shop, visitor and education center and café. You can also tour **Pinewood Estate**, a 1930s-style Mediterranean Revival home with French, Italian and Spanish antique furnishings.

The grounds that surround the bell tower draw visitors to Bok Tower Gardens

➕ 224 C2 ✉ 1151 Tower Boulevard, Lake Wales, I-4 west to Exit 55; travel 28 miles (45km) south to Lake Wales and turn left at CR 17A (Burns Avenue) ☎ 863/676-1408; www.boktower.org 🕐 Daily 8–6
💲 Inexpensive; under 5: free

🟣20 Kennedy Space Center

The Kennedy Space Center represents the most successful space base on earth. If you are even remotely interested in space travel, engineering, discovery, daring or heroism you owe it to yourself to see this place.

The **Kennedy Space Center Visitor Complex** offers a combination of tours, artifacts, IMAX films, and ingenious attractions. Surprisingly, a lot of local residents take it for granted. They shouldn't – and neither should you. Located less than an hour from Orlando's theme parks, this is where Americans were first, and have ever since been, launched into space. The great part of this history of exploration is that you can see it all. Up close.

Departing from the bus loop, just outside the entrance area and to your right, coach tours simplify most of the complex, almost immediately giving passengers close-up views of the enormous **Vehicle Assembly Building**. Built to accommodate Saturn V rockets, the VAB is 716 feet (218m) long, 588 feet (179m) wide, 525 feet (160m) high, and encompasses 129.5 million square feet (more than 12 million sq m) – the equivalent of nearly four Empire State Buildings.

Another stop is the **Launch Complex 39 Observation Gantry**. From the top of the six-story struc-

KSC's impressive Rocket Garden: Which one is your favorite?

ture, you'll get a Hubble-perfect view of the space shuttle launch pads.

Outside the **Apollo/Saturn V Center**, you'll see stands that are reserved for media and family members during launches. If you know when you'll be visiting, call ahead and request special passes that may grant you access to these seats – they offer a great view of the launch pads. Inside, the first exhibit is the **Firing Room Theater**, where the simulation of the launch of Apollo 8 pulls you into the drama of the program's first manned lunar mission. Until 1968, astronauts had only traveled 850 miles (1,370km) from earth and now Apollo 8 was aiming for a lunar orbit about 250,000 miles (400,000km) away. The Firing Room contains the actual launch control consoles used in 1968, and the drama is heightened by audiotapes from the launch. You'll actually believe you're witnessing the real thing when you hear "3, 2, 1… ignition… lift off!" followed by a ground-shaking, window-rattling launch of a Saturn V rocket, visible in the sky behind you.

The show exits to a magnificent hall where you'll encounter the biggest space souvenir of them all: An actual 363-foot-long (111-m) Saturn

V rocket. The 6.2-million-pound (2,800-tonne) spacecraft is longer than two space shuttles, 2.4 Statues of Liberty, nine 40-foot-long (12-m) tour buses, or a football field plus 20 yards (110m). Also in the hall is the transfer van that ferried astronauts to the launch pad, models of lunar modules suspended from the rafters, moon rovers on lunar dioramas, actual capsules from Apollo missions, and a moon rock that you can touch.

Do not miss the **Lunar Surface Theater**, which presents an emotional recreation of the lunar module Columbia landing on the moon.

Take the bus back to the main entrance and settle down for one of three **IMAX films** offered with admission: Tom Hanks' "Apollo 13, The Dream Is Alive", or "Space Station 3-D". If ever a film warranted the use of 3-D effects, this is the one. Shot by astronauts and cosmonauts, the super crisp and clear images will most likely make this the most realistic vision you may ever have of space travel. Absolutely stunning, this is a must-see.

Outside the theater, KSC has planted the impressive Rocket Garden, the collection of spare rockets and equipment that includes the

actual service arm that led to the Apollo 11.

A few feet away, a museum of **Early Space Exploration** focuses on the highlights of the early days of rocketry, and features an actual-size mock-up of Robert Goddard's 1926 liquid-fuel rocket – which is roughly the size of a rolled-up newspaper but powerful enough that it would, within four decades, lead to Apollo. There are also additional exhibits that bring you up to speed on the glory days of the Mercury and Gemini space programs.

Before you go, make sure you participate in the **Astronaut Encounter** (► 205). Believe it or not, every day an actual astronaut appears for a free question-and-answer session with guests.

By now you should have an appreciation of what America's space explorers have accomplished, so head over to the **Astronaut Memorial** where the names of those who have died are inscribed on the 60-ton (54-tonne) marble mirror. Pay your respects and, the next time you're looking at the stars, you can think of them and your visit to America's space center.

Space Facts

The Space Coast is an easy shot from Orlando via Highway 50 or the Beeline Expressway. Just head east for about 40 miles (65km) and follow the signs. About 6 miles (10km) from the KSC entrance is the **Astronaut Hall of Fame**, now a partner with KSC. This houses the world's largest collection of astronaut memorabilia and features hands-on activities, including a simulated moon walk, a chance to land the space shuttle via a video screen, and a contraption in which you can pull 4Gs.
A Maximum Access Badge is a two-day ticket valid for both the KSC Visitor Complex and the Astronaut Hall of Fame. This costs $33 for adults and $23 for children.

Kennedy Space Center 🚭 225 E3 ☎ 321/449-4400; www.kennedyspacecenter.com
🕐 Daily 9–5:30; last regular bus tour 3 hours before closing; closed certain launch dates
IMAX I and II Theaters 🕐 Daily 10–5:40
The Astronaut Hall of Fame 🕐 9–dusk
NASA Space Shuttle and Satellite launch hotline ☎ 800/KSC-INFO (572-4636)
Space Coast Office of Tourism ☎ 321/868-1126 or 800/936-2326

Where to...
Eat and Drink

Prices Expect to pay per person for a meal, excluding drink
$ under $25 **$$** $25–50 **$$$** over $50

As part of the general push to attract adult travelers, Walt Disney World® Resort has made an admirable effort to add diverse restaurants of high quality to appeal to discerning diners. Virtually all restaurants, however, do encourage dining with children and offer children's menus. In general, prices tend to be high, so choosing wisely is especially important. The following choices have been selected for the quality of the food and the fact that they offer pleasurable dining experiences for all ages.

Any restaurant that accepts reservations is a hot ticket. For information and reservations, tel: 407/939-3463. For those not staying on Disney property (or for those who just need a break), Orlando also has a wide variety of restaurants worth trying.

WALT DISNEY WORLD RESORT

▼▼▼▼ Arthur's 27 $$$

Arthur's 27 offers sophisticated international fare and creative, enticing desserts. Favorite dishes include a wonderful lobster bisque and chocolate macadamia mousse cake. One more selling point, after the food, is the romantic ambiance, complete with panoramic views (the restaurant is on the 27th floor), live piano music and excellent service.

➕ **229 B2** 🏨 **Wyndham Palace Resort and Spa, 1900 Buena Vista Drive (between Hotel Plaza Boulevard and Route 535)** ☎ **407/827-3450**

▼▼▼ Artist Point $$$

The Frank Lloyd Wright-inspired decor, like all replicas at Disney, is extremely well done at this restaurant, which specializes in the food and wine of the Pacific Northwest. The wine list, of more than 100 selections, is impressive in that many of the well-chosen bottles come from Washington or Oregon. The menu features specialty items such as elk, buffalo, ostrich and salmon. Certain dishes are soulful and tasty such as the cold smoked roast chicken; others such as the elk and rabbit sausage sound good but are ultimately disappointing.

➕ **229 A3** 🏨 **Disney's Wilderness Lodge**

▼▼▼ California Grill $$$

A fantastic view of the Magic Kingdom Park is one of the main draws at this California-style restaurant atop Disney's Contemporary Resort. The clientele is a mix of locals and tourists. The menu runs the gamut from brick oven-baked flatbreads to sushi and sashimi to fusion entrées such as tempura bonsai tuna or grilled beef filet with tamarind barbecue glaze. Unfortunately the food does not live up to the glowing reviews. Perhaps it remains a favorite because it was the first serious restaurant in the park. It does, however, have a good wine list of mostly California bottles.

➕ **229 A3** 🏨 **Disney's Contemporary Resort**

▼▼▼ Citrico's $$$

This sophisticated eatery at Disney's premier hotel property, Disney's Grand Floridian Resort & Spa (▲102), was conceived with a citrus theme in mind, which is reflected in the pleasing decor that makes full use of attractively bright orange and yellow tones. The French food is some of the best to be had in Disney – thankfully the original dreams of a citrus-based cuisine have been abandoned. Dishes such as zucchini and shallot soup with oak-grilled shrimp, or six-hour braised veal shank with orzo, are expertly prepared. There is also an excellent wine list.

➕ 229 A3 ⊠ Disney's Grand Floridian Resort & Spa

➤➤➤ Flying Fish Café $$$

Huge gold-scaled fish-tail sculptures act as columns at this trendy seafood restaurant. The open kitchen turns out full-flavored American food that borrows much of its inspiration from the Southwest. A good way to start is with the buttermilk fried oysters, followed by potato-wrapped red snapper or seared yellowfin tuna with shrimp-basmati rice and Peking sauce. In addition there are simple New York strip steaks,

grilled pork chops and homemade pasta. You'll want to stroll along the boardwalk after indulging in the highly recommended Vahlrona chocolate lava cake.

➕ 229 B2 ⊠ Disney's BoardWalk

➤➤➤ Fulton's Crab House $$–$$$

A real find. Located on a re-created riverboat, this comfortable restaurant provides exceptionally fresh seafood, a lively scene at dinner and pleasant serenity at lunchtime. The best dishes are from America's waters, especially shellfish. Stone crab claws are sweet and meaty, oysters are expertly shucked, and entrées such as lobster and Dungeness crab treated with due respect. The menu changes weekly.

➕ 229 B2 ⊠ Downtown Disney

➤➤➤ Narcoossee's $$$

Located in a boathouse a short walk from the lobby, this bustling yet cozy spot offers pretty views of the twinkling water outside. The inven-

tive, mostly seafood, menu is highlighted by Maine lobster, Fanny Bay oysters and wild Alaskan salmon. They also serve filet mignon as well as toasted coconut, or sautéed wild salmon with couscous. The wine list offers some great selections to complement the eclectic menu.

➕ 229 A3 ⊠ Disney's Grand Floridian Resort & Spa

➤➤➤ Portobello Yacht Club $$–$$$

It is easy to have a very good and reasonably priced meal at this Tuscan eatery if you stick to the selection of hearty pasta dishes – rigatoni with Italian sausage, crimini mushrooms, black olives, escarole and several more – or the pizzas. There are other traditional Italian dishes such as veal marsala and chicken Milanese. The restaurant is attractively styled with earth tones and nautical paraphernalia.

➕ 229 B2 ⊠ Downtown Disney

➤ Rainforest Café $$

This enormous restaurant is worth a visit for the sheer spectacle, as well as the refreshing smoothies and fruity cocktails. In addition to the lush tropical foliage overhead, complete with replicas of tropical birds and gregarious gorillas, there are huge tropical fish tanks, playful elephants, a giant volcano and a "real" rainstorm every few minutes. The dishes are all named to fit the theme, such as "rumble in the jungle." The restaurant only serves environmentally ethical food, such as line-caught fish. Also a good vegetarian selection.

➕ 229 B2/A2 ⊠ Downtown Disney Marketplace and Animal Kingdom

➤➤ Restaurant Marrakesh $$

The winding approach to this vast Moroccan restaurant, through a simulated souk, transports you to the Magreb. The dining room is adorned with Islamic mosaic tiles, tapestries and slim columns. The menu is a collection of favorites from the North African country, somewhat toned down for American palates, and features different types of couscous, traditional roasted lamb and fragrant mint tea. Belly-dancers and Moroccan music complete the illusion. There is a small selection of Moroccan wines.

➕ 229 B2 ⊠ Morocco Pavilion, Epcot

Rosie's All American Café $

With a dearth of adequate sit-down establishments at Disney-MGM Studios, it's best to opt for one of the fun fast-food kiosks located on Sunset Boulevard amid umbrella'd picnic tables. One of the best is Rosie's for reasonable hot dogs and barbeque. Also available are the huge, meaty smoked turkey legs that are sold from carts everywhere.

➕ 229 A2 ⊠ Disney-MGM Studios

Spoodles $$-$$$

The casual trattoria-like feel and superb Italian-inspired fare at Spoodles are very popular with families. The open kitchen, complete with a wood-burning oven, turns out truly impressive dishes – oak-fired quail with seeded wild rice and truffle honey, whole roasted *loup de mer* (a Mediterranean sea bass that is flown in specially for the restaurant), and seared dayboat scallops with warm root-vegetable salad and pistachio brown butter vinaigrette.

➕ 229 B2 ⊠ Disney's BoardWalk

Victoria & Albert's $$$

At this intimate, formal and very expensive restaurant, diners are greeted by servers in period dress and presented with personalized souvenir menus. Despite this slightly over-the-top approach, the restaurant serves good, classic Continental fare. The menu changes nightly and diners can choose from the regular six-course menu or upgrade to a menu which can include such luxurious items as terrine of foie gras, Russian caviar, lobster in Newburg sauce, succulent baby lamb, plenty of truffles, and elegantly sinful desserts. The dining room is somewhat staid and stuffy, but there is a "chef's table" in the kitchen where diners can enjoy dinner behind the scenes.

➕ 229 A3 ⊠ Disney's Grand Floridian Resort & Spa

OUTSIDE WALT DISNEY WORLD

The Boheme $$$

Located downtown at the gorgeous Grand Bohemian hotel, this is an elegant, artistic restaurant whose tag line reads: Seafood, steak, art, music. Very true. The Bösendorfer Lounge (named after the Imperial Grand Bösendorfer piano – one of only two in the world) is a great place for sipping a martini.

➕ 228 D5 ⊠ 325 S. Orange Avenue ☎ 407/581-4700

Café Tu Tu Tango $$

Artists at work are strategically placed throughout this colorful restaurant, so their motto of "food for the starving artist" is fitting. Although the menu has dishes that span the globe, those inspired by Mexican cooking seem to work best in the festive ambiance. There are picadillo and cheese empanadas, pizzas and barbecue ribs. All dishes are appetizer-size, so diners are encouraged to graze, tapas-style, and share.

➕ 229 C2 ⊠ 8625 International Drive ☎ 407/248-2222

Dux $$$

Named for the famous ducks that parade through the hotel lobby, this elegant restaurant is one of the most celebrated in the area. The contemporary menu offers an enticing mix of traditional French dishes and creative inventions such as the roasted veal chop with a pink artichoke-basil fricasee, garlic confit and *jus au naturel*. For vegetarians there's a medley of fresh vegetables served over risotto. The desserts are delectable, and the service attentive.

➕ 229 C2 ⊠ The Peabody Orlando, 9801 International Drive ☎ 407/345-4550

Hue $-$$$

One of the trendiest restaurants in Thornton Park, the artsy district east of downtown, Hue was named one of the 'Best New Restaurants in the World' by Condé Nast *Traveler* magazine and appeals to a growing number of trendy diners. Creative spins on traditional items lead to "progressive American" entrees such as tamari-roasted duck breast with sesame hoisin sauce. The setting is warm, active, and inviting.

➕ 228 D5 ⊠ 629 East Central Boulevard ☎ 407/849-1800

Manuel's on the 28th $$$

Don't let the spectacular views distract you from the excellent seasonal fare – abalone and shrimp in garlic sauce, top-quality meat and fish, and stellar desserts. The attentive service also makes it a perfect choice for a sophisticated evening.

➕ 228 D5 ⊠ 390 N. Orange Avenue (at West Livingston Street) ☎ 407/246-6580

Pebbles $$

There are several locations of this casual restaurant, which serves creatively interpreted American fare, and a fine selection of wines. The cheery decor, amiably efficient staff and reasonable prices make it a popular choice with the local lunch crowd.

➕ 228 D5 ⊠ 17 West Church Street (between South Orange and South Garland avenues) ☎ 407/839-0892
➕ 228 B2 ⊠ 12551 Route 535 (Hotel Plaza Boulevard), Lake Buena Vista ☎ 407/827-1111
➕ 228 E6 ⊠ 2516 Aloma Avenue, Winter Park ☎ 407/678-7001
➕ 225 D4 ⊠ 2110 West State Road 434, Longwood ☎ 407/774-7111

Themed Restaurants/Dinner Shows

With the emphasis more on entertainment than cuisine, people usually come for the shows rather than the often uninspired food. Call in advance, since show times can change.

Arabian Nights

A Bedouin show that includes a three-course prime-rib dinner served while you watch 25 feats of horsemanship, including a chariot race.

➕ 229 B1 ⊠ 6225 W. US 192 ☎ 407/239-9223 or 800/553-6116; www.arabian-nights.com ⏰ Daily 7:30 pm 💲 $$$ adults, $$ children 3–11

Capone's Dinner & Show

This show takes you to Prohibition-era Chicago, where you say a secret password and are ushered into Al Capone's Underworld Cabaret and Speakeasy.

➕ 229 C1 ⊠ 4740 W. US 192 ☎ 407/397-2378 or 800/220-8428; www.alcapones.com ⏰ Daily 8 pm 💲 $$$ adults, $$ children 4–12

Dolly Parton's Dixie Stampede Dinner & Show

This country-style show has singing, dancing, comedy, eight buffalo, a few ostriches and racing pigs, as well as fast-paced acrobatic horsemanship with 32 horses. A Southern-style four-course feast and audience participation make this show stand out.

➕ 229 C2 ⊠ 8251 Vineland Avenue ☎ 407/238-4455; 866/443-4943; www.dixiestampede.com 💲 $$$ adults and children

Medieval Times

Set in the Middle Ages, this meal is held with lords and ladies, noblemen and knights. You dine in a magical venue, with enough room to accommodate dozens of steeds and knights.

➕ 229 C1 ⊠ 4510 W. US 192 ☎ 407/396-1518 or 800/229-9300; www.medievaltimes.com ⏰ Daily 6:15 and 8:30 pm 💲 $$$ adults, $$ children 3–12

Sleuth's Mystery Dinner Show

In the tradition of popular murder mystery evenings, guests at Sleuth's dine on a four-course meal while working on one of seven mysteries.

➕ 229 C3 ⊠ 7508 Universal Boulevard, Exit 75A ☎ 407/363-1985 or 800/393-1985; www.sleuths.com ⏰ Times vary 💲 $$$ adults, $$ children

Where to... Stay

Prices Expect to pay per room per night
$ under $125 $$ $125–250 $$$ over $250

See page 42 for general information on hotels and resorts.

WALT DISNEY WORLD RESORT

▼▼ Disney's BoardWalk Inn and Disney's BoardWalk Villas $$$

The Atlantic Coast boardwalks of the 1940s were the inspiration behind this whimsical resort, located on Crescent Lake. The hotel spills onto an actual boardwalk – complete with old-fashioned vending carts and midway games – and the result is one of the most enchanting places on Disney soil. The lobby is filled with amusement park memorabilia, such as a model roller coaster, vintage posters and a fun-park-themed mural. Most of the rooms contain two queen-size brass beds and comfortably cozy furnishings; many also have balconies overlooking the lake. The villas range in size from spacious studios to three bedrooms, and most are equipped with kitchen and laundry facilities. The two facilities share a swimming pool that also makes use of the fanciful theme.

✚ 229 B2 ✉ 2101 N. Epcot Resorts Boulevard ☎ 407/939-5100

▼▼ Disney's Coronado Springs Resort $$

Located near Disney's Animal Kingdom Park, the Coronado borrows inspiration from Mexico and the American Southwest. The huge complex is relatively inexpensive (for Disney, that is) and offers accommodations that fall into three categories: Ranchos, cabanas and casitas (modeled on ranch houses), beach clubs and Mexican-style dwellings. The lobby, as well as all the rooms, feature Mexican tiles, earth tones and original art. There is a lake in the middle of the resort, and the pool is designed like an Aztec ruin, with a waterfall tumbling down the side of a pyramid. The one full-service dining option is the Maya Grill, serving good quality Mexican food; there is also an extensive food court.

✚ 229 A2 ✉ 1000 West Buena Vista Drive ☎ 407/939-1000

▼▼ Port Orleans $$

You can see a working cotton gin powered by a 32-foot (10-m) water wheel at this mammoth, mid-priced resort styled after an antebellum plantation. The lodgings are set amid such Southern foliage as azaleas and magnolia trees. There is a mansion area with 19th-century Southern architecture and a rustic bayou area with faux swamp houses. The rooms feature pretty quilts and, though on the small side, they are still comfortable. The swimming area is called "Ol' Man Island" and is located in the center of a creek.

✚ 229 B2 ✉ 1251 Dixie Drive, at Bonnet Creek Parkway ☎ 407/934-6000

▼▼▼ Disney's Grand Floridian Resort & Spa $$$

This hotel is modeled on the style of the grand resorts that proliferated in Florida at the turn of the 19th century. The spacious rooms continue the theme with papered walls, wood trim and stately bathroom fixtures. Many of the rooms have their own balconies. This hotel is billed as Disney's premier spot, so they have made an effort at truly excellent service. The public spaces are very pretty with paths winding through well-tended lawns, foliage and a lovely pool. In 1995 the property opened a full-service spa, making this the most luxurious choice on Disney property.

🚹 229 A3 ⊠ 4401 Grand Floridian Way (off World Drive) ☎ 407/824-3000

🍷🍷🍷 Disney's Wilderness Lodge $$–$$$

Disney even seems to have re-created the chill mountain air at this magnificent replica of a grand, turn-of-the-20th-century Northwestern lodge, complete with flickering lanterns that light the pine tree-lined entryway. The vast lobby has two authentic totem poles, Native American artifacts, a huge fireplace and comfortable leather Adirondack chairs and couches. The property, which really looks as if it's nestled in the wilderness, smells of pine, and the swimming pool is built into an enormous, albeit fake, rock formation. The rooms are comfortable and furnished in the Mission style; most have two queen-size beds. There is a restaurant, Artist Point

(▶ 98), that specializes in food and wine from the Pacific Northwest; the Territory Lounge, a lively bar that celebrates the Westward expansion of explorers Lewis and Clark; and a lobby restaurant, Whispering Canyon Café, where kids help to fight off hostile bandits during dinner.

🚹 229 A2 ⊠ 901 West Timberline Drive (off Cypress Point Drive) ☎ 407/824-3200

🍷🍷🍷 Disney's Yacht & Beach Club Resort $$$

These adjoining hotels evoke the feel of a grand Victorian coastal resort. Disney's Yacht Club is a spacious wooden structure with comfortable furniture and a huge wrap-around veranda, complete with big white rocking chairs. Disney's Beach Club is more casual but also takes full advantage of the coastal motif. The shared pool area features a natural-looking body of water that even has a sandy bottom, as well as a pool with real fish. The

rooms are light and airy with two queen-size beds or one king-size. Many have good views of the picturesque 25-acre (10-ha) lake. The Yachtsman Steakhouse offers prime aged beef, grilled to perfection. There is also a health club and a video-game arcade that has an attached ice-cream parlor.

🚹 229 A2 ⊠ 1700–1800 Epcot Resort Boulevard (off Buena Vista Drive) ☎ 407/934-8000

OUTSIDE WALT DISNEY WORLD®

🍷🍷 Holiday Inn Sunspree Resort Lake Buena Vista $

This popular, family-friendly hotel provides a wealth of kids' activities at a fraction of the price that you would pay at a Disney property. Children are greeted by the hotel's mascots, a pair of raccoons named Max and Maxine, and check in at their own desk, where they receive a bag of goodies. The rooms are of the dependable chain-hotel variety, but they are larger than average and

have kitchenettes. Families can also choose to book a "kids' suite", decorated in various themes that include an igloo and a boat.

🚹 229 B2 ⊠ 13351 SR 535 (off I-4) ☎ 407/239-4500

🍷🍷🍷 Hyatt Regency-Grand Cypress Hotel $$$

Located just over the Disney border, this luxury property offers many wonderful amenities in an indulgent setting. The resort boasts a top-rated 45-hole golf course designed by Jack Nicklaus, 12 tennis courts, an enormous pool with waterfalls, and a lakeside beach that stretches for almost a quarter mile (400m). The lobby displays an impressive collection of Asian art and has a tropical feel, complete with wildlife and palm trees. The rooms are elegantly appointed and plush, and they all have terraces. There is entertainment on the weekends in the lobby bar, several full-service restaurants, including the highly rated La Coquina and Hemingway's, both of which are popular with locals. There is also a full health club with a sauna and steam room.

☐ 229 B2 ☒ 1 Grand Cypress Boulevard (off Route 535) ☎ 407/ 239-1234 or 800/233-1234

👒👒👒 Peabody Orlando $$$

This hotel is most famous for the ducks that parade through the lobby each day. That aside, the Peabody is a sophisticated hotel in the middle of the pervading kitsch of Orlando's tourist area. The rooms are decorated in Southern style – the original Peabody is in Memphis, which is where the strange duck tradition began – and are light and airy with attractive pale wood furnishings. The top floors are the concierge level and extra amenities are offered. There is live entertainment in the lobby each night, and there are several full-service restaurants, including Dux (▶ 100).

☐ 229 C3 ☒ 9801 International Drive ☎ 407/352-4000 or 800/PEABODY

Where to...
Shop

Few people have ever left Walt Disney World® Resort without a souvenir. Each theme park has a primary gift shop and there are lots more boutiques, gift kiosks and strolling sales hosts anxious to get your money. Few things are inexpensive or useful, but after all you are on vacation. For the widest selection check out the Emporium at the Magic Kingdom, the Centorium at Epcot, Disney Outfitters at Disney's Animal Kingdom and, at Disney-MGM Studios, Mickey's of Hollywood (with a special visit to see the Tinseltown memorabilia at Sid Cahuenga's One-of-a-Kind).

The main shopping area, however, is Downtown Disney, a three-part collection of stores, restaurants, a theater, discos, sports bars, comedy clubs, blues bars, speakeasies and a Western saloon, divided into the **Marketplace, West Side** and **Pleasure Island.** Depending on your mood and your age, you will have to decide which of the three suits you. You can order anything at Walt Disney World® Resort through the mail (although you pay shipping costs); tel: 407/363-6200 for information. If you are a resort guest, most stores can deliver purchases back to your hotel.

Marketplace

The tamest of Downtown Disney's trio is Marketplace, a pleasantly casual shopping village that includes 20-plus stores and restaurants. The rambling **World of Disney** dwarfs other stores, with the largest selection of Disney merchandise anywhere, ranging from a $2 candy bar to a $13,500 diamond-encrusted

Pooh pin. There is also a huge **LEGO Imagination Center** and other toy stores, as well as stores specializing in resort wear, a glass shop and a kitchen supply store. Smaller themed stores are hidden down quiet lanes, and larger ones include **Ghirardelli Chocolates, Disney's Days of Christmas, Pooh Corner, Disney at Home** and the **Art of Disney.** Don't miss **Once Upon a Toy,** a huge store filled with Hasbro toys marked with Disney logos and characters.

West Side

On the West Side (▶ 107) there is the **Virgin Megastore,** with a huge selection of music; **Celebrity Eyeworks,** with fashion sunglasses and eyewear from designers such as **DKNY, Ray Ban** and **Calvin Klein;** and **Hoypoloi,** a unique gift shop with handmade Judaica, wind chimes, sculpture and Zen products. There is also the **Sosa Family Cigar Store; Magnetron** (which is good for anyone who owns a refrigerator or a piece of metal); **Starabilias**, which sells overpriced collectibles; and other spots for unusual gifts. **George's Guitar Gallery** has guitars ranging in price from $200 to $25,000.

Pleasure Island

Pleasure Island (▶ 106) boasts two clothing stores with trendy merchandise as well as places that sell music memorabilia. After 7 pm you have to pay to enter.

OUTSIDE WALT DISNEY WORLD®

Because Orlando is so geared toward tourists, the shopping areas are plentiful and easy to navigate by foot. Unlike many other cities, Orlando has outdoor shopping areas and neighborhoods where visitors can easily spend a pleasant afternoon. You can find just about everything, from souvenirs (no matter where you turn) to high fashion.

International Drive

International Drive stretches from Orlando to South Orange County and is most notable for the abundance of neon that adorns the strip malls on or near International Drive. (▶ 92–93). There are several mini-malls on or near International Drive.

Mercado (8445 International Drive, tel: 407/345-9337) is an open-air mall with stores, restaurants and a roving mariachi band in the evenings.

Belz Factory Outlet World (5401 W. Oak Ridge Road, between International Drive and I-4, tel: 407/352-9611) offers savvy shoppers savings of 30 to 60 percent in 170 stores with premium merchandise such as **Nike**, **Timberland**, **Calvin Klein**, **Tommy Hilfiger**, **Villeroy & Boch** and much more (▶ 92–93).

The Florida Mall

The Florida Mall, the largest mall in the tourist area, has more than 200 stores, including a huge Sears, and is located about 5 miles (8km) from International Drive (8001 S. Orange Blossom Trail, at Sand Lake Road).

Mall at Millenia

The three anchors at this huge upscale mall – Neiman Marcus, Bloomingdale's and Macy's – are exclusive to Orlando. Among the 170 stores are Gucci, Brookstone, Cartier, Tiffany and Orlando's only Apple store. Mall services include a concierge selling area attraction tickets, a post office and valet parking (take I-4 to Exit 78, tel: 407/363-3555; www.mallatmillenia.com).

Winter Park Village Marketplace

In one of the success stories of urban renewal, an old mall was bulldozed and a village put up in its place. It has a good mix of stores, restaurants, sidewalk cafés and a 20-screen movie theater. Evenings are very active and there's a good vibe here (take I-4 to Exit 88, head east 2 miles/3km to Route 17/92, turn right [south] and it's a quarter-mile on your left).

Winter Park

Winter Park is an affluent suburb of Orlando located about 40 minutes from Disney. The city's main drag is **Park Avenue**, which runs alongside picturesque Central Park. It offers adults the most sophisticated assortment of boutiques in the area. There are big names (**Banana Republic** and the **Limited**), as well as more exclusive clothiers. There are also other upscale chain stores (**Williams-Sonoma** and **Pottery Barn**). Many galleries selling unusual jewelry, gifts and artwork have opened right on Park Avenue or just off it on one of the many quaint side streets.

Of particular note is **Timohy's Books & Gallery**, located on Park, which sells jewelry, handmade clothing, ceramics and art books. There are also some good restaurants and cafés, including a Japanese sushi restaurant, a popular brunch café and a good Italian eatery, making Winter Park a very pleasant place to spend an afternoon. (🚇 228 E6. Take I-4 to Exit 45 east, then left on Park Avenue, tel: 407/644-8281; www.winterparkcc.org).

Where to...
Be Entertained

Orlando is full of entertainment options for children and adults, whether on or off Walt Disney World® Resort. There is also a lively nightlife, with most clubs and bars clustered together in the various entertainment complexes. Since Walt Disney World® Resort governs itself, its clubs are able to stay open later than other local bars. If you have the stamina, you could party until nearly 3 am. If you drive yourself, get here before 9 pm – any later and the parking lot fills quickly. Disney operators can provide a complete list of shows and cover charges. For information or reservations, tel: 407/939-3463.

What's On

Several publications provide comprehensive listings of what's happening around town. One of the best is the *Orlando Weekly*, a free paper that tells you what's happening every day of the week from music, to clubs, to theater, to sporting events, to galleries. The paper lists happenings that will appeal to a wide audience. If you want to go out and do anything from dancing to reggae to strolling through an art exhibit, this is your definitive source.

Running a close second is the *Orlando Sentinel*'s Calendar section, an insert that comes in Friday's newspaper. With movie listings, a concert calendar, restaurant reviews and announcements for a slew of free activities, it's worth getting.

Orlando Magazine is a monthly that runs articles about various activities in the city. There are often features that revolve around restaurants or bars that will tell you what's hot at the moment. In the back pages of the magazine is an "About Town" section that lists various happenings around Orlando. While the listings are not nearly as exhaustive as those in the *Orlando Weekly*, it is a good selection of what's out there. The Orlando/Orange County Convention and Visitors Bureau (tel: 407/363-5872) puts out an official visitors guide, which is a good source for information about the many attractions in the area other than Walt Disney World® Resort. The guide also has restaurant and shopping listings, but it does not give information on specific happenings such as concerts, shows or museum exhibits.

Disney Pleasure Island

The center for adult nightlife at Walt Disney World® Resort is Pleasure Island (tel: 407/934-7781), located within Downtown Disney. After 7 pm there is an admission charge to get onto Pleasure Island. You must be over 18 or accompanied by a parent to enter. Only those over 21 are permitted to drink. **Mannequin's** and **BET SoundStage Club** require all guests to be over 21. The admission fee is not required for dining.

Once there, visitors can hit most of the clubs free of charge. There are multiple entrances. The main ones are usually backed up, so enter from the Marketplace side and avoid a long wait. When you arrive here you will detect a portent of things to come: Cast members wearing earplugs to drown out the noise from stage shows and nightclubs. Pleasure Island will be very crowded on Thursdays, Fridays and Saturdays. Disney cast members get paid on Thursday afternoon and pack Pleasure Island to blow their money here on Thursday evening.

The theme for each evening is a New Year's Eve celebration, complete with a midnight countdown, confetti and fireworks. The subplot is a big party. There are huge tubs filled with chilled beer, kiosks where you can get a temporary tattoo, young ladies selling syringes filled with a liquor-based gelatin, and **Super Star Studios** where, after a syringe of 100-proof Jell-O, you won't mind warbling out your favorite song for a souvenir CD or video.

Then there are the clubs. At the **Pleasure Island Jazz Company**, the mood is decidedly intimate. Sitting at small tables in a 1930s-style speakeasy, you can sip a drink and listen to jazz soloists and combos.

Disney is nothing if not obsessed with themes, so they answered the rock 'n' roll call with the **Rock N Roll Beach Club**. The three-floor venue features pool tables, pinball, darts and music from the 1950s and '60s.

At **Mannequins Dance Palace**, the music is loud and Thursdays draws a gay crowd. **8-Trax** high-

lights the music and fashions of the '70s, but the **Adventurers Club** is a must. It re-creates a turn-of-the-19th-century explorers' club in rich detail, with a treasure trove of artifacts and trophies as well as actors regaling you with tales of their latest expedition. The **BET SoundStage Club** is funky and loud and pays tribute to all types of black music from old rhythm and blues to hip-hop.

If you want to laugh last (and loudest), save **The Comedy Warehouse** for evening's end. During five nightly shows, improv actors create squeaky-clean sketches based on suggestions from the audience. The clubs on Pleasure Island close at 2 am.

Disney West Side

One of the most popular spots on Pleasure Island is the huge **Planet Hollywood**, which serves lunch and dinner every day.

Without resorting to hyperbole, the **House of Blues** on West Side (next door to Pleasure Island) is the

greatest club in the world. Juke-joint decor, folk art, hot music and great Cajun food are presented so well it would be easy to stay the night enjoying a Mississippi Delta meal, listening to a singer in the restaurant and blues bar, grooving to live reggae in the lakeside Voodoo Garden, and wrapping up the night in the Music Hall, watching acts that include Brian Setzer, David Byrne, Steve Miller and Los Lobos.

More passive, but just as enjoyable, is **Cirque du Soleil® La Nouba**. A multimillion-dollar theater was built especially for this show. With the highest-priced ticket in town ($72–80), the 90-minute show – a fantastical circus that combines breathtaking acrobatics with New Age music, contortionists and impressive production values – is worth every penny. Reserve early to get better seats. Call for tickets and showtimes (tel: 407/939-7600).

Across the walk, **DisneyQuest** is a five-floor video/virtual-reality arcade filled with cutting-edge

computer games, team video sports and a virtual jungle cruise. It's fairly expensive (about $33 for all-day admission; $27 for children 3–9) so save it for a rainy day.

Next door, the **Virgin Megastore** has a selection as large as its prices. More than 150,000 music titles, 20,000 videos and DVDs, 2,000 software titles, and a bookstore are helping Richard Branson pocket another billion. Emilio and Gloria Estefan's **Bongo's Cuban Café** has an eye-catching design and borrows the style of Miami's South Beach.

Disney's BoardWalk

This is another pleasant entertainment destination. It does not attract the same throngs as Pleasure Island and is located in a more picturesque spot. There is an **ESPN Club** for sports fans, the **Big River Grille & Brewing Works** microbrewery, and a few stores and restaurants. Admission to the BoardWalk is free, but there may be cover charges for certain activities.

Universal Studios CityWalk

In 1999, Universal Studios opened CityWalk, a huge entertainment complex that is home to several new theme clubs, restaurants and stores. Among the most interesting are **Bob Marley – A Tribute to Freedom**, a reggae club and Jamaican restaurant that is modeled after Marley's home in Kingston; **Pat O'Brien's**, an exact replica of the famous New Orleans bar that also serves Cajun food; and **The Groove**, a huge dance club designed to look like a century-old theater.

As for dining, there is **Emeril's Restaurant Orlando**, which serves excellent Creole food created by the popular television personality Emeril Lagasse, as well as an NBA-themed eatery.

Admission to CityWalk is only $9 for entry to all clubs.

✚ **228 C4** ⊠ **6000 Universal Boulevard, off I-4 or International Drive, Exit 74A West Bound, 75A East Bound** ☎ **407/224-2600** ⏰ **Daily 11 am–2 am**

Pointe*Orlando

This entertainment complex is located near the convention center, on International Drive. The complex has 60 stores (including FAO Schwarz); a 20-screen movie complex, which has an IMAX theater; and an interactive science museum, **WonderWorks** (▶ 92). They also have a wide variety of restaurants, bars and nightclubs.

✚ **229 C3** ☎ **407/248-2838; www.pointeorlandofl.com**

Sports

Florida has become a major destination for sports fans eager to see baseball players in spring training, hoops stars and hockey. While Orlando has lagged behind other cities such as Tampa and Miami in the sports department, it is finally catching up and offers the avid fan ample entertainment.

The Orlando Magic

The only professional sports franchise in Orlando, basketball team the **Orlando Magic** continue to harbor high hopes for the playoffs.

✚ **228 D5** ⊠ **Orlando Arena, 600 W. Amelia Street, between I-4 and Parramore Avenue** ☎ **407/849-2020; www.orlandomagic.com**

Disney's Wide World of Sports™ Complex

Check out the events at this sports complex and you will find plenty to watch, everything from soccer and beach volleyball matches to tennis, cycling and rugby games. During spring training the facility is home to the Atlanta Braves. The team plays its spring training games before Disney spectators. There is also the interactive **NFL Experience**, which allows budding football stars to try passing, catching and kicking field goals.

✚ **229 A1** ☎ **407/363-6600**

Golf

Considering Florida is home to more golf courses than most other states, it should come as no surprise that Floridians take the game very seriously. You are never far from a good golf course in Florida. Unfortunately, many of the best courses are associated or attached to exclusive resorts and access is only granted to registered guests.

There are 125 courses in and around Orlando. Disney maintains the largest number of top-quality golf courses (99 holes) in the area; to find out about them you can dial one convenient number, 407/WDW-GOLF (939-4653) or 824-2270. The meticulously maintained, 18-hole championship courses on Disney property are the **Lake Buena Vista Course**, the **Osprey Ridge Course**, the **Eagle Pines Course**, the **Palm Course** and the **Magnolia Course**.

Every October, Disney plays host to the **National Car Rental Golf Classic**.

Fortunate guests at the **Hyatt Regency-Grand Cypress Hotel** (▶ 103) have access to 45 holes designed by Jack Nicklaus. For more courses, check www.orlandogolf.com.

Miami and the South

Getting Your Bearings

Some years back, crimes against tourists, combined with the exodus of Cuban prisoners and other "troublemakers" arriving via the Mariel Boatlift, put Miami low down on America's list of top tourist spots. That was then.

Ironically it was the cop show "Miami Vice" that helped the city clean up the streets. The nation started to see Miami in a different light. European fashion photographers realized Ocean Drive made a great backdrop, and entrepreneurs began refurbishing rundown art deco hotels. Miami, having realized the value of the tourist dollar, began cracking down on real-life criminals, and today it is one of the country's hotter cities, where people flock to see and be seen.

You are likely to spend the majority of your time not in Miami, but on Miami Beach, a narrow strand of islands slicing between Biscayne Bay and the Atlantic Ocean. Catch some sun in the middle of winter, join the café society on Ocean Drive, and stretch out beneath the coconut palms (really). If you are ready for the most exotic vacation you can take in mainland America, Miami Beach awaits.

While Miami has the lion's share of attractions, a drive north along the Atlantic coast will introduce you to another part of South Florida – one based on beaches, sprawling commercial growth and, most notably, one of the finest examples of planned communities of the 1920s (Boca Raton) and one of the most elegant examples of high society (Palm Beach).

Previous page: A South Beach lifeguard hut

If fantasies of palm trees, ocean breezes and warming sun flashed before you as you planned your Miami vacation, here's a good itinerary to follow:

Miami in Three Days

Above and below: South Beach

Day One

Morning Have breakfast at the News Café in 🖪 **South Beach** (800 Ocean Drive, tel: 305/538-6397). It's active and fun. The food is great, and the prices are fair. Bring your bathing suit and beach supplies because next you will walk across the street to **Lummus Park** (➤ 114), the most popular section of sand in Miami Beach, for your day in the sun.

Afternoon Brush off the sand and cross the street for a leisurely lunch at another of Ocean Drive's plentiful cafés.
Drop in at the **Art Deco Welcome Center** (1001 Ocean Drive, tel: 305/531-3484) and rent an audio walking tour of the **Art Deco District** (➤ 115–116 and 206–208).
After covering the Art Deco District, return to your hotel and rest up for a late night.

Evening Walk down the **Lincoln Road Mall** (➤ 115). There are plenty of restaurants, as well as street performers, local characters and interesting stores, cigar bars, bookstores and theaters. If you have energy, reserve time for a nightclub – or a nightcap at the weird and wonderful Delano Hotel (➤ 142).

Day Two

Morning Pack or pick up a picnic lunch and head to the islands. Take US 1 south through downtown and then get back in the water – this time at ❷ **Virginia Key** (➤ 122) and ❹ **Key Biscayne** (➤ 122). Learn to windsurf at Virginia Key, head out for deep-sea fishing, or take a bicycle trip around the **Bill Baggs Cape Florida State Recreation Area** (➤ 123).

Afternoon Enjoy your picnic or eat at the recreation area café, which serves beer, wine and meals ranging from hot dogs to lobster.

Leave the beach and head south on Miami Avenue to Coconut Grove's ❾ **Vizcaya Estate and Gardens** for a tour of the mighty bayfront estate (➤ 126).

Continue south and the road becomes Bayshore Drive. You will drive right into the heart of ❿ **Coconut Grove** (right) for a stroll around the village (➤ 117–119).

Evening At dusk, settle down for dinner at Café Tu Tu Tango (➤ 118). Wrap up dinner and drop in at a Coconut Grove bar, club, theater – or just enjoy a casual evening of window shopping.

Day Three

Morning Drive south on Brickell Avenue, turning onto Coral Way to reach ⓫ **Coral Gables** (➤ 126). Take a dip in the fabulous, thematic **Venetian Pool**.

Afternoon Head over to Miracle Mile for a sidewalk (pavement) shopping stroll (➤ 126). Head east to reach US 1 south and enjoy a natural afternoon at the ⓬ **Fairchild Tropical Gardens** (left), ⓭ **Miami Metrozoo** (➤ 128). Afterward, head north on US 1 for a snack/shopping break at the Shops at Sunset Place (Red Road – S.W. 57th Avenue – South Miami).

Evening After resting and freshening up at your hotel, return to your favorite South Beach restaurants and nightclubs for another late night.

◻ South Beach

Photogenic South Beach has been pictured so often, there's a chance you could navigate its streets based simply on the backdrops you have seen in fashion magazines.

Why is South Beach worth seeing? Because, quite accurately, SoBe (to those in the know) has proclaimed itself America's Riviera and because it is the most cosmopolitan area in the American South. Everything you have imagined is here in glorious Technicolor – art deco hotels, blue waters, green palm trees and colorful characters.

In the early 1980s the vintage hotels were run down, but dedicated preservationists rescued them from demolition, and the Miami Beach Architectural District became the first 20th-century district to be named on the National Register of Historic Places. More than 800 buildings are now on the roll.

Unlike Orlando's major attractions, there are no ticket lines to stand in or admission charges to pay. You can get right in on the action by starting your day at **Lummus Park**, the beachfront stretch that runs from 5th to 15th streets

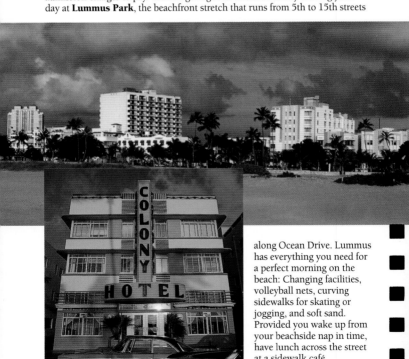

along Ocean Drive. Lummus has everything you need for a perfect morning on the beach: Changing facilities, volleyball nets, curving sidewalks for skating or jogging, and soft sand. Provided you wake up from your beachside nap in time, have lunch across the street at a sidewalk café.

Miami's signature piece: The art deco hotel

By early afternoon, you should be rested for a walk around South Beach. At the **Art Deco District Welcome Center** (1001 Ocean Drive, tel: 305/531-3484, daily 11–6) you will find postcards, posters, reproduction deco accessories and a taped tour of the **Art Deco District**. The tour lasts about 90 minutes (inexpensive), but if you'd prefer to save your cash, set off on your own to catch a few highlights. The home at 1114 Ocean Drive is where fashion designer Gianni Versace was gunned down in July 1997. Unfortunately, it has now become a strange attraction and some visitors pose on the steps where he died. This is not recommended.

At 10th Street, head two blocks west to reach Washington Avenue, a working-class street cluttered with delis, restaurants, clothing stores and nightclubs. Turn left and at the end of the block you will reach the **Wolfsonian–Florida International University** (1001 Washington Avenue, tel: 305/531-1001; www.wolfsonian.org). The one-time storage facility now houses a beautiful, artistic collection of more than 70,000 objects such as glass, ceramics, metalwork, furniture and ephemera – primarily industrial design artifacts from the late 19th century to the mid-20th century.

Head north on Washington past 14th Street (grabbing a snack at one of the many Cuban grocery stores) and turn left

Miami Beach's sands stretch for miles

on Espanola Way. Built as the entertainment complex for a long-gone hotel, this is where the young Desi Arnaz introduced the conga to America. The stores and youth hostel here give it character – especially Friday through Sunday when it becomes a venue for a collection of flea-market merchants.

A few blocks up Espanola Way, turn right on Plaza de España and head three blocks to the **Lincoln Road Mall**. Individually, there are few must-see stores here – but collectively the re-designed pedestrian mall has become a magnet for a cross-section of Miami residents and visitors.

Turn left (west) and take a break at the **Van Dyke Café** (846 Lincoln Road, tel: 305/534-3600). From its outdoor tables you can watch the people who are watching you. Afterward, head west to Lenox Avenue, turn around and follow the opposite side

SOUTH BEACH: INSIDE INFO

Top tips Save the Wolfsonian for Thursday night when **admission is free**.
• South Beach is a large area to cover on foot. Look for the **ELECTROWAVE** (tel: 305/843-9283), a fleet of electric trolleys that charge 25 cents and cruise all over South Beach, picking up at 30 spots throughout the district (hours vary).
• **Inline skating** is all the rage in SoBe. There are many skate-rental stores in the area; ask your hotel for the nearest one if you want to glide along the beach and act like a local.
• Look for parking garages on Collins Avenue at 7th and 13th streets, on Washington Avenue at 12th Street, and west of Washington at 17th Street. If you park on the street, **feed the meter or risk a ticket**.
• Crimes against tourists have dropped significantly, but don't be foolish. **Avoid back streets** and areas too far removed from the central tourist areas.

Hidden gems If you like your coffee thick and black and your sandwiches flat and hot, order up a **Cuban tinto** (a potent espresso) and a **Cuban sandwich** at any ramshackle sidewalk window in SoBe.

of the mall, enjoying the eclectic collection of stores, theaters, restaurants and bars. When you reach Collins Avenue, turn left and drop in at the **Delano** (1685 Collins Avenue, ➤ 142). A weirder hotel you will never see. Walk back to the pool area and you'll feel you have traveled through the looking glass – not surprising considering the *Alice in Wonderland*-inspired surrealism.

Wrap up the evening people-watching and dining at an Ocean Drive restaurant, and if you have the stamina check out a SoBe club.

Miami Beach's glorious sands

TAKING A BREAK
Ghirardelli's Soda Fountain & Chocolate Shop (801 Lincoln Road, tel: 305/532-2538) is an air-conditioned oasis where you can sit down with a sundae, chocolate soda, soft drink or candy.

10 Coconut Grove

In the 1800s, this small bayside community became a haven for artists, intellectuals and writers. Following World War I, more people in *Who's Who in America* listed Coconut Grove as their winter residence address than anywhere else.

Today, more than a half century after that, the same holds true – but tourists have been added to the mix.

Even on a quiet evening in Coconut Grove, the center of the village is jumping – but why? There's no single defining venue that attracts the gathering throng; yet almost nightly without fail a combination of teenagers, students from the nearby University of Miami, couples and business travelers converge at the intersection of McFarlane Road, Grand Avenue and Main

Highway. Most likely, they are lured by the choices of entertainment: Sports bars, rock 'n' roll clubs, trendy restaurants, movie theaters, bookstores, themed restaurants, juke joints, dive bars, boutiques and galleries – all concentrated within a few blocks of the village's epicenter.

The extensive landscaped formal gardens of the Vizcaya estate

---

Vizcaya Estate and Gardens ✚ 230 B3 ✉ 3251 S. Miami Avenue ☎ 305/250-9133; www.vizcayamuseum.org 🕐 House daily 9:30–4:30; garden daily 9:30–5:30 💵 Inexpensive
Miami Museum of Science and Planetarium ✚ 230 B3 ✉ 3280 S. Miami Avenue ☎ 305/646-4200 museum; 305/646-4420 for 24-hour Cosmic Hotline; www.miamisci.org 🕐 Daily 10–6 💵 Inexpensive
Café Tu Tu Tango ✚ 230 B2 ✉ 3015 Grand Avenue, Suite 250 (CocoWalk) ☎ 305/529-2222; www.cafetututango.com/miami/

Bear in mind you shouldn't dismiss the area's daytime appeal. If you have a full day to spend in Coconut Grove, you will find action in the sunlight before turning your attention to the evening's activities.

Arriving around noon allows time to see what needs to be seen in Coconut Grove. The popular attraction for visitors is **Vizcaya Estate and Gardens** (► 126). As in other castle tours, you will be led from room to room and shown pieces of furniture and works of art as you hear tales about the owner, but the tour is dull in comparison to the architecture. Once you can cut loose from the group, wander around the grounds on your own, walk over to the gardens and relax within the courtyard of the main house. Not much else to do, but it's pretty in here.

Returning to the village via South Bayshore Drive, you'll see the **Miami Museum of Science and Planetarium** on your right. If you're looking for a museum centered around hands-on experiments for children and adults or a wildlife center that houses native Florida snakes, turtles, tortoises and birds of prey, this is the place to come. At night there's a rock 'n' roll laser light show in the planetarium.

Back in the village, a great place to take a break anytime is **Café Tu Tu Tango** at CocoWalk. The interior is designed like an artist's studio, it serves creative entrées/appetizers and has a balcony overlooking the village, perfect for a Coconut Grove day.

The crowds begin trickling in around 7 pm and most gather at **CocoWalk**, a three-story entertainment complex comprising restaurants, bars, stores, a multiplex theater and vendors selling miscellaneous merchandise (cigars, beads, incense, herbs, etc.) from pushcarts (barrows).

If you would like an evening of passive entertainment, pull up a bar stool and commence an evening of people-watching. On the second level there are three drinking establishments to choose from. At **Hooter's** waitresses in tight T-shirts and luminescent shorts serve bar food and beer; **Fat Tuesday** is an outdoor bar serving beer and multiflavored 150-proof-plus daiquiris.

Coconut Grove
– arguably the
prettiest village
in the city

Within the **Streets of Mayfair** (2911 Grand Avenue, tel: 305/448-1700), you'll find 100,000-plus books in **Borders Books, Music and Café**. Book-browsing can be fun, but attending **The Improv Comedy Club** (3390 Mary Street, tel: 305/441-8200) may be even more entertaining. Be warned: The fortress-like setting doesn't encourage shopping.

If you are an experienced traveler, you may want to avoid the touristed spots and hang with the locals. There are several bars and taverns in the Grove, each with a slightly different theme. Try the **Sandbar Grill** (3064 Grand Avenue, tel: 305/444-5270), a popular sports bar that also serves Baja California cuisine. The **Tavern in the Grove** (3416 Main Highway, tel: 305/447-3884) has been a bar for decades, and is a favorite for students from the University of Miami as well as local showbiz and sports celebrities. **Mr. Moe's** (3131 Commodore Plaza, tel: 305/442-1114) is a beer and full liquor bar with an easygoing open-air atmosphere.

Art is everywhere and everything in Miami

COCONUT GROVE: INSIDE INFO

Top tips If you arrive on a weekend night, **don't fight for a parking space** in the village. Just follow signs to parking lots a few blocks away (inexpensive).
• Coconut Grove's **"can't miss"** is the village itself.

Ones to miss If touring houses and museums reminds you that you have turned this into a working vacation rather than a relaxing one, **skip Vizcaya and the Miami Museum of Science and Planetarium**. It's better to take it easy than force yourself to see these two.

Hidden gem About a half-mile (800m) south on Main Highway, you will pass Devon Road and the **Plymouth Congregational Church** (tel: 305/444-6521; call ahead to arrange a tour). The coral rock church resembles a Mexican mission, set in a deep wooded hammock with beautiful grounds and gardens.

Hooter's 🚩 230 B2 ✉ 3015 Grand Avenue Suite 250 (CocoWalk) ☎ 305/442-6004
Fat Tuesday 🚩 230 B2 ✉ 3015 Grand Avenue (CocoWalk) ☎ 305/441-2992
Streets of Mayfair 🚩 230 B2 ✉ 2911 Grand Avenue ☎ 305/448-1700 ☎ Sun–Thu 11 am–10 pm, Fri–Sat 11 am–10 pm
Sandbar Grill 🚩 230 B2 ✉ 3064 Grand Avenue ☎ 305/444-5270

19 Everglades National Park

There's no question that the Everglades doesn't share the majesty of other parks, such as Yosemite and Yellowstone. However, if you'd like to see a natural phenomenon and Florida in its close to native state, this is the place to be.

At 1.5 million acres (6 million ha), the **Everglades National Park** is roughly the size of Rhode Island and Delaware combined, but for decades it was viewed as disposable property. Developers eager to turn land into cash spent years draining it to create room for farms and houses before environmentalists pointed out that this was, in fact, a river that filters water, prevents flooding and is a major habitat for wildlife and plant life. President Harry Truman dedicated, and thereby protected, the Everglades National Park in 1947.

Among the Everglades activities: Airboat tours and bird-watching

The park is open year round, with peak tourist season occurring between December and April when it's dryer and cooler (summer is hot, wet and mosquito-plagued).

From Miami, head southwest and look for State Road 9336, which leads you to the **Ernest F. Coe Visitor Center** ($10 per vehicle for 7-day pass), where you can watch an introductory film and pick up brochures on the wide-ranging activities of the park. Whether you start your visit here or at another visitor center, you'll be able to obtain information about the park because each offers many, if not all, of these services: guided tours (by jeep, tram or airboat); orientation films on the park's history and environmental composition; brochures, books, film, postcards, insect repellent (a must); hiking trail maps; restaurant (or snacks and soft drinks); a marina, bicycle and canoe rentals; schedule of events.

The rangers here have also developed a variety of events and tours designed to appeal to a range of visitors. **Scheduled tours** may cost an additional fee, but they include bird walks; canoe trips; shoreline strolls; bayside talks; hammock walks (a hammock is a stand of trees); boat tours; Everglades tours and tram tours.

For wildlife viewing, head to the Anhinga Trail, Snake Bight, Chokoloskee Bay, Loop Road, or Turner River Road. A wildlife-viewing tram tour leads to **Shark Valley** and a 65-foot (20-m) tower that gives an aerial view of the sawgrass prairie's birds and alligators.

If you're a thrillseeker, the 99-mile (160-km) **Wilderness Waterway** is a canoe/kayak trail through mangrove islands with several shorter loops, including 5.2 mile (8.3km) Nine-Mile Pond, and 2-mile (3-km) sections on Noble Hammock, Mud Lake and Hells Bay. You'll need navigational charts for this, and permits if you decide to rough it and camp for the night.

Traditional tribal living on display at the Miccosukee Indian Village

In the midst of all of this, the **Miccosukee Indian Village** (tel: 305/223-8380; www.miccosukee.com/mivillage.html) is a permanent, inhabited display of how this Native American tribe, which retreated to the Everglades rather than be deported to a western reservation in the 1800s, still lives. Granted sovereignty in 1962, they give craftwork demonstrations. Airboat rides, alligator wrestling and a tour of the cook *chickee* are also part of the experience. In the museum are photographs of tribal members from generations past, native attire, and paintings and sculptures by tribal members. A third room highlights the relationship beween the Miccosukee and the Mississippi Band of Choctaw Indians.

Wherever you roam, heed the advice of the rangers, who caution guests to never attempt to touch or feed the docile-looking manatees, turtles and raccoons. Many have lost their fear of people and see a snack instead of a finger. Above all, give plenty of room to the alligators and snakes you'll encounter, since venom and sharp teeth will win out over your jogging shoes. Above all, have fun.

Everglades National Park ⊞ 227 D2 ⊠ 40001 State Road 9336, Homestead ☎ 305/242-7700; www.nps.gov/ever or www.everglades.national-park.com

EVERGLADES NATIONAL PARK: INSIDE INFO

Top tips There are five visitor centers where you can get information, sign up for tours, and pick up supplies. The closest to Miami is the **Ernest F. Coe Visitor Center** (tel: 305/242-7700), west of Homestead and Florida City. On the eastern side of the park are the **Royal Palm** (tel: 305/242-7700), 4 miles (6.5km) west of the main entrance station and near the Anhinga Trail, and **Flamingo** (tel: 941/695-2945). The latter location, near the foot of the last road in South Florida, is 38 miles (61km) southwest from the main entrance at the southern end of the park. **Shark Valley** (tel: 305/221-8776) is on the northeast border of the park, by Big Cypress National Preserve and the Loop Road. **Gulf Coast** (tel: 941/695-3311), the gateway for exploring the Ten Thousand Islands, is in the northwest corner of the park in Everglades City. All are open daily from 8–5.

At Your Leisure

❷ Virginia Key

South Beach is busy; downtown is crowded. So it's worth $1 to enter the Rickenbacker Causeway, cross over the bridge and settle down on Virginia Key. On the sliver of waterfront just past the tollbooths you can park your car and join the locals who gather for tailgate parties and to ride wave-runners. **Sailboards Miami** has a concession here and they claim to be able to teach anyone to windsurf in two hours. Restrooms are available, but there's no restaurant.

Sailboards Miami, Windsurfer Beach
➕ 230 C3 ☎ 305/361-7245;
www.sailboardsmiami.com
🖳 Moderate per hour, expensive per two-hour session with lesson

❸ Miami Seaquarium

SeaWorld has cornered the Central Florida market on oceanic attractions, but this old-timer satisfies South Florida. Shows revolve around sea lions, dolphins and a killer whale – although some animal-rights activists point out the whale's tank is too small. But there's a lot more than just the shows, including a tropical-reef aquarium and rescued manatees. If you've got the cash (very expensive), you may want to consider swimming with the dolphins during a two-hour session at the **Water and Dolphin**

Exploration program (WADE) – reservations are suggested.
➕ 230 C2 ✉ 4400 Rickenbacker Causeway ☎ 305/361-5705;
www.miamiseaquarium.com 🕙 Daily 9:30–6; last entry 4:30 🖳 Moderate (parking extra: inexpensive)

❹ Key Biscayne

If you can ignore the residential nature of Key Biscayne, you will find that nature itself dominates this island. Two parks comprise most of the key.

Crandon Park

Crandon Park covers more than 1,200 acres (485ha). One of the nicest public golf courses around is the **Crandon Park Golf Course** (6700 Crandon Boulevard, tel: 305/361-9129, very expensive), which spreads across a tranquil tropical setting. Also within the park is the long-titled **Marjory Stoneman Douglas Biscayne Nature Center** (tel: 305/361-6767), where you can take a tour that includes walking on a path to view grass beds to study sea cucumbers, seahorses, crabs and shrimp. There are tennis courts, ball fields, skating and jogging paths, but skip those and head to the

Crystal clear water + fantastic fish = incredible dives

Spend the day at Bill Baggs Cape Florida State Recreation Area

2-mile-long (3-km) beach, where the sand is soft and the parking is easy.

🛉 230 C2 ⊠ 4000 Crandon Boulevard
☎ 305/361-5421 ⏰ Daily 8–dusk
✋ Inexpensive

Bill Baggs Cape Florida State Recreation Area

Perhaps the nicest beaches on Biscayne Bay are at the very end of Crandon Park Boulevard. This park offers every convenience imaginable. It will make you want to quit your job, sell your house, move to Miami and start weaving hats out of palm leaves. When you get tired of doing nothing but lying on the beach like a jellyfish, there's a café, playground, boardwalk, picnic cabanas, bridle paths, bicycling, skating, kayaking, fishing piers and the

Cape Florida Lighthouse (circa 1846). Clean and pleasant, this is the kind of place you picture when you visualize leisurely Miami.

🛉 230 C2 ⊠ 1200 South Crandon Boulevard ☎ 305/361-5811
⏰ Daily 8–dusk ✋ Inexpensive

2 Virginia Key

3 Miami Seaquarium

4 Key Biscayne

Deep-sea Fishing

If you have the time and the interest (but note that it is very expensive), you can go deep-sea fishing. At **Crandon Park Marina** fleets of deep-sea fishing boats await enthusiasts ready to catch sailfish, kingfish, dolphin (the fish), snapper, wahoo, grouper and tuna. Chances are you can keep half your catch (the captain keeps the rest). Don't let a charter captain sell you a fishing license – charter boat licenses cover all passengers so it's not necessary. If you want to, go it on your own – rent a boat and go fishing, waterskiing or head off to a nearby island for a picnic.

🛉 230 C2 ⊠ Crandon Park Marina, 4000 Crandon Boulevard ☎ 305/361-1281;
www.miamidade.gov/parks ⏰ Daily 8–6 ✋ Very expensive (half-day charter)

For more information about deep-sea fishing and a range of other sports, contact the **Florida Sports Foundation** (2964 Wellington Circle North, Tallahassee 32308, tel: 850/488-8347).

5 Parrot Jungle Island

Founded in 1936, this attraction relocated to a new 19-acre (7.7-ha) home on Watson Island in June 2003. There are 3,000 exotic animals, over 362 species of parrot and 500 species of plants, as well as snakes, turtles, flamingos, panthers, monkeys and alligators at this wildlife park, which is centered on stage shows and displays.

➕ 230 C3 ✉ 1111 Parrot Jungle Trail, Watson Island ☎ 305/258-6453; www.parrotjungle.com ⏰ Daily 10–6 ♿ Moderate

Celebration cruises past Millionaires' Row and the Venetian Islands.

➕ 230 B3 ☎ 305/445-8456 ⏰ Daily 11, 1, 3, 5, 7 ♿ Inexpensive

Island Queen, Island Lady, Pink Lady

These double-decker tour boats carry passengers on a 90-minute bilingual narrated tour that cruises past the Port of Miami and Millionaires' Row.

➕ 230 B3 ☎ 305/379-5119; www.islandqueencruises.com ⏰ Daily 11–7, departing hourly ♿ Inexpensive

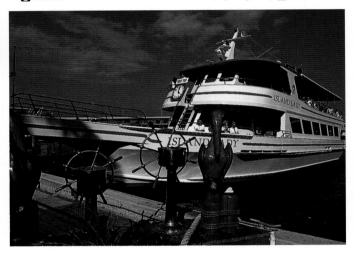

6 Boat Tours

Nothing beats the beautiful aquamarine waters of Miami. If you don't have $100,000 to spend on a high-powered boat, a few dollars will at least get you on the waves for a pleasant ride. If you can schedule this at dusk, you may catch the fabled "Moon Over Miami" rising above the horizon. The Bayside Marketplace (401 Biscayne Boulevard), which borders Biscayne Bay in downtown Miami, is home to several sightseeing cruises that provide refreshments as well as tour guides who can tell you what you're looking at. Check out:

Floribbean Hospitalities

The air-conditioned, 150-seat

Sightseeing cruises on Miami's bays are an inexpensive excursion

Heritage of Miami II

This double-masted, 85-foot (26-m) topsail schooner sails around Biscayne Bay past Coconut Grove, Vizcaya and the homes of several celebrities such as Sly Stallone. Remember, this one is a sailboat.

➕ 230 B3 ☎ 305/442-9697 (often on extended charters, so call ahead) ⏰ Hours vary, call ahead ♿ Inexpensive

7 Miami-Dade Cultural Center

If you're a traveler who likes indulging in art, books and history, then you can't do much better

than this. The 3-acre (1.2-ha) down-town complex encompasses the Miami Art Museum, the Historical Museum of Southern Florida and the Main Public Library.

Miami Art Museum
The highlights here are a permanent collection and major touring exhibitions of art-work by interna-tional artists, focus-ing on work completed after 1945.
➕ 230 B3 ✉ 101 W. Flagler Street ☎ 305/375-3000 🕐 Tue–Fri 10–5, Sat–Sun noon–5 ♿ Inexpensive

Historical Museum of Southern Florida
This is where you can see what Florida was like before tourism arrived. Whether you're interested in Native Americans, the Spanish conquistadors, or the transformation of a mosquito-ridden swampland into a subtropical paradise, you can find all the information you want right here.
➕ 230 B3 ✉ 101 W. Flagler Street, Miami ☎ 305/375-1492; www.historical-museum.org 🕐 Mon–Sat 10–5 (also 3rd Thu), Sun noon–5 ♿ Inexpensive

Cigars are still rolled by hand at Little Havana's El Credito

Main Public Library
If you need a place to read and think, the Main Public Library has nearly four million books and all the space you need to enjoy a little solitude. A great retreat if you're here on business.
➕ 230 B3 ✉ 101 W. Flagler Street, Miami ☎ 305/375-2665; www.mdpls.com 🕐 Mon–Sat 9–6 (Thu until 9; also Sun 1–5 Oct–May)

8 Little Havana
There is a definite difference between vacation perception and reality. If you talked to a travel agent, you would probably deduce that Little Havana is a festive Latino community that lives the carefree spirit of pre-Castro Havana. Don't be fooled. An assortment of ramshackle motels and cluttered store-fronts line the busy boulevard that slices through the center of the district.

Aside from a few monuments, there's not much to see. A few high-lights include **El Credito** (1106 S.W. 8th Street, tel: 305/858-4162 or 800/726-9481), where Cuban workers roll cigars by hand for the occasional celebrity smoker (customers include Robert DeNiro and George Hamilton) and the regular folks who just like a good cigar.

For contact with a foreign culture, drop by Domino Park, also known as Maximo Gomez Park (Calle Ocho and S.W. 15th Avenue), where elderly Cuban men gather to play dominoes, have a drink and talk about the good old days before the revolution.

➕ 230 B3 ✉ S.W. 8th Street (Calle Ocho), Miami

❾ Vizcaya Estate and Gardens

This estate gets a lot of mileage out of its magnificent facade and larger-than-life architecture, but you'll either love it or hate it. Chicago industrialist James Deering originally built his 34-room winter residence on Biscayne bayfront. The home is beautiful, albeit slightly sterile due to the paintings, sculptures, antiques and furniture from the 15th through 19th centuries. Leave the guided tour when you can, and spend more time on your own in

Venetian Pool: Denman Fink's fantasy swimming pool

the 10-acre (4-ha) formal gardens or by the water. This will take about an hour.

➕ 230 B3 ✉ 3251 S. Miami Avenue, Coconut Grove ☎ 305/250-9133; www.vizcayamuseum.org ⏰ Daily 9:30–5 (house), 9:30–5:30 (garden) 🖐 Inexpensive

⓫ Coral Gables

In the early 1920s, George E. Merrick envisioned an American Venice, so he built it. After adding 1,400 acres (567ha) to the 160 acres (65ha) of vegetable fields and citrus groves he inherited, Merrick created his ideal city based on Mediterranean images. The result is this community located a few miles – and worlds – away from Miami.

➕ 230 A3 ✉ Coral Gables Chamber of Commerce, 360 Greco Avenue, Suite 100, Coral Gables ☎ 305/446-1657; www.gableschamber.org

Miracle Mile

Should shopping be your thing, this strip of bridal boutiques, antique shops, bookstores, jewelry galleries and other independent merchants makes passing some time with the locals worth considering. **Books &**

Books, one block north of the Miracle Mile, is a treat (296 Aragon Avenue, tel: 305/442-4408).

➕ 230 B3 ✉ Coral Way between S.W. 37th Avenue (Douglas Road) and S.W. 42nd Avenue (Le Jeune Road)

Venetian Pool

If you can carve out some free time to relax, do it here. This stunning work of art makes hotel pools look like ordinary swimming holes. Artist Denman Fink turned an old rock quarry into a Venetian canalscape, and the fantasy aquatic village attracted movie stars, big-band leaders and beauty queens – whose vintage photos are displayed here. You will have no regrets about coming here – even if you can't swim. The convenient snack bar, lockers and showers make this a welcome retreat.

➕ 230 A3 ✉ 2701 DeSoto Boulevard, Coral Gables
☎ 305/460-5356
🕐 Days and hours vary by season, call ahead 💲 Inexpensive, parking free

A simple room in the 34-room mansion known as Vizcaya

there. Built in the 1920s, this 278-room showplace is an architectural masterpiece. Although it fell on hard times for decades and served as an army hospital in World War II, it was carefully restored in 1992. The lavish Moorish-style lobby, adorned with antiques and chandeliers, has a hand-painted ceiling. Outside, the palatial balcony and grand pool are stunning. Now owned by the city of Coral Gables, the hotel is operated by Westin. Wander around at your leisure, and if you're here on a Sunday afternoon, take a guided tour. Ask about the Everglades Suite (also known as the Al Capone Suite), where former President Clinton stayed when visiting Miami.

➕ 230 A3
✉ 1200 Anastasia Avenue ☎ 305/445-1926; www.biltmorehotel.com
🕐 Daily; tours Sun 1:30, 2:30 and 3:30 pm

Map labels:
DOLPHIN EXPRESSWAY
TAMIAMI TRAIL
WEST MIAMI
Little Havana **8**
Coral Gables **11**
Vizcaya Estate **9**
SOUTH MIAMI
Coconut Grove **10**
Biscayne Bay

Biltmore Hotel

Why is a 16-story re-creation of Seville's Giralda Tower sitting in the middle of a residential neighborhood? Because George Merrick wanted it

Coral Gables Merrick House and Gardens

If you're here on a Wednesday or Sunday and you have time, then drop by the boyhood home of George

Merrick. A 10-minute video presentation is a good introduction to his life as well as to this Old Florida home, which has been restored to its early 1900s appearance. On display in the homestead are family heirlooms, antique furnishings, photographs and artwork. Take a lazy walk around the tropical grounds and try to imagine what it was like for Merrick growing up here.

🔢 230 A3 ✉ 907 Coral Way
☎ 305/460-5361 🕐 House: Wed and Sun 1–4 or by appointment 💰 Donation

🔢 Fairchild Tropical Gardens

The name "tropical garden" conjures up images of an exotic paradise with brilliantly colored plants and flowers. At Fairchild, named for David Fairchild, a prominent tropical botanist and resident of Miami, it's more like an understated landscape with various shades of green and a few tinges of color. There are 11 lakes, a hothouse, and flowering plants such as orchids, mountain roses and bougainvillea. Several areas are very picturesque, and special events including theatrical and musical performances, enhance the natural setting. Go here with the understanding that A) you should wait for the on-the-hour tram tour instead of hoofing it across the 83-acre (33.5-ha) park, and B) you won't find a Hawaiian paradise of flowers.

🔢 230 A2 ✉ 10901 Old Cutler Road, Coral Gables ☎ 305/667-1651; www.fairchildgarden.org 🕐 Daily 9:30–4:30; closed Dec 25 💰 Inexpensive

Fairchild Tropical Gardens, an 83-acre (33.5ha) oasis, is named after the renowned local botanist David Fairchild

🔢 Miami Metrozoo

This place deserves to be among the top zoos in America, especially since the animals aren't caged – they're protected from visitors by a moat. More than 700 creatures are given room to enjoy simulated natural habitats in this 290-acre (117-ha) site. Star attractions are the **Tiger Temple**, with its splendid rare white Bengal tigers; the permanent **koala exhibit**; and **African Plains**, which features giraffes, zebras and ostriches.

Children can also get close up to a variety of animals at **PAWS** (a petting zoo) and at the **Ecology Theater**, which features Florida's native animals. A **Wildlife Show** has trained animals demonstrating natural behavior on cue.

🔢 227 E3 ✉ 12400 S.W. 152nd Street ☎ 305/251-0401; www.zsf.org 🕐 Daily 9:30–5:30, last entry 4 💰 Inexpensive; 45-minute tram tour inexpensive

Metrozoo gives animals such as this Bengal tiger relatively free rein

Farther Afield

Miami to Palm Beach

If you can escape the gravitational pull of South Beach, you may find yourself driving up Collins Avenue (also known as A1A) toward north Miami. At first you may not notice many differences since you'll still see a series of art deco hotels that gradually fade in favor of taller, boxier, uglier condominiums.

Thankfully, you don't have to look at the condos. On your left is **Indian Creek** and on the opposite shore are beautiful homes that were built in the 1920s. The contrast between modern condos and these classic homes is striking, and crossing a bridge into these old neighborhoods,

1950s, here's your answer. Famed Miami architect Morris Lapidus created this large and ostentatious 1,200-room grand dame to appeal to high rollers who were flying south for the winter. It reflects a part of Miami's past that is largely overshadowed by the success of South Beach, but it's worth a stop to see a hotel that looks like a city.

The Fontainebleau was so successful that the following year Lapidus was asked to design another hotel. The **Eden Roc**, a few doors north, was his response. Smaller than the Fontainebleau, the nautical-deco Eden Roc is classier, looking like a steamship heading out to sea. Inside is just as nice. Lapidus pointed out,

Miami's magnificent Fontainebleau Resort, known locally as "the Big Blue"

you'll enjoy several blocks of low-key sightseeing.

Back on Collins Avenue at 44th Street, where the road bends to the left, is the "modern French provincial" **Fontainebleau Resort**. If you lie awake at night wondering what kind of hotels they were building in the

"If ever I designed an elegant movie set as a lobby for a grand hotel, this was it."

From here, the grand hotels stop and are followed by a nondescript stretch of A1A until you reach 91st Street and the back-to-back towns of Surfside and Bal Harbour.

Surfside is popular with French Canadians, who frequent the beaches between 88th and 96th streets. Perhaps they're also drawn to the real neighborhood, which has gift shops, pharmacies, restaurants and other working-class businesses filling in the storefronts along Collins Avenue.

A few blocks north, **Bal Harbour** is Miami's last gasp of grandeur, a "square mile of elegance." Former Senator Bob Dole owns a condo here, as do other millionaires who treasure their access to the ultra-exclusive **Bal Harbour Shops** at 9700 Collins Avenue. The 100-plus stores and boutiques are anchored by the largest Saks Fifth Avenue in Florida. Drop by if you simply can't return home without a trinket from Gucci, Cartier, Chanel, Tiffany & Co. or Neiman Marcus.

Just north of this salute to materialism, Miami switches gears with more natural pursuits. At **Haulover Beach Park** (10800 Collins Avenue, tel: 305/947-3525, inexpensive), the county has provided a range of outdoor activities as well as the rare clothing-optional beach. There are barbecue grills, tennis and volleyball courts, exercise paths, kite and kayak rentals, charter fishing excursions and a nine-hole golf course – but all of these require clothing.

If you can't get enough of the great outdoors, farther north you can make a left on N.E. 163rd Street to enter the **Oleta River State Recreation Area** (3400 N.E. 163rd Street, tel: 305/919-1846, inexpensive). Less dressy than Haulover, it's the largest urban state recreation area in Florida (1,043 acres/422ha) and emphasizes camping, kayaking, canoeing and fishing. Popular with people who prefer a more rustic retreat, in the winter it also attracts dolphins, ospreys and manatees.

A few miles later you'll leave Miami-Dade County and enter Broward County. Along A1A there's not much to look at with the exception of the Atlantic Ocean, which isn't a bad deal at all. Then again, you may have to catch glimpses of it between the towering condos that line the waterfront.

Collins Avenue is long gone, and when you reach the town of **Dania**, A1A takes a sharp left and joins US 1, also called Federal Highway, for a few miles. The reason you should stop here is because the best buys in Florida aren't in regular malls but in antiques shops. There are antiques shops and stands here in great numbers, which makes spending a day of treasure hunting fairly easy – although you have to realize this isn't a quaint shopping district but a busy highway.

14 Fort Lauderdale

After you pass I-595, look for the 17th Street Causeway, where you turn right and return to A1A, the lovely road that lets you ride beside the seaside. You're in **Fort Lauderdale** now, which is sometimes called America's Venice. There are more than 250 miles (400km) of navigable waterways that crisscross the city, and thousands upon thousands of private boats are docked along these canals.

Highway A1A is either called Atlantic Boulevard or Ocean Drive here. Either way, stay on this road and between Las Olas Boulevard and

Sunrise Boulevard you'll find the center of Fort Lauderdale's beachfront activities. A low, wavy white wall threads its way between the road and the beach. It's a slow drive through this section, not so much because there's a lot of traffic but because cars slow down for pedestrians walking over to the beach and filtering in and out of sidewalk cafés and stores. Male drivers tend to slow down even more for the women in bikinis who roll past on skates.

If you can pull yourself away from the rolling bikini display, another side

Fort Lauderdale has one of the liveliest beaches along this stretch of the coast

Fort Lauderdale – America's Venice, minus the gondoliers

of Fort Lauderdale can be seen by returning to Las Olas Boulevard and driving west. Along the way you'll see some expensive homes and boats along the New River. The boulevard then turns into a district of art and history museums, and the **Las Olas Riverfront**, an entertainment, dining and shopping complex, with outdoor cafés, picnic tables and park benches. The **Riverwalk** promenade is what its name implies – a pleasant place in which to take a gentle stroll along the waterfront.

15 Boca Raton

When their town was incorporated in 1925 at the height of the Florida land boom, Boca Raton's city fathers commissioned famed society architect Addison Mizner to plan a world-class resort community. Although the end of the boom squelched most of his plans, one of Mizner's projects – **City Hall** – was completed in 1927. It still bears the original footprint of the Mizner design, and was constructed using ironwork, tile and woodwork supplied by Mizner Industries. Restored to its former elegance, today it serves as home of the **Boca Raton Historical Society**. Boca remains an affluent city anxious to show off its wealth, and it does so at places like **Mizner Park**, a shopping and residential district where upscale boutiques, art galleries, jewelers and cafés set the scene for concerts by top-name performers. Relax in the amphitheater, or on the grass and enjoy.

Boca Raton Historical Society
✚ 227 F4 ✉ 71 North Federal Highway ☎ 561/395-6766; www.bocahistory.com

Mizner Park
✚ 227 F4 ✉ 500 S.E. Mizner Boulevard ☎ 561/362-0606; www.miznerpark.org

Pink is the color in ritzy Mizner Park

16 Palm Beach and West Palm Beach

Making Boca Raton look like the poorhouse is **Palm Beach**, which, for more than a century, has been the favorite winter playground for America's wealthiest families. Palm Beach is largely the creation of Henry M. Flagler, who first saw the future of Florida tourism in the late 1800s. Flagler was in his 50s when he opened up the state to tourism by building the Florida East Coast Railway to deliver travelers to the doors of resorts in St. Augustine, Daytona, Palm Beach, Miami and Key West.

The **Flagler Museum** (One Whitehall Way, tel: 561/655-2833; www.flagler.org) is located in Whitehall, a mansion he built for his wife, and while the museum displays much of Flagler's possessions (such as his private railroad car), the biggest display of his wealth and vision is a few blocks away at **The Breakers** (One South County Road, tel: 561/655-6611; www.thebreakers.com).

Originally built by Flagler, it was rebuilt twice after the first two burned down, and today's version (► 144) was modeled after Rome's Villa Medici. In 1926, 75 Italian artisans arrived to complete the magnificent paintings on the ceilings of the 200-foot-long (61-m) main lobby and first-floor public rooms. Today's rates may be daunting, but you can walk around the lobby and public area for free and get a sense of the size, style and elegance Flagler brought to Palm Beach.

Easier on the wallet is **Clematis Street** (tel: 561/833-8873), a popular gathering spot for locals. Located in downtown West Palm Beach along Flagler Drive and bordering the Intracoastal Waterway, the 20-square-block district is the acknowledged arts and entertainment center of the area, with more than 50 bars and restaurants, frequent live entertainment, free trolley service and parking in some locations.

More upscale is **City Place** (700 S. Rosemary Avenue, tel: 561/366-1000; www.cityplace.com), a complex of stores, restaurants and movie theaters

The palm-shaded entrance to Palm Beach

created in a European town-center style. Although relatively new as a complex, one building they did recycle is the **Harriet Himmel Gilman Center** – a concert venue formerly known as the First United Methodist Church.

If you really need to visit an art museum, the **Norton Museum of Art** (1451 S. Olive Avenue, tel: 561/832-5196; www.norton.org) claims to be Florida's largest. As you're measuring the interior, take a look at the 19th- and 20th-century paintings and photography from American, European and Chinese artists such as Matisse, Miro, Gauguin, Monet, Picasso and O'Keefe.

Greater Fort Lauderdale Convention & Visitors Bureau
🚹 227 F5 ✉ 1850 Eller Drive, Suite 330 ☎ 954/765-4466; www.sunny.org

Palm Beach County Convention & Visitors Bureau
🚹 227 F5 ✉ 1555 Palm Beach Lakes Boulevard, Suite 800, West Palm Beach 33401 ☎ 561/233-3000 or 800/833-5733; www.palmbeachfl.com

🔟 Big Cypress National Preserve

Located 50 miles (80km) from both Miami and Naples, **Big Cypress National Preserve** covers more than 700,000 acres (280,000ha) and contains a mixture of pines, hardwoods, prairies, mangrove forests, cypress strands and domes. White-tailed deer, bear and Florida panther roam the park, sharing it with tropical linguus tree snails, royal palms and cigar orchids. This is a wonderful place to witness biological diversity, and the camping, canoeing, kayaking, hiking, and birdwatching provide more reasons to stick around and experience a preserved section of wild Florida.

In Clewiston is the **Seminole Indian Reservation** (tel: 800/683-7800; www.seminoletribe.com; Tue–Sun). The Ah-Tah-Thi-Ki Museum shows 'We Seminoles', a film that chronicles the tribe's struggles to survive, and presents artifacts and cultural displays that explain how they hunted, cooked, traveled, married, told stories and worshipped. Other activities include the chance to spend the night in an authentic *chickee* (covered shelter).

Big Cypress National Preserve
🚹 227 D3 ✉ Tamiami trail (US 41) ☎ 239/695-1201; www.nps.gov/bicy 🕐 8:30 am–4:30 pm 💲 Free

Mangroves in Big Cypress: A vital plant system

Miami to Key West

🔞 Biscayne National Park

Southeast of Miami, off the road that leads to the Keys, is **Biscayne National Park**. About 95 percent of the park is underwater, so start at the visitor center (on dry land) to learn about the park through exhibits, films and scheduled events. You can sign up for snorkeling and dive trips, and island excursions. If you prefer to travel solo, canoes and kayaks can be rented (inexpensive) to get you on the water and up close to the mangrove shoreline. The safest route may be guided glass-bottom boat tours (moderate) that last three hours and reveal a flood of sea turtles, dolphins, tropical fish and coral reefs. Getting you even closer are dive trips (snorkel,

A whole new underwater world: Biscayne

scuba and night) that depart from the marina to living coral reefs, although windy conditions may change the destination to a quiet bay. Snorkeling (inexpensive) includes your equipment and instruction; two-tank scuba dives (expensive) are offered on weekends only and require certification and equipment rental; one-tank night dives (expensive), which reveal

a hidden world beneath the waves, are held only once a month.

November through May, campers can catch a lift (moderate) to **Elliott Key** or **Boca Chita Key** for an evening (inexpensive) as a castaway. Elliot has freshwater, and both have showers, campsites, restrooms, trails and a swimming area. Be prepared for raccoons, mosquitoes and nearly invisible insects called "no-see-ums."

> **Biscayne National Park** ➕ 227 F2
> **Biscayne National Park Visitor Center**
> ➕ 227 E2 ✉ 9700 S.W. 328th Street,
> Homestead ☎ 305/230-1100 or
> 305/230-7275; www.nps.gov/bisc

🔟 The Keys and Overseas Highway

On a map, the **Florida Keys** (➕ 227 D1) are one of the country's most recognized features. If you've made it as far as Miami, chances are you're going to go on to reach the southernmost point of the continental United States.

You can refer to the general tour (➤ 209), but there are several more places to visit en route where you can scuba dive on living coral reefs, spot rare bird species nesting on remote islands, kayak in serene backwaters and hike among divergent tropical flora in dense hammocks.

On Key Largo (at MM 102.5), the major attraction is the **John Pennekamp Coral Reef State Park** (➤ 210, tel: 305/451-1202; www.pennekamppark.com), the first and finest underwater preserve in the nation. It covers 75sq miles (195sq km) and is a refuge to 55 varieties of coral, more than 500 species of fish, and shipwrecks from the 1600s. The draw here is diving, pure and simple.

At the park you can rent a canoe, kayak, and even swim fins, snorkel and a mask. After you sign up for a snorkeling or scuba charter, board a boat for the shallow reefs and see a colorful flow of tropical fish ablaze in the clear waters. One of the most popular features of the park is the "Christ of the Deep" statue. Just 11 feet (3.4m) below the surface, it's easily accessible and an underwater photo beside it makes a great souvenir.

Kick back, relax and enjoy the Keys' life

Marathon, the largest key, is also one of the least scenic, although it is home to the **Dolphin Research Center** (MM 59, tel: 305/289-1121; www.dolphins.org), known for its dolphin swims (expensive). A tour may have to suffice. **Crane Point Hammock** (MM 50.5, tel: 305/743-9100; www.cranepoint.org), is a 63-acre (26-ha) historical and archeological site that contains evidence of pre-Columbian and prehistoric Bahamian artifacts and was once the site of an entire Indian village.

After Marathon, the **Seven Mile Bridge** is an engineering marvel that parallels the railroad track built by Florida pioneer Henry Flagler. From the impressive span you'll have a glorious view of the Florida Straits. Later, at MM 33 at Big Pine Key, the **National Key Deer Refuge** (tel: 305/872-2239; www.nationalkey-deer.fws.gov) is a 9,200-acre (3,725-ha) expanse of mostly undeveloped pine lands where the diminutive Key deer

(less than 3 feet/90cm tall) live. Once there were fewer than 50 deer remaining before extinction, and today there's an estimated 600 Key deer located on Big Pine and No Name Keys.

A few more miles and you'll cross the last bridge into the most playful island of all: **Key West**. If you drink swim or dive you'll love Key West. If not, you may still enjoy it anyway. Then again, you can never be too sure how you will take mainland America's southernmost island. Once it was Florida's largest and wealthiest city, and through the years it has been home to pirates, fishermen, dropouts, authors, artists and hippies. When singer Jimmy Buffett spread the word about this remote island, wealthy escapees arrived to change Key West into a generic beachfront community. But many native Key Westers – or "Conchs" (pronounced "conks") – are not ready to give up their individuality. You can still find places, people and customs that thrive despite attempts to change them. When you arrive in Key West on US 1 (the only way to get on and off the island), you'll be at Roosevelt Boulevard. Turn right, go up a few blocks and you'll see the **Key West Welcome Center** (38 N. Roosevelt Boulevard, tel: 305/296-4444 or 800/284-4482; www.keywest welcomecenter.com), which is a smart first stop for brochures, as well as reservations for lodging, snorkeling and diving excursions, sunset sails, and tickets for train and trolley tours. You can also try the Chamber of Commerce (402 Wall Street, tel: 305/294-2587; www.keywestchamber.org).

It's a good idea to start with a tour. Although there's a variety of tours here (historic homes, vegetation, ghosts), boarding the **Conch Tour Train** (Mallory Square, tel: 305/294-5161; www.historictours.com) is an

navigate some places the train won't fit. Unlike the train tour, you can board and reboard at a dozen stops along the way.

In addition to trolley tours, you can try the in-depth walking or bicycling tours of **Island City Strolls** (tel: 305/294-8380; www.seekeywest.com). The guides of **Ghost Tours of Key West** (tel:305/294-9255; www.haunt-edtours.com) are dead serious about their work, and play the part by dressing like undertakers while taking you to the favorite haunts of the island.

After your tour returns to Mallory Square, you're at the center of activity in Key West. From here, you can begin a walking tour of the surrounding streets. Everything worth seeing is within a few blocks of here.

Pretty Mallory Square is at the heart of things

excellent way to get an overview of the entire island. You can board it here or, better yet, continue on Roosevelt and follow the signs to Mallory Square at the northeast tip of the island.

The Conch Tour Train has survived despite – or because of – its kitschy quality. After you board the tram, guides who know Key West inside out take you on a 90-minute tour of the island, explaining sites such as the **Audubon House**, **City Cemetery** and the **Southernmost Point**. If you see a place you'd like to explore, you might have better luck with the **Old Town Trolley** (6631 Maloney Avenue [office only], tel: 305/ 296-6688; www.historictours.com), which also takes a 90-minute tour but can

The **Mel Fisher Maritime Museum** (200 Greene Street, tel: 305/294-2633; www.melfisher.org) is a tribute to Mr. Fisher, who, after years of searching, discovered the wrecks of the *Nuestra Señora de Atocha* and the *Santa Margarita*. Both ships were carrying gold and emeralds. Among the displays is a 6-lb (2.7kg) gold bar and a 77-carat uncut emerald.

Just as impressive is the **Harry S. Truman Little White House Museum** (111 Front Street, tel: 305/294-9911). America's 33rd president fell in love with Key West and came here to escape from presidential pressure. If you know anything about Truman, you'll appreciate the sincerity of the tour. The guided walk through this simple two-story house affords access to nearly every room.

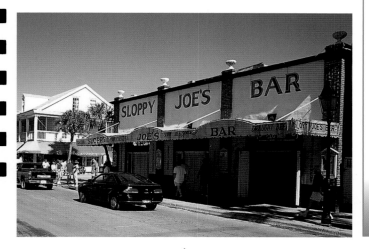

The **Curry Mansion** (511 Caroline Street, tel: 305/294-5349; www.curry mansion.com), a magnificent historic home/bed-and-breakfast, lures people in through heavy advertising. If you're an architect or it's raining, go inside. If not, save your money.

Believe it or not, you may even consider missing the **Hemingway Home and Museum** (907 Whitehead Street, tel: 305/294-1136; www.hemingway home.com). You will see where the author wrote *For Whom the Bell Tolls*, *To Have and Have Not* and *A Farewell to Arms* from a second-story writing room, but tours are often crowded and guides may push tours to pack more people in.

You'll probably have more fun on a snorkeling excursion, parasailing ride, or a tall ship cruise aboard one of the charter boats that depart from the Harbor Walk at the end of William Street. The *Fury* catamaran (tel: 305/294-8899 or 800/994-8898; www.furycat.com) is a safe bet. The huge, steady boat departs from the Hilton Marina, sails out a mile or so and serves free champagne, beer, wine, and soda along the way. It also offers an earlier snorkeling/sunset cruise combination.

One thing you can't miss in Key West is the **Sunset Celebration**, with the biggest party of all at **Mallory**

The fabled Sloppy Joe's, a favorite watering hole with visitors

Square. Arrive at least a half hour before sunset and you'll see the true side of Key West: skilled street performers juggling fire, balancing kitchen ranges on their faces, walking tightropes, and performing impossible tricks on bicycles.

Watching the sunset by boat, just off Key West

Where to Stay in Key West

There are several bed-and-breakfasts in town. One of the nicest is the **Island City House** (411 William Street, tel: 305/294-5702; www.islandcity house.com), which comprises three large buildings hidden within a tropical garden. A pool and free Continental breakfast complement the large and comfortable rooms.

For a wider selection of inns, hotels, motels or guest houses, remember to check with the **Key West Welcome Center** (38 North Roosevelt Boulevard, tel: 800/284-4482) or visit www.keywestinns.com for a list of inns.

Following sunset, most people return to their hotels to clean up and return later for the "Duval Crawl." Duval Street is the main shopping section of the town with several blocks of stores, bars and restaurants, as well as attractions like **Ripley's Believe It or Not!** (527 Duval Street, tel: 305/293-9694), a quirky museum filled with oddities like shrunken heads and an artistic re-creation of the Birth of Venus made out of 66 slices of browned toast.

There are dozens of fine restaurants, art galleries and gift shops along here, but drinking is big business and the real draws are two of Key West's 582 bars. **Sloppy Joe's Bar** (201 Duval Street, tel: 305/294-5717; www.sloppyjoes.com) is legendary.

Around the corner, **Capt. Tony's Saloon** (428 Greene Street, tel: 305/294-1838) is the site of the original Sloppy Joe's Bar, and is more authentic and less touristed.

At the south end of the island, the **Key West Lighthouse** (938 Whitehead Street, tel: 305/294-0012; inexpensive) was built in 1847. The 86-foot-tall (26-m) structure was decommissioned in 1969, but you can still visit it and the Keeper's Quarters and museum.

Street performances become more spectacular as the sun sets

Top tips
• If you're not used to driving in America, US 1 is not the place to learn. Narrow lanes and speeding drivers make the only highway in and out of the Keys fairly nerve-wracking. Drive defensively, and keep your headlights on to be seen.
• Despite being surrounded by ocean, Key West has few good beaches. One is the beach at the **Fort Zachary Taylor State Historic Site** (accessed through the Truman Annex), another is **Smathers Beach** near the southeast tip of the island near Key West International Airport.
• On your way south along the Keys, plan on making numerous stops along the way. Even though you think you'll only be going to Key West, you'll find plenty to see in Largo, Marathon, and Moradas.
• Peak season is from the beginning of February through May, and again from October through December. **It's slow and very hot in June and July.** Make reservations.

Where to...
Eat and Drink

Prices Expect to pay per person for a meal, excluding drink
$ under $25 $$ $25–50 $$$ over $50

Miami (particularly Miami Beach) has undergone a major renaissance since the late 1980s. This is especially evident in the restoration of South Beach's Art Deco District, where throngs of beautiful people stroll (and rollerblade) along Ocean Drive. Food can be a bit of a hit-or-miss proposition as many restaurants in the area are driven by trends, not quality, and prices overall are very high. Don't despair, though, because there are many wonderful restaurants that turn out impressive food. And if nothing else, dining in Miami is always a scene.

MIAMI

⬤⬤⬤ Chef Allen's $$$

Allen Susser has been producing some of Miami's most exciting food for more than a decade. The restaurant is modern, filled with clean lines and features a glass-encased kitchen. The menu makes full use of the bountiful array of ingredients available in southern Florida, and thus the seafood dishes are particularly inspired. As a whole the New World food is excellent, if at times overly creative. Be sure to save room for one of the dessert soufflés.

➕ 230 C5 ⬛ 19088 N.E. 29th Avenue (between 191st Street and Biscayne Boulevard), Aventura ☎ 305/935-2900

⬤⬤ China Grill $$$

The New York branch of China Grill practically invented Pan Asian cooking more than a decade ago, and the more recent Miami outpost does the cuisine proud. The huge restaurant is located on an otherwise quiet corner that oozes colorful South Beach glitz. Try incredible faux-Chinese fare such as dumplings filled with broccoli rabe or grilled Australian lamb with mandarin orange sauce. There is always a wait for a table, but the bar area is a great place to people-watch. For the more literary minded, there are passages from Marco Polo's travel diaries inlaid in a colorful mosaic.

➕ 230 C3 ⬛ 404 Washington Avenue, Miami Beach ☎ 305/534-2211

⬤⬤ Crystal Café $$$

A romantic and elegant, somewhat private, European-style restaurant. There are fewer than 20 tables here, which means the attentive waiting staff can guide you through the ever-evolving menu of "New Continental" cuisine – chicken paprikash, veal marsala, duck l'orange and more. The more modern take on Old World classics reflects the restaurant's creative direction under popular chef/owner Klime Kovaceski. The atmosphere, awards and ambience have earned Crystal Café a dedicated Miami Beach following. Reservations.

➕ 230 B3 ⬛ 726 Arthur Godfrey Road ☎ 305/673-8266

The Forge $$$

For the regulars at the Forge, there is no other steakhouse in Miami. The cathedral-like space contains a wacky mix of stained glass, high-backed chairs and contemporary accents. Steak is excellent and comes in varieties and cuts you didn't know existed. Continental specialties are also prepared here. There is an excellent wine list and a wine room for private dining.

✚ 230 C3 ⊠ 432 Arthur Godfrey Road (41st Street), Miami Beach ☎ 305/538-8533

♥ Islas Canarias $

There is always a crowd at this cheery family-run Cuban restaurant in Little Havana. On Sunday afternoons (after church), entire families savor home-style cooking that includes rich stews, fried plantains, fried pork, and rice and beans. A cup of *café con leche* or a fresh fruit shake helps wash it all down delightfully. If you don't speak Spanish, just look around the room and point to the dishes you want to order.

✚ 230 B3 ⊠ 285 N.W. 27th Avenue, at 3rd Street ☎ 305/649-0440

♥♥ Joe's Stone Crab Restaurant $$$

Customers are happy to wait for an hour, or sometimes two, to get into this legendary South Beach eatery. Since 1913, the restaurant has been serving its legendary stone crabs, with the fresh briny taste of having been just plucked from the water that has become almost as famous as the crabs. The claws are served cold with a tangy mustard sauce and the meat is sweet and delicious; pure pleasure. The stone crab claws are very expensive, but don't try to save by ordering one of the other entrées. If you've bothered to wait so long for a table, you might as well splurge. The Key lime pie is tart and rich, far and away the best dessert available. The restaurant closes from mid-May to October, when the crabs are out of season. It is also closed for lunch on Mondays during the season, but you can order from the take-out store and eat on the outdoor patio. The restaurant even ships its famous crabs all over the world, at a price.

✚ 230 C3 ⊠ 227 Biscayne Street (Washington Avenue), Miami Beach ☎ 305/673-0365

♥♥♥ Nemo Restaurant $$–$$$

The scene at Nemo's is white hot – which is usually an indicator of overpriced, inedible food and spacey service. Luckily Nemo's seems to be the exception that proves the rule! The Asian-accented food is light and often zestly spiced. Salmon comes wok-charred and served with a salad of sprouts and pumpkin seeds. The hearty country bread comes with a delicious bean dip. The outdoor patio is quite lovely with graceful arching trees – only beware of hard seed pods that can sometimes fall on you while you dine.

✚ 230 C3 ⊠ 161 Collins Avenue, at 1st Street, Miami Beach ☎ 305/532-4550

♥♥♥♥ Norman's $$$

Norman Van Aken is deservedly considered one of the top chefs in the state, and every night his stylish restaurant is packed with regulars from the Coral Gables neighborhood. The prices are high, even by Miami standards, but Van Aken manages to come up with such unusual and creative combinations that nobody complains. The menu is lengthy, making it difficult to choose between dishes such as pancooked peeky toe crab cakes with West Indian guacamole and Turks and Caicos cracked conch chowder with saffron, toasted coconut, star anise and "clouds." To beat the indecision, opt for the seven-course degustation menu so you can sample a little bit of everything. Some find the food a little too contrived, but it is certainly never boring.

✚ 230 A3 ⊠ 21 Almeria Avenue, between Douglas and Ponce de León Boulevard, Coral Gables ☎ 305/446-6767

♥♥♥ Pacific Time $$$

Pacific Time blends some of the most exciting cooking in southern Florida with a scene to match. The menu is true Pacific Rim with every dish an homage to its Asian roots. There is delicious mandarin duck salad with crisp wontons, bamboo steamed lobster tails, sweet sake-roasted sea bass, good Asian-style noodles and lots of spice. The decor is modern Key West in style, with ceiling fans, original art and a pleasant patio deck.

♯ 230 C3 ⌧ 915 Lincoln Road, Miami Beach ☎ 305/534-5979

☞☞☞ Smith & Wollensky $$$

Once it was difficult finding a great piece of meat in South Beach. But it is all about the steak at this haven for carnivores. Beef is available in various cuts and styles – filet mignon, sirloin, prime rib, au poivre – and all are prepared exactly as ordered (beware, though, rare here means "still mooing"). All items are à la carte, so the bill can add up when you order tempting side dishes such as creamed spinach, hash browns and fried onions. As if great steak weren't enough, the restaurant also has a magnificent view of South Beach and cruise ships on their way out to sea.

♯ 230 C3 ⌧ 1 Washington Avenue, at Collins Avenue, Miami Beach ☎ 305/673-2800

☞☞☞ Wish $$–$$$

Designed by Todd Oldham, Wish is pretty, sexy and tasteful all at the same time. The open-air patio, covered by great big white umbrellas, is a particularly pleasant spot to dine. The indoor dining room is smaller but equally fun, with velvet banquettes and hand-blown glass ceiling fixtures. The food is well prepared and borrows elements from around the globe. There are duck and ginger spring rolls, tortilla soup, risotto, and beluga caviar for those who are willing to splurge.

♯ 230 C3 ⌧ 801 Collins Avenue, Miami Beach, in The Hotel ☎ 305/674-9474

BOCA RATON

Mark's at the Park $

Fancy and representative of Boca's style and class is this highly regarded restaurant created by South Florida favorite chef Mark Militello. Exuding relaxed, laid back elegance and featuring a menu comprised of Militello's signature contemporary cuisine, the sleek bistro specializes in grill-oriented contemporary American cuisine. Dishes include Russet potato goat cheese tartlet with bitter greens and spiced walnuts, along with less formal options: Salads and pasta dishes as well as pizzas from the wood-burning oven.

♯ 227 F4 ⌧ 344 Plaza Real, Mizner Park ☎ 561/395-0770

FORT LAUDERDALE

☞☞ Casablanca Café $$

Although Sam isn't on the piano, this oceanside restaurant features live music. There is an interesting eclectic "new Floridian" menu that mingles Continental, such as filet mignon in mushroom sauce, with contemporary dishes including warm macadamia nut goat cheese salad. The service is friendly and the atmosphere comfortable and less pretentious than in other South Florida spots.

♯ 227 F4 ⌧ Corner of FLA A1A and Alahambra Street ☎ 954/764-3500

PALM BEACH

Bice Ristorante $$–$$$

Although most outposts of this trendy Italian chain offer excellent food, at the Palm Beach location it's the clientele that makes dining exciting. The area's wealthiest residents seem to treat this like their own private dining room, hopping from table to table to say hello and chat with their friends. Many of them prefer the outside patio dining. The food is contemporary Italian, with specialties from ultrachic Milan such as risotto, grilled dishes and roasted game in season among the best offerings.

♯ 227 F5 ⌧ 313½ Worth Avenue ☎ 561/835-1600

Where to... Stay

KEY LARGO

▼▼ The Fish House Restaurant $

Another nautical theme, but with an impressive ability to create seafood in a variety of ways. Spice up your life with fish prepared charbroiled, fried, Creole-style, pan-seared, or Jamaican jerked. The spices and choices make it worth the wait for a table, although outdoor seating helps ease the anxiety of waiting – as does the homemade Key lime pie. All is served in a fun, friendly, and casual "Keys style" atmosphere.

🚹 226 B1 ⊠ MM 102.4 102401 Overseas Highway ☎ 305/451-4665; www.fishhouse.com

KEY WEST

▼▼ Jimmy Buffett's Margaritaville Cafe $

There's a difference between real Key West dining and a chain restaurant run by a multi-millionaire, but if you're a Buffett

fan you may want to drop in and try the fish sandwiches, yellowfin tuna, Key West pink shrimp, ribs, beers...and the margaritas. Just kick back, have fun and enjoy great local food and listen to live bands.

🚹 226 B1 ⊠ 500 Duval Street ☎ 305/292-1435; www.margaritaville.com

▼▼ Mangoes $$

Although most restaurants in the Keys highlight fish and seafood, some of the freshest, most creative and the best-prepared is offered at this bustling eatery. Mangoes is known for "Floribbean" cuisine that blends Caribbean influences, local seafood and a touch of the Mediterranean. Conch chowder with lobster dumplings, fire and ice shrimp with cucumber-tomatillo relish, and local snapper are among the best choices. Also worth trying are the delicious pizzas, cooked in the hardwood-fired oven

🚹 226 B1 ⊠ 700 Duval Street ☎ 305/292-4606

MIAMI

Delano $$$

Wow! That's all you'll be able to utter the first time you walk through the lobby (imagine oversize beds, fur-covered chaises, 20-foot-high (6-m) mirrors and oddly hung wood paneling) of this ultra-chic hotel. Pass through billowing white curtains to the Alice-in-Wonderlandesque lawn, over to the impressive eternity pool, which is *the* place to sun on South Beach. There's only one way to describe the rooms: White. (Even the electronic equipment is bleached.) More than a hotel, it's an experience, designed by the eccentric Phillip Starck. A

word of advice: Skip the highly touted Blue Door restaurant. It may look cool, but it's an overpriced extravagance. Agua, the rooftop spa, is a great place to de-stress.

🚹 230 C3 ⊠ 1685 Collins Avenue, Miami Beach ☎ 305/672-2000 or 800/555-5001; www.ianschragerhotels.com

▼▼▼ The Hotel $$–$$$

This hotel is a fashion statement in its own right. Designed by Todd Oldham, the four-story, 52-room boutique property is a fantasy of cloud patterns, mosaic tiles, hand-blown glass and an overall casual beauty. The comfortable rooms feature modern amenities, and even the unusual robes were designed by Oldham. There is an impressive rooftop pool that overlooks the ocean, complete with changing areas, a juice bar and a fitness facility.

⏏ 230 C3 ☒ 801 Collins Avenue, Miami Beach ☎ 305/531-2222 or 877/843-4683; www.thehotelofsouthbeach.com

▼▼ Indian Creek Hotel $$

It truly feels like walking into the past in this restored hotel, which was built in the 1930s. All of the details are perfect, like the wood paneling on the walls and the period artwork. The rooms are not luxurious, but they are nostalgically cool, with an air of history that is somehow romantic. The hotel is past South Beach to the north, so it affords a much quieter stay and lower prices than you would find on the main drag. There is a nice pool and a courtyard.

⏏ 230 C3 ☒ 2727 Indian Creek Drive, Miami Beach ☎ 305/531-2727; www.indiancreekhotel.com

▼▼ ▼▼ Loews Miami Beach Hotel $$$

Located right on the beach, this is one of the largest hotels in South Beach. It offers modern services such as valet parking that are hard to find in the smaller art deco hotels of the area. The comfortably furnished rooms are relatively large. The pool area, however, is one of the most impressive in town. There are plenty of palm trees and chaise longues, a kidney-shaped pool and a hot tub. The best part is that its deck connects directly to the beach. There are two restaurants, the stylish Gaucho Room and the more casual Preston's.

⏏ 230 C3 ☒ 1601 Collins Avenue, Miami Beach ☎ 305/604-1601 or 800/235-6397; www.loewshotels.com

▼▼▼▼ Mandarin Oriental $$–$$$

The city's only AAA Five Diamond Hotel, this is in one of Miami's most prestigious commercial and residential locations. The exterior is shaped like the company's fan logo and

every room has a water view. Rooms and suites are crisp, clean and exotic, displaying a gentle Asian touch with earth tones and bamboo. A martini bar, pool area, private beach and five-star restaurant make this a serious consideration.

⏏ 230 B3 ☒ 500 Brickell Key Drive ☎ 305/913–8288; www.mandarin oriental.com

▼▼ ▼▼ Sonesta Beach Resort Key Biscayne $$$

This first-class resort is located across the bay from Miami on picturesque Key Biscayne. Guests need never leave as they love tennis, snorkeling, fishing, kayaking, golf or simply sunbathing on a beautiful stretch of oceanside sand. There are three-bedroom villas for those interested in complete seclusion, as well as three full-service restaurants and a fabulous tiki bar on the premises.

⏏ 230 C2 ☒ 350 Ocean Drive, Key Biscayne ☎ 305/361-2021 or 800/766-3782; www.sonesta.com

BOCA RATON

▼▼▼ Marriott Boca Raton $–$$

With all the modern amenities and luxuries that you would expect of a hotel of this kind, this is a first-class place, conveniently located and easily accessible. The 256 well-appointed guest rooms are large, spacious and feature modern furnishings and contemporary decor. The hotel boasts an outdoor swimming pool (with poolside bar and grill) with whirlpool, and a fitness facility.

⏏ 227 F4 ☒ 5150 Town Center Circle, Boca Raton ☎ 800/950-1363; www.marriott.com

FORT LAUDERDALE

▼▼▼ Lago Mar Resort Hotel & Club $$

This family-owned property has been renovated to update the rooms (most of which are suites) and public areas. Located on the water, it is ideal for people traveling with children.

📍 227 F4 ⊠ 1700 S. Ocean Lane
☎ 954/523-6511 or 800/255-5246;
www.lagomar.com

PALM BEACH

🦞🦞🦞 The Breakers $$$

If you intend to travel in style and jet-set luxury, this is the place to do it. In keeping with the town's character, The Breakers is an elegant resort with outstanding service that caters to your every need. After a fire in 1925 destroyed much of the building, 75 Italian artisans were hired to rebuild the hotel in the style of Rome's Villa Medici. In less than a year, and at a cost of around $7 million, work was complete. Opulence is the key here – marble staircases, crystal chandeliers and big closets. The hotel is close to the main shopping attractions of the city and has a fine restaurant.

📍 227 F5 ⊠ 1 S. Country Road
☎ 561/655-6611 or 800/833-3141;
www.thebreakers.com

KEY LARGO

🦞🦞 Westin Beach Resort $$-$$$

This four-story resort, nestled in a hardwood-tree hammock, has all the usual modern amenities, plus windsurfing, charter fishing, parasailing and a boat dock. Suites, with refrigerators, are twice the size of standard rooms.

📍 227 E2 ⊠ MM 97, 97000 South
Overseas Highway ☎ 305/852-5553

KEY WEST

🦞🦞🦞 Pier House Resort & Caribbean Spa $$$

This elegant resort offers a sophisticated respite from the frenzied main strip in Key West. The rooms vary in design – some have balconies, others have water views. The spa rooms feature large whirlpool bathtubs, and massage and other spa treatments are first-class.

📍 226 B1 ⊠ 1 Duval Street
☎ 305/296-4600; www.pierhouse.com

Where to... Shop

Tiny string bikinis, muscle Ts and designer gear are often worn in Miami, especially on South Beach, and they are all available for purchase throughout the city. Because of Miami's reputation as a jet-set destination and the constant stream of youthful inhabitants, the shopping tends to be much more interesting than it is in other parts of the state, especially when it comes to clothing. Most major designers have outlets in the area, and many funky independent clothiers cater to the club-hopping crowd. Like everything else in South Beach, shopping is a major scene.

South Beach

Looking frumpy in the Art Deco District is simply not the done thing. This is a land of beautiful people with perfect bodies dressed in today's latest styles. Some who arrive with a suitcase full of clothing that would be perfectly acceptable in their home town feel the need to revamp their wardrobe after they arrive, especially if they have any inclination to explore the club scene. Head to Collins and Washington avenues and you will find everything from haute couture and youthful clubwear to outlandish accessories and retro vintage styles.

Also in South Beach is the pedestrian promenade **Lincoln Road**. The redeveloped strip hosts occasional outdoor concerts and farmer's markets and is home to a wide variety of restaurants, cafés and galleries, as well as a plethora of stores selling everything imaginable. Strolling and window-shopping up and down the road is a pleasurable experience.

Environmental Lifestyle Store

(932 Lincoln Road, between Jefferson and Michigan avenues), and **Browne's & Co.** (841 Lincoln Road) sell New Age aromatherapy, hair and beauty products.

Aventura Mall

This trendy mall (19501 Biscayne Boulevard, tel: 305/935-1110; www.shopaventuramall.com) is a long haul from South Beach, but if you make the journey, you'll find a Burdines, Macy's and Bloomingdale's, as well as many stylish boutiques. There's valet parking and a free shuttle service from some Miami Beach and downtown Miami locations.

Bal Harbour

One of the premier shopping malls in the country is located just north of Miami Beach in the exclusive neighborhood of **Bal Harbour**. Visit the **Bal Harbour Shops** (▶ 130; 9700 Collins Avenue, tel: 305/866-0311; www.balharbour-shops.com) to bask in the opulence

and moneyed splendor that is exuded from the dozens of premier boutiques. Throughout the three-floor mall you can purchase serious jewels and watches at Bulgari, Georg Jensen, Cartier, Tiffany & Co. and Tourneau, or spend thousands on top designer fashions at Neiman Marcus, Saks Fifth Avenue, Giorgio Armani, Prada, Chanel and Versace. There are also more affordable stores, if you dare to be seen in them, such as Gap and Banana Republic. Opening hours for the malls are generally Mon–Fri 10–9, Sat 10–7, Sun noon–6, but there are exceptions.

Coconut Grove

In addition to Bal Harbour, there are lots of other malls in the area that house mostly chain stores.

CocoWalk (3015 Grand Avenue at Virginia Street, Coconut Grove, tel: 305/444-0777; www.cocowalk.com) is a three-level, outdoor mall with a tropical feel and plenty of lively restaurants and bars, as well as a

movie theater. There are more than 40 stores ranging from expensive clothiers, shoe stores and jewelers to T-shirt shops and kiosks that sell funky jewelry, gifts and the like. CocoWalk was conceived as much more than just a shopping mall; there's a strong cultural and entertainment component here.

South Miami

The Falls (8888 S.W. 136th Street, off US 1/S. Dixie Highway, tel: 305/255-4570; www.shopthefalls.com) is a huge, outdoor mall with a Macy's and Bloomingdale's, in addition to **Coach**, which sells beautiful leather goods; **Sephora**, a huge cosmetics and fragrance emporium; **Bombay Company**, for furniture; **The Disney Store**, with enough stuff to please kids of all tastes; **Brooks Brothers**, with clothing for the well-dressed man; and many, many more.

Loehmann's

Loehmann's, the famous discount women's clothing store that origi-

nated in Brooklyn, New York, is the centerpiece of **Loehmann's Fashion Island Mall** (2855 N.E. 187th Street, at Biscayne Boulevard, tel: 305/932-0520, Mon–Sat 10–9, Sun noon–6). The Loehmann's here also sells men's clothing, shoes and home furnishings, all at discounted prices. The mall also boasts other stores selling designer fashions and shoes, a jewelry exchange, home furnishing stores, a 16-screen movie theater and a choice of restaurants.

Festivals and Markets

There are several outdoor flea markets and festivals in Miami that run different times of the year. They are great fun to stroll through to find unusual merchandise and see colorful people. The **Art Deco Weekend** (Ocean Drive from 5th to 15th streets, tel: 305/672-2014) is a street festival that happens for four days each January, and it is one of the liveliest events of the year. The street is crammed full of vendors selling all types of vintage merchandise, as well as food kiosks and clothing booths. The festival stays open until midnight and the atmosphere is happy and eclectic, and sometimes feels more like a party than a place to shop. The **Outdoor Antique and Collectibles Market** (16th to 17th streets, between Lenox and Washington avenues/Lincoln Road, tel: 305/673-4991) runs the first and third Sunday from October to May. Here serious antiques tempt collectors.

For handmade international crafts and funky used clothing, the **Espanola Way Flea Market** (Espanola Way, between Washington and Drexel avenues) is the place. The small market is open Friday through Sunday and is always lots of fun.

Down in Key West, the prices are high and the selection ranges from tacky souvenirs to stuffed toy manatees. If you really must use your credit card to feel as if you've had a vacation, look for cigars or local crafts (kites and glasswork) in the stores along Duval Street.

Where to...
Be Entertained

Nightlife is supreme in Miami, where the club scene is seriously hot and the people are super cool. Ask at your hotel or pick up a copy of *Miami New Times*, a free alternative newspaper that has the latest information on the best clubs in town. You'll find it in kiosks around SoBe.

If you are staying in one of South Beach's cool hotels, ask the staff what's on. Otherwise consult one of the many publications that devote pages and pages to the club scene, such as *Channel* and *Ocean Drive*, both available free in most hotels. A lot of clubs cater to a thriving gay culture, and there is a plethora of colorful drag shows. Many clubs set up velvet ropes and have huge bouncers and stylish door people who monitor the guest list and decide which fashionable people will get to go inside. While this can seem very intimidating, it is rare to be turned away completely; simply wait your turn and try to look like you belong. Be sure to call ahead to check cover charges.

Nightclubs

For celebrity DJs and a hip mix of house, trance and progressive music, go to **crobar** (1445 Washington Avenue, tel: 305/531-5027) and consider yourself at the very center of South Beach cool. Not so much a nightclub as a real SoBe relic, **Mac's Club Deuce** (222 14th Street, tel: 305/531-6200) is an old bar where you can grab a beer, shoot some pool, listen to the jukebox and watch the Miami models who swing by. Open till 5 am. **Salvation** (1771 West Avenue between Alton Road and Dade Boulevard, tel: 305/673-6508), predominantly a gay club on Saturday night, is fun for all regardless of sexual orientation because of the bone-shaking dance music that emanates from the DJ's turntables. **Jimmy's at Cuba Club** (432 41st Street, tel: 305/604-9798) is next to the elegant Forge restaurant. This classy nightclub has plush furniture, a walk-in humidor with private cigar storage, and a see-and-be-seen vibe with lots of locals. **320** (320 Lincoln Road, tel: 305/672-2882) has a cozy, clubby atmosphere that draws a VIP mix of glamour folks.

Miami is America's gateway to South America, and appropriately the Latin music scene is one of the most happening in the country. It's possible to salsa dance, hear live music or see flamenco dancers within the city's confines. **Yuca** (501 Lincoln Road, at Drexel Avenue, tel: 305/532-9822) is a popular Latin-influenced restaurant.

A Little Havana mainstay, **Casa Panza** (1620 S.W. 8th Street, between S.W. 16th and 17th avenues, tel: 305/643-5343) is a great place for drinks while watching live music and beautiful flamenco dancers. Open till 4 am.

Power Studios (3791 N.E. 2nd Avenue, at N.E. 37th Street, tel: 305/576-1336) is a lively entertainment complex that caters to everyone, with a jazz and blues room, a rock and dance floor and an art gallery.

Cinema

While it may seem that Miami is all about partying, there are many outlets for those seeking loftier cultural activities. Several movie theaters show foreign and independent movies exclusively, with the occasional revivals thrown in for good measure. Among the best is **Alcazar Cinematheque** (235 Alcazar Avenue, between Le Jeune Road and Ponce de León Boulevard,

Coral Gables, tel: 305/446-7144). Check local newspapers for listings.

Theater, music and dance

For theater lovers there are several good venues that consistently put on quality productions.

For glitzy musicals with show-stopping numbers, check out the **Actors Playhouse** (280 Miracle Mile, between Ponce de León Boulevard and Salzedo Street, Coral Gables, tel: 305/444-9293; www.actorsplayhouse.org).

For excellent thought-provoking and sometimes avant-garde plays, head to **New Theatre** (65 Almeria Avenue, Coral Gables, tel: 305/443-5909; www.new-theatre.org).

The mission of the **Bridge Theater** (Dezerland Cabaret, 8701 Collins Avenue, Miami Beach, tel: 305/886-3908) is to present works by Hispanic playwrights in English to attempt to bridge the cultural gap that exists between the city's American and Latino populations.

Miami is a wonderful city for dance, and aficionados can enjoy performances that range from classical ballet to unusual modern ensembles. The best way to find out what's happening is to contact the **Florida Dance Association** (tel: 305/867-7111; www.fldance.org) and ask for a copy of its Florida Dance Calendar.

From October to May **New World Symphony** (Lincoln Theater, 541 Lincoln Road, at Pennsylvania Road, tel: 305/673-3331 or 800/597-3331; www.nws.org) puts on a grand array of concerts to showcase its immense talent.

The **Florida Grand Opera** performs classics such as *La Boheme* and *The Marriage of Figaro* at the Dade County Auditorium (2901 W. Flagler Street, at S.W. 29th Avenue, tel: 305/854-1643; www.fgo.org).

The **Florida Philharmonic Orchestra** performs at the Gusman Center for the Performing Arts (tel: 800/226-1812 – box office; www.floridaphilharmonic.org).

Key West

In the spirit of the island's most famous resident, Ernest Hemingway, drinking and beachcombing are the two major pastimes in this resort town. As a gay mecca, Key West has a number of fun dance clubs that fill up on weekend nights and provide entertainment for a mixed crowd. Key West is informal, so don't hesitate to venture out in your shorts and flip-flops.

Sports

Miami has always been proud of its thriving football culture – the Dolphins are the only NFL team to ever have an undefeated season, and the University of Miami Hurricanes dominated college football in the 1980s and 1990s. Each year the city hosts the Orange Bowl for college teams, and the city's Pro Player Stadium was the site of the 1999 Super Bowl. Football aside, Miami has never been as much of a sports city as Chicago or New York. In recent years, however, the city has flourished in this department with the addition of ice hockey, basketball and baseball teams. Tickets for all Miami sports events can be bought over the phone with a major credit card, by calling Ticketmaster on tel: 305/350-5050.

Football

The Dolphins' 1972 undefeated season is legendary. However, in recent years the team has not been much of a dominating force. Nonetheless it is always great fun to attend a pro football game – season-ticket holders throw elaborate tailgate (car-boot) parties and go all out.

✚ 230 B5 ⊠ Pro Player Stadium, 2269 N.W. 199th Street, North Dade ☎ 1-888/FINS-TIX; 888/346-7849; www.miamidolphins.com

The University of Miami's football team, the Hurricanes, may be even more popular than the Dolphins. They play in the renowned Orange Bowl and have racked up an impres-

sive championship record during the past two decades.

College sports are often more intense than professional sports, with revved-up fans, marching bands, cheerleading squads and athletes who are still young enough to really care about the game. A Hurricanes game is no exception.

✚ 230 B3 ⊠ Orange Bowl, 1501 N.W. 3rd Street, between N.W. 14th and 16th avenues ☎ 305/643-7100; www.hurricanesports.com

Basketball

Under former New York Knicks coach Pat Riley, the Heat was transformed into a dominating force in the game of basketball. Superstar center Alonzo Mourning, one of the league's top scorers, led the Heat to the playoffs for three consecutive seasons. Today, the team plays home games at the new Bayside American Airlines Arena.

✚ 230 B3 ⊠ Miami Arena, 701 Arena Boulevard ☎ 305/530-4400; www.miamiheat.com

Ice Hockey

In 1992, the NHL said that entrepreneur H. Wayne Huizenga could bring a team to South Florida. Although they haven't been as successful as his World Series-winning Florida Marlins baseball team, the Florida Panthers are gaining respect as fast, aggressive competitors with a lot of defensive skill on the ice. The team is fan-friendly and likes to encourage new fans.

✚ 227 E4 ⊠ National Car Rental Center, 1 Panther Parkway, Sunrise ☎ 954/835-7000; www.floridapanthers.com

Baseball

The Marlins (www.flamarlins.com) came from behind in 1997 to win the World Series after only five years in the league. To achieve this feat, the team's owner sank major amounts of money into recruiting top-notch players to lead the team to victory. Amazingly, they repeated the feat in 2003, when they won the World Series a second time.

Pro Player Stadium, also home to the Dolphins (▶ Football), is known for the 434-foot-deep (132-m) home-run zone that makes it very difficult for players to hit over the fence.

Golf

There are more than 50 public and private golf courses in Miami, but many of the best are attached to resorts and limited to registered guests. Among them, the famous **Blue Monster** course at the top-ranked Doral Golf Resort and Spa (4400 N.W. 87th Avenue, at N.W. 41st Street, tel: 305/592-2000; www.doralresort.com) by the airport ranks the highest. If you are staying at the **Fairmont Turnberry Isle Resort and Club** (19999 W. Country Club Drive, tel: 305/932-6200; www.turnberryisle.com), you can play on two Robert Trent Jones courses. The **Biltmore Hotel** in Coral Gables (1210 Anastasia Avenue, tel: 305/460-5364) has a challenging course that is open to the public.

Tampa Bay Area

Getting Your Bearings

Although Tampa's preservationists have faced an uphill battle (as witnessed by empty lots where historic homes once stood), they have managed to save enough of their city to reveal a coastal town that isn't driven solely by tourism.

At the turn of the 20th century, however, the troika of tourism, shipping and cigars made Tampa a cultural and commercial center. Yet as decades passed, the bloom came off the rose as Miami and Palm Beach became the state's favored winter playgrounds, Walt Disney chose Orlando as his new kingdom, and Tampa and neighboring St. Petersburg shifted to a haven for retirees. In the last decade, both cities have been busy polishing their images. Professional sports teams attract national attention, once-blighted neighborhoods are being transformed into attractive walking villages, and beaches continue to be a top attraction (➤ 14–16).

Clearly, the pace here is significantly quieter than in Orlando or Miami. Options for entertainment range from the lone theme park (Busch Gardens) to abundant museums, antiques districts and some of the best beaches in the state.

From Tampa south, the Gulf Coast waters become ever more beautiful and the towns equally picturesque. While there's traffic to contend with along the highway that skirts the coast, it's worth the effort to visit towns such as Sarasota and the twin paradises of Sanibel and Captiva.

Previous page: Tarpon Springs: Florida's first – and only – sponge diving center
Page 151: Greek gift shop, Tarpon Springs

At Your Leisure

Farther Afield

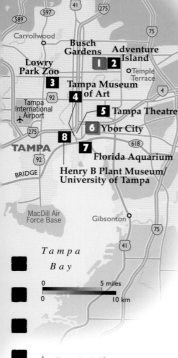

★ Don't Miss

Tampa Bay Area in Three Days

Three days in Tampa should provide enough time to experience the area's cultural offerings, laze on any of the powder-sand Gulf beaches and allow two nights to sample the nightlife of Hyde Park (civilized) and Ybor City (decadent).

Day One

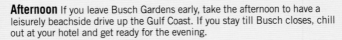

Morning Drive I-275 to Busch Boulevard and follow signs to ❶ **Busch Gardens** (tel: 813/987-5082, ➤ 154–157). An early arrival ensures no waiting on "can't-miss" rides (like Montu, right). (Check with your hotel for hours – they vary.)
Beat the lunch crowd and take a long break at the Crown Colony Restaurant at the entrance to the **Edge of Africa**.

Afternoon If you leave Busch Gardens early, take the afternoon to have a leisurely beachside drive up the Gulf Coast. If you stay till Busch closes, chill out at your hotel and get ready for the evening.

Evening Drive up Bayshore Boulevard, then west on Swann Avenue to enter **Old Hyde Park Village** (➤ 176) for dinner at an outdoor café. Walk around the surrounding 1920s Arts and Crafts community.

Day Two

Morning The Gulf Coast has hundreds of miles of beaches (➤ 14–16). Southern beaches are fine, but if you head north on Highway 699 to the lovely ❶⑥ **Clearwater Beach** (➤ 160), the powdery sands will crunch beneath your feet.
  If you've settled down at Clearwater, grab lunch at Pier 60, then return to tanning.

Afternoon If you want extra time in Tampa, head east. Take 60–90 minutes to hit the ⑧ **Henry B. Plant Museum** (➤ 162–163; Victorian), the ④ **Tampa Museum of Art** (➤ 161; pop to abstract to classical) or the ⑦ **Florida Aquarium** (➤ 162).

Evening Have a very exclusive dinner at Bern's Steak House (➤ 173), the restaurant with the largest wine list in the world and steaks to die for.

Alternatively, drive back to downtown and head to the ⑤ **Tampa Theatre** (➤ 162). One of the most beautiful movie palaces in the world, this time machine will take you back 70 years. Then it's an evening in ⑥ **Ybor City** (bottom left, ➤ 158–159). By the time you arrive, the madding crowd will be there to energize you into overdrive.

Day Three

Morning Take I-275 south to St. Petersburg and arrive at the ⑬ **Salvador Dalí Museum** (left, ➤ 166) when they open their doors. Beating the crowds allows you to appreciate the works of this madman/genius without interruption.

The ⑫ **Florida Holocaust Museum** (➤ 165) presents this horrifying episode with quiet dignity.

Afternoon Take a break and have lunch at the waterfront Renaissance Vinoy (501 5th Avenue N.E., tel: 727/894-1000). The hotel opened in 1925, was completely renovated in 1992 and looks better than it ever did.

Don't ask why the ⑪ **Florida International Museum** is in St. Petersburg – just be thankful it is. Exhibits are world class and presented with an eye on creativity (➤ 164).

For a change of pace take a walk down to the end of the St. Petersburg Pier. Less touristy are the abundant antiques shops on 4th Avenue. Catch a Tampa Bay Devil Rays baseball game if possible (played at St. Petersburg's Tropicana Field, April to October; www.devilrays.com).

Evening If you're feeling energetic, head over to BayWalk, the downtown entertainment complex with a 20-screen movie theater, stores, cafés and restaurants.

Busch Gardens

Busch Gardens, a slice of Africa thrust into the heart of urban American sprawl, has attracted tourists from around the world for more than 40 years. It's a heck of a lot of fun.

Busch Gardens is a major theme park squeezed on all sides by chain restaurants and strip malls. But when you walk through the African arches, hear the syncopated drumbeats, and see tribal masks and brass goods stacked high in the bazaar, you'll swear you've left Florida. If you're on a schedule, you may be tempted to breeze through the park hitting only highlights and getting back to the beach. Resist the temptation. This is worth a full eight hours.

The parking lots open a half hour before the park, so arriving early is a smart option that allows time to reach the entrance, review the park map and beat the crowds. After parking, you'll take a tram to the ticket booth/entrance.

If you know what tickets you need – better yet, if you've purchased them in advance – you'll be ahead of the game. Once you're inside, pick up a park map and entertainment schedule.

Meeting some of the menagerie of animals at Busch Gardens

Morning
Busch Gardens' regions have been given African names. The majority of guests tend to move to their right to reach Egypt and its popular roller-

Getting There
From Orlando westbound on I-4, exit north on I-75. Take the Fowler Avenue Exit 265 and follow signs to Busch Gardens. From Tampa, follow I-275, take Exit 33 (Busch Boulevard) and follow signs to the park.
➕ 224 B2
☎ 813/987-5082 or 800/4-ADVENTURE;
www.buschgardens.com
🕐 Daily 9:30–6, extended hours summer, holiday and weekend ✋ Very expensive; combined ticket available ➤ 81

coaster, Montu, as well as the safari-like Edge of Africa. It's tempting, but you'll save time and avoid lines by starting at the far left side of the park.

Once through the turnstiles (lavatories on your left), you'll pass through the Moroccan village. Turn to your right and bypass the Myombe Reserve. Don't panic and think you're missing everything – you'll have your turn later.

By starting at the **Skyride**, you can ride above the 65-acre (26-ha) **Serengeti Plain**, catching a glimpse of giraffes, zebras, lions, gazelles, impalas, lemurs, buffaloes, rhinos, ostriches, hippos, baboons and wildebeests – while obtaining aerial reconnaissance of the park's layout.

This gives you a lift above the increasing crowds and saves your feet on a one-way trip to the **Congo** region of the park. Since this is the far left corner of Busch Gardens, you'll have reached the park's farthest point in less than an hour. Leave the Skyride and head to your right to reach Montu's roller-coaster counterpart, **Kumba**. The highlight of this ride is three seconds of weightlessness courtesy of a spiraling 108-foot (33-m) vertical loop. Height restrictions may prevent smaller kids from riding Kumba, but smaller and slower coasters such as Congo's **Python** and Timbuktu's **Scorpion** provide equal opportunity to thrill them. Try to hit Congo early in the day to avoid the high-noon crowds that flock here to cool off on the water-based attractions. At the **Congo River Rapids** you sit in a circular, 12-person raft. Hang on tight as you fly through the whitewater. This must-see attraction is accompanied by neighboring **Stanleyville's** slower **Stanley Falls** (a log flume ride) and the **Tanganyika Tidal Wave**.

Hold on to your hats! It's not just the animals that make Busch Gardens a wild place

A new arrival is R.L. Stine's **Haunted Lighthouse**, a 4-D movie (a 3-D movie with sensory effects). Stine, a children's author, created this movie that revolves around a shipwreck, dead kids, and live kids trying to help them. You may want to see it because it's new and there are occasionally scary and/or funny moments, but other than that you won't need to see it again.

With a few thrill rides to your credit, continue your clockwise walk through the park. **Timbuktu** is filled with exotic, carnival-style rides and arcade games geared toward younger teenagers. It's not worth stopping if your time is short.

The next region, **Nairobi**, has no rides but you'll feel compelled to stop when you see the elephants and tortoises. It should be around noon now and you'll have reached the Skyride Station where you began the day.

Rhino Rally, on the east side of Nairobi, is a safari/thrill ride by Range Rover through five animal habitats. The safari part is a look at elephants, white rhinos, antelope, alligators, cape buffalo, zebras, gazelle and wildebeest. The thrill part is when your vehicle has to cross river rapids after a pontoon bridge is washed out. Then the comedy part is the quick one-liners tossed out by the safari guide. Topping the thrills, fun and wildlife is when the whole contraption is swept downriver before the safari can continue. Too much fun – don't miss it.

TAKING A BREAK

Grab a snack at a food kiosk or allow time for a leisurely lunch at the **Crown Colony Restaurant**, themed as an outpost of the British Empire, with cricket bats, polo mallets and vintage photos of Queen Victoria covering the walls. Unlike mass-produced theme park food, entrées here are tasty, portions large, and prices unusually fair. It's worth the few extra dollars to be able to enjoy table-side service, dine on the balcony and look over the Serengeti Plain.

Afternoon

After lunch you'll run into the flood of guests who began their day on the right side of the park. You've already covered more than half of the park with little interruption. The Crown Colony Restaurant is at the entrance to the circular **Edge of Africa**, a walk-through attraction. At the entrance, walk to your left and you'll reach an area where you'll be only a pane of glass away from baboons, hippos, crocodiles and most of the other animals you saw earlier from the

Skyride. If your timing is right, you may catch the lions wolfing down chunks of chicken or the hippos swallowing a vegetarian platter. If this is the closest you'll get to Africa, you may want to go on the half-hour jeep safari across the **Serengeti Plain** (moderate).

The walking path boomerangs back past flamingos, and within a few seconds you'll encounter a massive wall that seems to have come from the Valley of the Kings. This is **Egypt**, home of the **Montu**, the largest inverted rollercoaster in the Southeast. If you can ignore the screams of terrified passengers, work your way into the line. Unlike traditional sit-up-and-yell rollercoasters, this one will have you spinning upside down, plunging into tunnels and shrieking as you fly through the steel

Gwazi

Bolt together 236 miles (380km) of lumber, add two tracks, six fly-bys and speeds up to 50mph (80kph) and you've got Gwazi. Like most rides in Florida, this has a theme – here it's the mythological animal with a lion's body and a tiger's head battling it out between two coasters that come perilously close to one another. Gwazi completes Busch Gardens' trio of rollercoasters (Kumba and Montu are the other two) and is Florida's first dueling wooden roller coaster and the Southeast's largest and fastest wooden coaster.

maze at up to 60mph (97kph). If you doubt it's fast, check out the warning sign: "If you wear a prosthetic limb, make sure that it is firmly secure."

After this, you've done nearly every must-see ride – but you still haven't experienced the **Myombe Reserve**. This is home to chimps and gorillas – animals that command your attention even when they're doing nothing more than sleeping on mounds of hay or pacing behind glass before a large crowd.

Now the only things left to see are performances ranging from ice shows and 1950s musicals to bird and dolphin shows. Fun shows to watch, but only if your schedule allows. Try not to miss their newest show, **KaTonga**, performed inside the beautiful Moroccan Palace Theatre. The storyline of a celebration of African folklore involves huge and colorful puppets, rhythmic music and African-inspired dance created by Broadway producers. Near the front of the park, **Bird Gardens' Lory Landing** is a walk-through aviary where you can pay $1 to feed nectar to birds.

If you're traveling with kids, chances are they'll be dragging by now. They may come back to life when you take them to **Land of the Dragons**. At this elaborate kids-only fantasy land, the little ones can run like maniacs through treehouses, elevated boardwalks and fairy-tale cottages.

You should just about have reached the end of the road by now – time to go home and take a rest before deciding how to spend the evening.

BUSCH GARDENS: INSIDE INFO

Top tips If you plan to visit Universal Orlando, SeaWorld Orlando and Wet 'n Wild Orlando, see page 81 for details of the **Orlando Flex Ticket options**.

• If you feel you haven't had enough time at Busch Gardens, a **Next Day ticket** to the park costs $10.95. As the name implies, it's only good the following day.

• Most of the rides (especially Congo River Rapids) promise significant drenching, so wear something that will dry quickly or take a change of clothes with you.

• Don't wear heels or sandals – you may get your feet wet on the water rides. **Sneakers are the best bet** for comfort and safety.

• Even though the food here can be inexpensive, you can bring in your own provisions – just not in a cooler. **Backpacks and water bottles are allowed.**

6 Ybor City

So tranquil during the day, Ybor (pronounced Eebor) City needs to be tranquilized after dark. This is not a quaint Spanish village. The former capital of Tampa's cigar-making industry has been transformed into a boulevard of body-piercing parlors, coffee houses, beer joints, cigar bars and a fabled restaurant.

A few years ago, Ybor City was just another run-down neighborhood. Then, people with money saw a gold mine, bought the buildings, raised the rents and brought in new businesses to reap the rewards. That said, you won't find the spectrum of stores that were here a few years ago, but there are still plentiful reasons to visit Ybor City. Ybor is a National Historic Landmark District, and Barrio Latino, the area's watchdog group, makes sure buildings remain true to their Spanish/Cuban heritage.

And a fairly impressive heritage it is. Before the turn of the 20th century, when others saw only a heavily wooded and mosquito-infested clump of nothing, Key West cigar-maker and entrepreneur Don Vicente Martinez Ybor visualized the Cigar Capital of the World. Spaniards and Cubans, Italians, Jews and Germans began arriving for the steady work and wages that were offered.

Although it was primarily known to smokers, Ybor City's profile was raised when Teddy Roosevelt and his Rough Riders used Tampa as their point of embarkation to Cuba in the Spanish-American War. As soldiers and the press descended on Tampa, they discovered a thriving ethnic community in the heart of Central Florida. Shopkeepers lived above their stores on La Septima (7th Avenue) and the citizens gathered at casinos and their mutual aid societies.

If you arrive during daylight, a good place to get started is the **Ybor City State Museum**, housed in the old La Ferlita Bakery (1818 E. 9th Avenue, tel: 813/247-6323; www.ybormuseum.org; daily 9–5, inexpensive). Here you will get an interesting intro-

Intricate Spanish tile-work can be found throughout Ybor City

Ybor City Chamber of Commerce
224 B2   1514 1/2 8th Avenue   813/248-3712; www.ybor.org

duction to Ybor's beginnings, heyday, decline...and resurrection. Presentations include artifacts from the cigar factories, pictures and a 10-minute video on the history of the district. A restored cigar worker's home, La Casita, has been furnished in period and can be viewed (Tue–Sat 10–3).

Try dinner at the **Columbia Restaurant**, founded in 1905 and still in business (▶ 173). Ornate, handpainted tiles, several dining rooms (including a courtyard) and good service reflect the best of Spain. When Ybor City was a stop on the Havana–New York–Tampa entertainment circuit, the Columbia would feature flamenco dancers and classical guitarists – and they still do. There are free floor shows Monday through Saturday.

If you're around after dark, by 10 pm the streets become home to a wide selection of people, from bikers and bikers' chicks to punks and Rastafarians. To cater to the cross-section of culture, Ybor has opened clubs for just about every taste. Most of these are found along E. 7th Avenue. **Centro Ybor** (1600 E. 7th Avenue, tel: 813/242-4660; www.centroybor.com), is a typical entertainment complex with trendy stores and restaurants and a 20-screen movie theater. There is also a large number of soul clubs, R&B dives, country saloons, gay bars and techno-pop dance halls.

Ybor City's business is now cigars and tourism

YBOR CITY: INSIDE INFO

Top tips HARTLine (www.hartline.org) runs a Mon–Fri **lunchtime trolley service** from Tampa to Ybor City, approximately every 15 minutes from 11 am–2 pm. The fare is $1.25. Stops are about every two blocks.
• On weekend nights, **7th Avenue becomes a pedestrian mall**. Park outside that area if you plan to arrive early and stay late. Meters are enforced from 8 am–3 am Mon–Sat. Metered parking is available on side streets.
• Don't travel too far off 7th Avenue; **it's not particularly safe**.
• Want to walk on Cuban soil in the U.S.? Ybor City's El Parque Amigos de Marti Park **belongs to Cuba**.

16 Tampa Bay Area Beaches

The Gulf stays pretty calm most of the time. With that peace of mind, you can relax on sands that, for the most part, are soft and sugary and will persuade you to extend your leisure time on the beach (► 14–16).

There are 7 miles (11km) of undeveloped beaches southwest of downtown St. Petersburg at **Fort DeSoto Park**, and North Beach is a consistent favorite with locals. There are facilities here, the fort, a fishing pier and other activities to keep you occupied when you get tired of tanning. Most visitors think they'll have better luck on St. Pete Beach. Perhaps, but when you reach the beaches along Highway 699 (also known as Gulf Boulevard), stingrays often skim in the shallows. Hotels here suggest you do the "stingray shuffle" (carefully shuffling your feet on the surface of the sand) to scare them away – which is not a pleasing thought if you just want to dive in and splash around like a maniac.

Several miles north you'll find a beach that's not rocky or stingray-plagued. **Treasure Island** is a typical Florida beach town with everything you need for a good day of sunning and swimming. There's plenty of parking, facilities and a

The "Pink Palace." St. Petersburg's landmark Don CeSar

snack bar, and if you need more supplies there are several grocery stores within a short walk. You can rest here, or keep exploring.

North past John's Pass Village and Boardwalk in Madeira Beach, communities such as **Redington Shores**, **Indian Rocks Beach** and **Belleair Shores** have hidden entrances to beaches that provide more privacy – all good choices if your motivation is to experience seaside serenity.

The mother of all beaches is **Clearwater Beach**, and bright blue cabanas suggest a scene from the French Riviera. The beach is wide and wonderful. You're never too far from essentials, and there are fishing charters and parasailing boats departing from the marina. At the end of the day, you can walk down to Pier 60 to partake in the daily sunset celebration.

At Your Leisure

Tampa

2 Adventure Island

Gulf waters are smooth and salty, which makes this high-energy freshwater water park more popular with some folks. Aquatic thrills will find you plunging seven stories down a water slide at the Tampa Typhoon, shooting the flume at Runaway Rapids, and rocketing twisty tubes at Calypso Coaster and Key West Rapids. The 30-acre (12-ha) water park has nearly two dozen slides, heated pools, a wave pool, volleyball courts and snack bars. It takes about 5 hours to make the rounds, and although there are places to snack you may want to pack your own food and drinks.

🔢 224 B2 ✉ 4500 Bougainvillea Avenue, adjacent to Busch Gardens, Tampa Bay (➤ 154–157) ☎ 813/987-5600; www.adventureisland.com 🕓 Feb–Oct, hours vary 💷 Moderate. Parking inexpensive

3 Lowry Park Zoo

You could travel the world over to see four continents of wildlife, or you can just come here. From the Asian Domain to Primate World, roughly 1,600 animals call these natural surroundings home. There are baboons, lemurs, chimps and tigers. The Florida Wildlife Center showcases natives such as alligators, panthers and black bears. The Manatee and Aquatic Center is one of only three rehabilitation centers in Florida. Plump, cute-as-a-button sea cows spend their days swimming in a huge aquarium. At the interactive Lorikeet Landing you can invite birds to feed out of your hand. One more to look for is the new 6-acre (2.5ha) Safari Africa exhibit, which features zebras, elephants, giraffes and warthogs.

🔢 224 A2 ✉ 1101 W. Sligh Avenue, I-275 to Exit 48, follow signs ☎ 813/-935-8552; www.lowryparkzoo.com 🕓 Daily 9:30–5 💷 Inexpensive

Tampa Museum of Art houses a mighty diverse collection

4 Tampa Museum of Art

Art lovers who fancy eclectic collections of classical and contemporary art will enjoy pottery and busts from the classical period of Greece and Rome, and the traveling shows that range from pop art, abstract oils and sculptures to the traditional images of Ansel Adams. The tour will take an hour or so, with a few minutes spent in the gift shop and the gallery that overlooks the Hillsborough River and the University of Tampa.

🔢 224 B2 ✉ 600 N. Ashley Drive (entrance on Twiggs off Ashley) ☎ 813/274-8130 🕓 Tue–Sat 10–5 (also Thu 5–8), Sun 1–5 💷 Inexpensive; 5 and under: free

5 Tampa Theatre

Built in 1926, this restored architectural masterpiece is one of the most picturesque movie palaces in Florida. Once facing extinction, the faltering theater was bought by the city in 1973 for $1. Through grants and fundraisers, it was restored to its original splendor and is listed on the National Register of Historical Places. Unlike today's run-of-the-mill multiplexes, the interior theme of this atmospheric theater is a Florida Mediterranean courtyard on a moonlit night. Stars sparkle overhead, Roman statues frame flowering balconies, vintage sconces and decorative columns accent elaborate mosaic tilework (244,185 floor tiles to be exact, says a staff member). With so much beauty surrounding you, it may be hard to watch the screen. Showing are first-run foreign films or, on weekends, classics such as "Casablanca," "Gone With the Wind"

The University of Tampa, with its distinctive onion-domed minarets

7 Florida Aquarium

Your 90-minute tour of Florida ecosystems begins here. With more than 10,000 oceanic and freshwater animals plus plants and the new Caribbean-themed family friendly outdoor exhibit "Explore-A-Shore," it offers an instant education on the diverse ecosystems existing outside the theme parks. Exhibit placards give only limited information, so fish fanciers may want to take the taped tour for more details and flexibility, or catch up with staff members, who host various presentations throughout the attraction. The parking lot is about a quarter-mile (400m) away, so drop your group off first.

🔲 224 B2 ⊠ 701 Channelside Drive
☎ 813/273-4000; www.flaquarium.org
🕐 Daily 9:30–5; closed Thanksgiving and Dec 25 📷 Inexpensive

Tampa Theatre. Its exterior belies the splendid interior

or "A Hard Day's Night." Like many old buildings, this one has a friendly ghost. Foster "Fink" Finley, the projectionist, died on the job after 35 years on the job and is occasionally said to come back to check on things.

🔲 224 B2 ⊠ 711 Franklin Street
☎ 813/274-8981; www.tampatheatre.
com 🕐 Daily 7:30 pm; Sat–Sun, matinée times vary 📷 Inexpensive

8 Henry B. Plant Museum/ University of Tampa

Built in 1891 as a labor of love by railroad magnate Henry B. Plant, the Tampa Bay Hotel was Florida's first

Florida Aquarium's Coral Reef Gallery

all-electric, steam-heated, fireproofed, elevator-equipped hotel. Its quixotic and exotic blend of Moorish revival architecture, accented by cupolas, domes, keyhole arches, broad verandas and onion-domed minarets, each crowned with a crescent moon, makes this Tampa's most visible vintage landmark and a National Historical Landmark. After Plant's death in 1899, the $3 million Victorian resort was purchased by the city in 1904 for $125,000. Tours of the museum, in one of the old hotel's wings, begin with a short video, "The Tampa Bay

Florida Aquarium, one of the most impressive aquariums in the United States, is set under a futuristic glass canopy

Hotel: Florida's First Magic Kingdom," and rooms are themed to reflect popular Victorian pastimes.

Next door, the University of Tampa houses the hotel's grand rotunda, salon, and music and dining rooms.

Tour sheets are available in French, German, Italian, Japanese, Portuguese and Spanish.

➕ 224 A2 ✉ 401 W. Kennedy Boulevard ☎ 813/254-1891; www.plant museum.com ⏰ Tue–Sat 10–4, Sun noon–4 💲 Inexpensive

Florida before photography. A beautiful piece at the Museum of Fine Art

St. Petersburg

⑨ St. Petersburg Museum of History

If you want to see what happened here in the 500 years before you arrived, you might find the blend of history and culture at this museum interesting. Located at the entrance to the Pier (➤ 166), the small history center is highlighted by a display of the Benoist Airboat, the first scheduled commercial airline in the world. In 1914, one passenger could pay $5 and catch a 23-minute lift from St. Petersburg to Tampa and save six hours of driving muddy roads that encircled the bay. More recent displays show St. Pete during its 1950s heyday through bathing-beauty shots, archival photographs and postcards.

🚩 224 A2 ⊠ 335 2nd Avenue N.E.
☎ 727/894-1052; www.museumof historyonline.com ⏰ Mon–Sat 10–5, Sun noon–5 💲 Inexpensive

⑩ Museum of Fine Arts

This is the sort of aesthetically appealing museum preferred by traditional art enthusiasts. Its library-quiet formality complements the permanent high-end fine art selections such as Monet's "Houses of Parliament," O'Keeffe's "Poppy," Renoir's "Girl Reading" and Berthe Morisot's "La Lecture," which are prominently displayed alongside works by Rodin, Cézanne and Gauguin. There are also oil landscapes reflecting the Hudson River School style, French furniture, a smattering of contemporary works and visiting shows. Give yourself an hour or so, and if you need a break, step outside to the open-air courtyard or into the gift shop.

🚩 224 A2 ⊠ 255 Beach Drive N.E.
☎ 727/896-2667; www.fine-arts.org
⏰ Tue–Sat 10–5, Sun 1–5
💲 Inexpensive; 6 and under: free

⑪ Florida International Museum

What was once St. Petersburg's largest department store now houses one of Florida's most impressive museums. Florida International Museum draws blockbuster touring shows. Exhibitions create an interactive learning experience, drawing visitors into episodes of history through life-size re-creations, multimedia presentations and displays of significant artifacts.

In addition to its excellent revolving exhibits, FIM has a permanent exhibit "The Cuban Missile Crisis". This exhibition highlights the tense events of October 1962 during the Cuban Missile Crisis. You can go back to a 1962 classroom to practice "Duck and Cover"; see how a nation learned about civil defense; feel the tension of the war coming closer while watching President Kennedy address the nation on a vintage

Above: Pictures of Holocaust survivors fill a wall at the Holocaust Museum
Left: Experience life during the Cuban Missile Crisis: Part of the permanent collection at the Florida International Museum

The focal point of the museum, however, is a powerful reminder of the Holocaust: Auschwitz Boxcar No. 113-0695-5, used to transport Jewish people to the concentration camps. In the process of moving the boxcar to this location, a child's ring from the 1940s fell from the cracks and is now on display. Be prepared for some emotional moments.

🕂 224 A2 ✉ 55 5th Street S., at 1st Avenue S., I-275 to Exit 10, right at first stoplight (5th Street N.), cross Central Avenue, museum is on right
☎ 727/820-0100 or 800/960-7448
🕐 Mon–Fri 10–5, Sat–Sun noon–5, last entry 4 💲 Inexpensive. Parking free

television, and step down into a community fallout shelter complete with emergency supplies and equipment.
🕂 224 A2 ✉ 100 2nd Street N.,
☎ 727/822-3693 or 800/777-9882;
www.floridamuseum.org 🕐 Mon–Sat 11–5, Sun noon–5; tours every 10 minutes
💲 Inexpensive; 5 and under: free

🔢 Florida Holocaust Museum

Ordinarily, museums are places of beauty evoking pleasant emotions. Holocaust museums aren't. They are usually unsettling, sometimes disturbing. The Florida Holocaust Museum is no different. One subtle change in presentation, however, is a message of hope that permeates the displays. The first floor takes you through the Holocaust with personal tales told by survivors – some of whom are now local residents. The second-floor art gallery showcases traveling exhibits and art of the Holocaust, while one floor above is an education center.

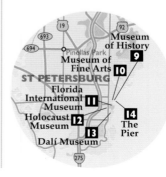

Visitors to the Salvador Dalí Museum can see the most comprehensive collection of the artist's works

⑬ Salvador Dalí Museum

Dalí's dreamlike, surrealistic paintings continue to intrigue even casual observers, and the museum shows a chronological journey of his life travels, from the early landscapes he drew as a talented 14-year-old to some of the last drawings he worked on while wasting away in Spain. Most works, however, show Dalí at his peak. This is the most comprehensive collection of the artist's works you'll find anywhere in the world and has eight of his sixteen masterpieces including the *Hallucinogenic Toreador* and *Discovery of America by Christopher Columbus*. Check out the *Disintegration of the Persistence of Memory*, the self-explanatory *Lobster Telephone* and the *Venus de Milo with Drawers*. Come early, before busloads of people arrive, and then browse the delightful gift shop offering a selection of Dalíesque books, videos, postcards, T-shirts and jewelry.

➕ 224 A2 ✉ 1000 3rd Street S., I-275 South, Exit 9, follow signs for 175 East until 4th Street S., right to 11th Avenue S., left one block to 3rd Street S. ☎ 727/823-3767; www.salvador dalimuseum.org 🕐 Mon–Sat 9:30–5:30 (also Thu 5:30–8), Sun noon–5:30 💲 Inexpensive; 9 and under: free

⑭ The Pier

The Pier is one of the most recognized landmarks on Florida's west coast. It is a complex of specialty stores, an aquarium, restaurants and various attractions, housed in a five-story inverted pyramid, with fine views from its observation platform. In winter, HMS *Bounty* docks here.

➕ 224 A2 ✉ 800 2nd Avenue N.E. ☎ 727/821-6164 🕐 Mon–Sat 10–10, Sun 11–8

Progress Energy Park

While major league baseball games are played about a mile (1.6km) away at Tropicana Field, during Spring Training – which takes place each March – the Devil Rays play at Progress Energy Park, a few blocks from the Pier. Tickets to watch the team in action cost between $9 and $15, less than for a major league game.

⊞ 224 A2
✉ 180 2nd Avenue S.E.
☎ 727/825-3250

15 Fort DeSoto Park

This is one of Florida's best beach and camping bargains. More than 1,100 acres (445ha) on five interconnected islands provide the perfect blend of activities and relaxation, from the shaded, 235-site waterfront campground to the magnificent beaches on the southern tip of the peninsula. Camping sites, if you can get one, include grills and picnic tables with nearby showers and lavatories. Day-trippers can forget the tents and set up a picnic near East Beach only a few miles away, or head east for an incredible view of the

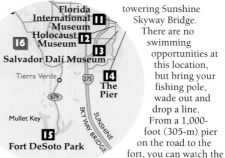

towering Sunshine Skyway Bridge. There are no swimming opportunities at this location, but bring your fishing pole, wade out and drop a line. From a 1,000-foot (305-m) pier on the road to the fort, you can watch the comings and goings of barges and sizeable ships as they exit the Gulf and pull into Tampa Bay. Up the road, the remains of Fort DeSoto provide a glimpse into history. The fort overlooks Egmont Key's historic lighthouse. If you save the best for last, North Beach is *the* beach to hit.

⊞ 224 A2   ✉ 3500 Pinellas Bayway S.
☎ 727/582-2267   💵 Moderate (cash only). Camping reservations must be made in advance; call 727/582-2267 (moderate); cash only

Fort DeSoto, named after the Spanish explorer, was built in 1898 to protect the Gulf shipping lanes during the Spanish-American War

Fort DeSoto Canoe Outpost
☎ 727/864-1991; www.canoeoutpost.com
🕐 Mon–Fri 10–5, Sat–Sun 9–5
💵 Moderate per canoe/kayak per day

17 John's Pass Village & Boardwalk

You'll see this either as a tacky tourist trap or a neat, Cape Cod-like waterfront fishing village with a Key West twist. This is a haven for seafood restaurants, gambling cruises, gift shops and an armada of wave-runner concessions clustered along the north bank. The pseudo village includes ice-cream parlors, T-shirt emporiums,

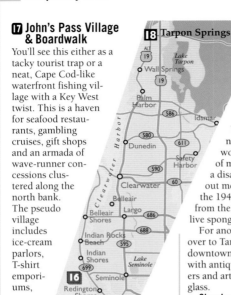

nature-themed art galleries and the requisite bait and tackle stores. Boats set sail for sightseeing tours along the Intracoastal and romantic sunset cruises, but if you want to do it yourself rent a wave-runner, jet ski, three-passenger jet boat or another cutting-edge water toy. Hint: With so much competition, try striking a bargain (and watch for come-on prices that exclude additional charges). If you have time to fish, charter captains will take you out for snapper, kingfish, barracuda and amberjack, which you can take to the Friendly Fisherman restaurant to be cleaned, filleted and cooked for a nominal fee (provided you caught it from one of their boats).

➕ 224 A2 ✉ 12901 Gulf Boulevard East, Madeira Beach ⏰ Daily

18 Tarpon Springs

It's as if Poseidon had plucked this village from the Greek islands, placed it on Florida's west coast, then added

a host of tacky T-shirt, shell and sponge stores.

Greek divers came to Tarpon Springs around the turn of the 19th century to harvest a natural bounty of sponges. Today, the city boasts of having the largest natural sponge market in the world, with annual revenues of more than $5 million, despite a disastrous blight that wiped out most of the sponge beds in the 1940s. A sightseeing cruise from the sponge docks includes a live sponge-diving exhibition.

For another look at the city, drive over to Tarpon Avenue and visit the downtown area, which is brimming with antiques and craft shops, jewelers and artists who work with stained glass.

Chamber of Commerce ➕ 224 A3
✉ 11 E. Orange Street (corner of Alternate Highway 19 and Orange)
☎ 727/937-6109;
www.tarponsprings.com

Natural sponges, gathered from deep waters, are trimmed into shape before going on sale

Farther Afield

Sarasota to Naples

The most scenic route to Sarasota is via the Sunshine Skyway Bridge. Follow I-275 south from Tampa and St. Petersburg, where it hooks up with I–75. Head south until you reach University Parkway, which heads west straight into the heart of Sarasota.

🔟 Sarasota

Once recognized primarily as the winter home of the Ringling Brothers Circus, Sarasota is now known as home to a lot of retirees. Add to the mix students from the **Ringling School of Art and Design** and you have an impressive degree of diversity. The two factions meet at the area's most visited attraction, the **John and Mable Ringling Museum of Art**.

The museum, located at the intersection of University Parkway and US 41, was part of the Ringlings' legacy, a supplement to their winter home, **Ca' d'Zan**. Upon his death in 1936, John Ringling bequeathed the entire estate and his impressive art collection to the people of the state of Florida.

There are more than 500 years of art here, with bronze replicas of ancient Greek and Roman sculptures as well as paintings by Rubens, Bonheur, Alfred Stevens and other artists. If you like art, you'll love this; if not, you may want to skip it and head over to the Circus Museum or the mansion. Three architects worked on this project and the result is a Venetian-style, eclectic, $1.5 million masterpiece.

After recovering from your art attack, drive south down US 41 to the John Ringling Causeway, turn right and you're heading to the beaches and **St. Armands Key**, the best place to get a feel for the area. In addition to restaurants, sidewalk cafés and courtyards with antique statuary, **St. Armands Circle** is a world-renowned center of trendy stores (tel: 941/388-1554). The best part of St. Armands Circle is that it's only a few blocks from one of the nicest stretches of beach in Florida. The sunsets here are fantastic – perhaps the best in Florida – and if you can't get enough of the free show, then drive north on

The rare art museum that's a work of art in itself

Highway 789, where there are small motels and beachside cottages. If you check with the tourist center (tel: 941/955-8187; www.sarasota chamber.org), they'll tell you about opera, ballet, plays and golf tournaments, but it's far more pleasing just to lie on the beach and watch the sun.

John and Mable Ringling Museum of Art
🚌 224 A1 ✉ 5401 Bay Shore Road
☎ 941/359-5700; www.ringling.org
🕐 Daily 10–5:30 💲 Inexpensive; 11 and under free – but free for all on Sat

When you leave Sarasota, US 41 is the best road south, and the next town of any size is **Venice**. Although the name conjures images of a cultural Italian city, this is actually urban sprawl separated by a series of canals and bordered by nice beachfront at Nokomis and North Jetty Park.

20 Fort Myers
There is one place worth seeing. Exit off US 41 at McGregor Boulevard, head west and about a mile (1.6km) down is the **Edison-Ford Winter Estates**. This is where Thomas A. Edison spent his winters working on the phonograph and teletype, and planting new plants in an effort to create a new source for rubber. The nice thing is that his laboratory is exactly as he left it, right down to the beakers and bottles. His home across the street is a great example of what an Old Florida house was like, nice and airy with wide windows and a broad veranda where he could sit and enjoy the Caloosahatchee River flowing at the end of his yard.

It's all low key, but his home (and Henry Ford's house next door), plus the laboratory and sprawling banyan tree, make it worth the stop.

No computers in sight at Edison's house. The great man used his head

The draw here is shark's teeth, which wash ashore with great frequency (minus the shark). Farther south, **Caspersen Beach** is the longest beach in Sarasota County and relatively unscathed by modernization.

From here, US 41 continues south to Fort Myers, but the ride isn't that spectacular. In fact, it gets pretty busy with heavy traffic and stoplights over the 70 or so miles (112km).

Edison-Ford Winter Estates
🚌 226 B4 ✉ 2350 McGregor Boulevard, Fort Myers ☎ 239/334-3614; www.edison-ford-estate.com
🕐 Mon–Sat 9–5:30, Sun noon–4
💲 Inexpensive

21 Sanibel and Captiva
Off the coast of Fort Myers are two of Florida's loveliest islands. **Sanibel** (🚌 226 B4), on the south, is the larger of the two, but there is scant commercial development here since nearly two-thirds of the island is

protected from future development. That said, don't miss the **J.N. "Ding" Darling National Wildlife Refuge** (tel: 941/472-1100, inexpensive), where you can take a guided tour among the 6,000-acre (2,430-ha) habitat of roseate spoonbills, pelicans, osprey and alligators. Rent a canoe or kayak and paddle beside mangrove trees and estuaries that are also explained in fascinating detail. There are several public beaches on the island, and the calm waters, white sands and shady trees make sunbathing a must. Also, unusual Gulf currents make this one of the world's best destinations for shell collectors, so when you're not filling up souvenir buckets for yourself, visit the **Bailey–Matthews Shell Museum** (tel: 941/395-2233, inexpensive). Exhibits reveal the role seashells have played in ecology, medicine, literature, religion, art and as a food source. Sounds boring, but it's not. Not at all.

A few miles north, the island of **Captiva** (⊞ 226 B4) is more laid back and luxurious than Sanibel. Take a beach break at Blind Pass (the small river that separates the islands), and work your way up the lone road to the village, where there's a small grocery store, several nice art, clothing and gift galleries, and two popular top-drawer restaurants. The waterfront **Mucky Duck** (tel: 941/472-3434) is renowned for its Key lime pie and sunset views, and the **Bubble Room** (tel:

Shelling is a prime activity on Sanibel and Captiva

941/472-5558) is equally famous for its food as for a fun and colorful interior that looks like an exploded toy chest. From **South Seas Resort**, a grand resort on the north end of the island, charter boats leave for neighboring islands such as Cabbage Key, the inspiration for Jimmy Buffett's anthem, "Cheeseburger in Paradise." If you can only see two islands in Florida, Sanibel and Captiva are sure to captivate you.

Lee Island Coast Visitor and Convention Bureau ⊞ 226 B4 ✉ 2180 W. First Street, Suite 100, Fort Myers ☎ 239/338-3500 or 888/231-6933; www.leeislandcoast.com

Sanibel-Captiva Islands Chamber of Commerce ⊞ 226 B4 ✉ 1159 Causeway Road, Sanibel ☎ 239/472-1080; www.sanibel-captiva.org

Bradenton
Sarasota **19**
Nokomis
Venice
Arcadia
Port Charlotte
Punta Gorda
Gulf
of
Mexico
Sanibel and **21** **20** Fort Myers
Captiva
Naples **22**

22 Naples

Yet another wealthy Florida community, Naples (about 165 miles/265km south of Tampa) has several points of interest for travelers. First, perhaps, is downtown itself. The **Fifth Avenue South** shopping district is a broad, tree-lined avenue of fashionable shops, art galleries and European bistros. You can get a good overview of this and the town's historic districts on a 2-hour sightseeing tour with **Naples Trolley Tours** (tel: 239/262-7300) that rolls around town in a replica of a 1907 Cincinnati trolley. **Caribbean Gardens** (1590 Goodlette–Frank Road, tel: 239/262-5409; www.caribbeangardens.com) is a zoo that began in 1919 as a 52-acre (21ha) botanical park. The gardens still remain and, since the late 1960s,

and almost 200 bird species. A 2.25-mile (3.5-km) boardwalk meanders through the nation's largest old-growth cypress forest and a tropical jungle of ferns, orchids and wildflowers.

Since Naples was established as a port town (note the tribute to Napoli, Italy), its greatest claim to fame is beaches that form mile after mile of the Gulf Coast. Ask locals about their favorites, or call the beaches directly for information. Among your choices are **Naples Beach**, which features the popular 1,000-foot (305-m) fishing pier, **Lowdermilk Park** (tel: 239/434-4698), **Vanderbilt Beach** (tel: 239/597-6196), **Delnor–Wiggins Pass State Recreation Area** (tel: 239/597-6196), **Clam Pass Park/Beach** and **Lely Barefoot Beach**. Most beaches have facilities that include showers,

Chic and photogenic, Naples' historic district

they've added animals, boat rides, lectures, live shows and a petting farm.

Fifteen miles (24km) east of I-75, the **Corkscrew Swamp Audubon Sanctuary** (375 Sanctuary Road West, tel: 239/348-9151, inexpensive) is an 11,000-acre (4,500-ha) preserve that's considered the crown jewel of the National Audubon Society's sanctuary system. One of the world's most popular destination for birders, photographers and wildlife watchers, the park is home to hundreds of alligators

lifeguards, grills, picnic tables and pavilions, boat ramps, observation towers, restrooms, bath house, public parking, snack bars, boardwalks, fishing and gear rental, and beach chairs. When making your choice, also consider that some are remote while others may offer convenient access to nearby hotels.

Naples Chamber of Commerce
🎯 226 B4 ✉ 895 Fifth Avenue South,
Naples ☎ 239/262-6141;
www.napleschamber.org;
www.naples-florida.com

Where to...
Eat and Drink

Prices Expect to pay per person for a meal, excluding drink
$ under $25 $$ $25–50 $$$ over $50

TAMPA

Tampa's location right on the water made it a booming port town, open to influences from all over the world. As with the rest of Florida, it maintains strong ties with the Spanish and Cuban roots of many of its inhabitants. This is evident in much of the food, especially in Ybor City. There is also a wide variety of restaurants well worth trying. Prices tend to be fairly reasonable, even in some of the trendier places.

🍷🍷🍷 Armani's $$$
Perched atop the Grand Hyatt Tampa Bay (▶ 175), Armani's offers stunning, panoramic views of Tampa. The setting is serene, with taupe and black accents. The fare is traditional Italian – think *osso buco*, *cioppino* and homemade pastas – with several creative dishes including bresaola with black truffles, veal topped with crab and lobster, and pepper-crusted, seared tuna. Opposing the view, the focal point of the room is an extensive antipasto bar. There is also a comfortable outdoor terrace, which lets you take even better advantage of the view.

Jacket required for men. No jeans or tennis shoes (trainers).
✚ 224 A2 ☒ Hyatt Regency Westshore, 6200 Courtney Campbell Causeway ☎ 813/281-9165

🍷🍷 Bernini of Ybor $$–$$$
Low-key, romantic dining with superb, artfully presented dishes. The menu features traditional Italian cuisine with an edge, including a mouthwatering braised lamb shank with redcurrant and Marsala sauce, and an amazing fillet of beef with Gorgonzola and sun-dried tomato demiglace. The menu changes daily. This place is popular with locals. Ask for an upstairs table and look down on the dining area.
✚ 224 B2 ☒ 1702 E. 7th Avenue, Ybor City ☎ 813/248-0099

🍷🍷🍷 Bern's Steak House $$$
Bern's is a restaurant that defies description. The decor is somewhere between a museum and a bordello, and there's a series of rooms with red walls, gold accents, plaster sculptures, 12-foot-high (3.5-m) mirrors and mediocre artwork. The menu is a lesson in beef; the various cuts of steak and the aging process are described in minute detail. The wine list is held to be the most extensive in the world (really) with more than 6,000 different labels, the prices of which offer surprisingly good value. Guests get a tour of the kitchen after dinner before being escorted to the private dessert rooms upstairs. This restaurant is more than worth it for the sheer spectacle; as for the food, stick to steak (the rib eye is a favorite) and you will have a memorable meal. But be careful of the locale: Take a cab here and stay on the premises.
✚ 224 B2 ☒ 1208 S. Howard Avenue ☎ 813/251-2421; www.bernsteakhouse.com

🍷🍷 Columbia Restaurant $$
Opened in 1905, this family-owned Spanish restaurant is a Tampa legend. The original corner cafe has expanded to a huge space that seats

more than 1,500 people. One of the nicest dining rooms is located in the center of the restaurant and has been designed to look like the courtyard of a Spanish hacienda, complete with palm trees and a fountain. Other rooms are darker and decorated with Spanish tiles. On some nights there is live entertainment and dancing. The menu offers Spanish and South American favorites – passable tapas, good *caldo gallego* (a bean soup with chorizo and greens), paella and traditional *arroz con pollo* (chicken with rice). Heavy on the garlic and the tourists, dinner is nevertheless satisfying.

✚ 224 B2 ⊠ 2117 E. 7th Avenue, Ybor City ☎ 813/248-4961

Jim Strickland's Old Meeting House $

This local diner hasn't changed much since it opened in 1947 – the formica tables have a cozy patina, the portions of hearty American fare are still large, the prices are still

cheap and Harold still makes the ice cream every day by hand. It's good, old-fashioned simplicity at its most charming, with daily specials such as Salisbury steak with onions and gravy and two vegetables. Treat yourself and ask about the Milkshake of the Week.

✚ 224 B2 ⊠ 901 S. Howard Avenue ☎ 813/251-1754

✑ Kojak's House of Ribs $

A good place for an inexpensive BBQ, as well as a place to hang out with locals in a casual setting, Kojak's has tables inside and outside, and the mood is always festive. Not only is the food a draw, but the drive up Bayshore Drive offers a nice glimpse of downtown Tampa.

✚ 224 B2 ⊠ 2808 Gandy Boulevard ☎ 813/837-3774

✑✑✑ Le Bordeaux $$$

Step into this lovely bistro and you are immediately transported to the French countryside. The decor is

pretty and romantic with lace curtains, painted walls and individual table lamps. The high-quality French food complements the decor. Favorite dishes are cassoulet, braised rabbit, escargot and boeuf en croûte. The adjoining Left Bank is a delightful café where you can have appetizers and dessert around a lovely covered pool while you listen to first-rate jazz.

✚ 224 B2 ⊠ 1502 S. Howard Avenue ☎ 813/254-4387

✑ Lonni's Sandwiches $

Part of a chain of take-out shops/cafés, Lonni's is a favorite among locals for interesting, healthy sandwiches on homemade bread – the wild-rice bread is known across the state. The staff is incredibly friendly and helpful and will gladly describe the nuances of Ron's Sunny Bird (turkey with cream cheese, sunflower seeds, sprouts, mayonnaise and honey dressing) or any of the other tasty concoctions on offer. Also available are soups and salads,

healthy muffins and low-fat baked goods. A good place to pack a picnic.

✚ 224 B2 ⊠ 513 E. Jackson Street ☎ 813/223-2333

✑✑✑ Mise en Place $$

Dozens of votive candles light the way through this dark, sophisticated New American restaurant. The large space is divided into several smaller rooms. Chef Marty Blitz serves up creative cuisine from a huge menu that has no fewer than 20 appetizers and 15 entrées. The food is fairly priced, if sometimes overwrought, and there is a five-course tasting menu that offers good value.

✚ 224 B2 ⊠ 442 W. Kennedy Boulevard ☎ 813/254-5373

ST. PETERSBURG

✑✑ DISH $

It's a pleasure to find a restaurant that's breaking new ground. Mongolian barbeque inspired this

Where to... Stay

Prices Expect to pay per room per night
$ under $125 $$ $125–250 $$$ over $250

TAMPA

Holiday Inn Statefair Downtown $$

This moderately priced hotel is conveniently located right next to the Tampa Bay Performing Arts Center and is only a short distance from the Tampa Museum of Art. The rooms have decent wood furniture and good-size bathrooms. The rooms on the upper floors can have beautiful views and many rooms have microwaves. There is a lively bar and two full-service restaurants.

➕ 224 B2 ⊠ 111 W. Fortune Street, Tampa ☎ 813/223-1351 or 800/513-8940

Grand Hyatt Tampa Bay $$$

The most upscale hotel in town, this elegant property is just a stone's throw from Tampa Airport. The service is attentive and friendly, and the amenities – such as Armani's (► 173), the pool, the fitness center and the nature walk – are first rate. The rooms are comfortable and spacious, if a little dated. In keeping with the hotel's urban feel, the business and meeting facilities are carefully thought out.

➕ 224 A2 ⊠ 6200 Courtney Campbell Causeway, Tampa ☎ 813/874-1234 or 800/233-1234

Wyndham Harbour Island Hotel $$$

Located on its own island (Harbour Island), a small development just off the mainland, this hotel is convenient to the convention center and downtown Tampa. The rooms are spacious and the service is friendly and helpful. The hotel is also attached to a small mall with restaurants and shops, and a business complex. It provides easy access to the fitness trail and recreational walk along Bayshore Boulevard.

➕ 224 B2 ⊠ 725 S. Harbour Island Boulevard, Harbour Island ☎ 813/229-5000 or 800/WYNDHAM

ST. PETERSBURG

Don CeSar Beach Resort & Spa $$$

Known as the "Pink Palace," this grand resort and spa is one of the best on the Gulf coast. It boasts two swimming pools (one with an underwater sound system), a beautiful beach with different watersports

approach to dining. Take a plate, load up on raw meats and/or fish and an assortment of vegetables and sauces, then pass it to one of the chefs, who cook the ingredients to create an outstanding, exotic meal. The experience is fun and novel.

➕ 224 A2 ⊠ 197 2nd Avenue N. (Baywalk) ☎ 727/894-5700

Fourth Street Shrimp Store $

You'll know this fun and inexpensive eatery when you get near it, because it looks like the outside wall has been graffitied beyond recognition. On closer inspection you will realize the mural of people eating and having a good time has been put there by the management to encourage people to come inside. The colors and fun don't stop inside the warehouselike space. A seafood counter at the entrance displays the fresh shrimp and other seafood you will enjoy in huge portions.

➕ 224 A2 ⊠ 106 4th Street N. ☎ 727/822-0325

equipment rentals and a spa where you can have your cares massaged and wrapped away.

✚ 224 A2 ☒ 3400 Gulf Boulevard, St. Pete Beach ☎ 727/360-1881

♨♨♨ Renaissance Vinoy Resort $$$

About a half-hour southwest of Tampa, this impressive hotel maintains the feel of the 1920s when St. Petersburg was a premier tourist destination. The hotel went through a major restoration in the early 1990s, and now all of the rooms, many overlooking the bay, are equipped with every modern convenience, including TVs in the bathrooms. There is a wonderful waterfall on the property that spills into one of the hotel's pools, as well as tennis, golf, a marina, a fully equipped workout facility, day spa and salon. There are also three restaurants and outdoor dining.

✚ 224 A2 ☒ 501 5th Avenue N.E. (Beach Street), St. Petersburg ☎ 727/894-1000 or 800/HOTELS-1

Where to...
Shop

TAMPA

Malls have been springing up around Tampa, including The Shops at Channelside, a downtown waterfront dining and shopping spot that is easily explored on foot, and Westfield Shoppingtown Citrus Park, north of downtown Tampa. International Plaza, near the airport, boasts Lord & Taylor, Neiman Marcus and Nordstrom as anchors. Other popular yet charming places to drop a dollar include Old Hyde Park Village, a redeveloped area in the center of one of Tampa's historic neighborhoods, and the lively Centro Ybor in Ybor City.

Centro Ybor

Ybor City's most popular gathering spot is a family-friendly shopping, dining and entertainment complex. Highlights include GameWorks, featuring interactive games and a nightclub/restaurant, the Improv Comedy Club, a 20-screen Muvico Theater (where you can enjoy martinis, beer, wine and a light café menu), and Big City Tavern for New American cuisine. Don't miss the Ferdie Pacheco Gallery.

✚ 224 B2 ☒ 1600 E. 8th Street
☎ 813/242-4314;
www.centroybor.com

Old Hyde Park Village

This outdoor shopping area is located in the middle of Hyde Park, a quaint residential area that dates back to the late 1700s. The pretty streets of this village are home to a wide variety of stores, restaurants and cafes. Notable among the chain stores are Brooks Brothers, Ann Taylor, Williams-Sonoma, Godiva, Chico's, Tommy Bahama and Pottery Barn Kids. There are also many privately run boutiques that sell an eclectic array of goods – jewelry, hand-blown glass, Mexican pottery, toys and original clothing.

✚ 224 B2 ☒ Swann and Dakota avenues, off Bayshore Boulevard ☎ 813/251-3500

WestShore Plaza

This huge, airy mall is exactly what you would expect from a Florida shopping center, from the valet parking to the palm trees and marble decor. There are more than 100 fashionable stores such as Victoria's Secret, Bebe, Nine West, American Eagle Outfitters, and department stores such as Saks Fifth Avenue, JC Penney and Dillards, as well as nail and hair salons, electronics outlets, kitchenware shops and a 14-screen movie theater. The Tampa Bay Devil Rays have a store here where you can buy baseball paraphernalia.

There is a giant food court that has everything from French to Japanese, and there are several restaurants in the complex. For a special treat, try a cone at Tanya & Matt's Ice Creamiest.

➕ 224 A2 ⊠ 250 Westshore Boulevard ☎ 813/286-0790: www.westshoreplaza.com

The Shops at Channelside

Located next to the Florida Aquarium along the downtown waterfront, this new shopping and entertainment complex offers a mix of specialty stores and restaurants.

➕ 224 A2 ⊠ 615 Channelside Drive ☎ 813/223-4250

On Beach Drive, trendy shops offer clothing, tableware and art. Antiques can be found on Central Avenue between 12th and 13th streets at the **Gas Plant Antique Arcade** (1246 Central Avenue, tel: 727/895-0368), where more than 100 dealers peddle their wares at what is considered the largest antiques show on the west coast of Florida.

Where to...
Be Entertained

TAMPA

Some of the more happening spots in downtown Tampa can be a little hard to find because, other than 7th Avenue in Ybor City, there is not really a central neighborhood with visible nightlife. If you look, however, there is something for everyone on Tampa's night scene, and several free publications give all the inside information you need.

Inside Tampa is a free paper concerned mostly with covering news in the downtown area, but the second page is devoted to "doing downtown," a weekly listing of events, concerts, theater, movies, sports and museum exhibits. These listings are more geared toward popular high culture than down-and-dirty venues. At the other end of the spectrum is *Ink19*, an off-beat monthly devoted to West Florida's music scene. The center spread is a calendar of the month's concerts, mostly alternative music. Lying somewhere between the philosophies of these two papers is the *Weekly Planet* with a calendar that describes many of the week's more cultural entertainments, from Native American dance performances to the city's best Super Bowl party.

In the past few years Tampa has been making an effort to upgrade the image of Ybor City and attract more people. The result is a proliferation of bars and restaurants that line 7th Avenue. During the week the strip is relatively quiet, but on weekend nights it teems with people and the atmosphere is not unlike a large college fraternity party. One spot to check out is **The Rare Olive** (1601 E. 7th Avenue, tel: 813/248-2333), a classy martini-and-cigar club with jazz, reggae, funk, dance music and a lively mixed crowd.

Downtown Tampa has its share of friendly bars and hotspots. **Four Green Fields** (205 West Platt, tel: 813/254-4444) is a neighborhoody Irish pub with a welcoming crowd, live Irish folk music and a great selection of beers. **Newk's Café** (514 Channelside Drive, tel: 813/307-6395), a seafood restaurant and bar, has a post-business crowd, but perhaps the most reliable nightlife is at **Centro Ybor** (1600 E. 8th Avenue, tel: 813/242-4660), home to several nightspots, including **Adobe Gila's** (tequila), **Barley Hopper's** (beer), the **Improv Comedy Club** (laughs) and **Big City Tavern** (wines and ale).

For up-to-the-minute information about what's going on in St. Petersburg, look for the Friday "Weekend" section of the St. Petersburg Times or the free weekly Daily Planet tabloid. In addition to live music concerts and nightclubs, you might want to take in a movie at **Muvico Baywalk 20** (151 2nd Avenue North, tel: 727/502-0965), which has stadium seats and digital sound. Or try cutting the rug at the **Coliseum** (535 4th Avenue North, tel: 727/892-5202), a 75-year-old ballroom with weekly Big Band Tea Dances.

Sports

Given the climate, it is something of an anomaly that Tampa, and Florida in general, has become so enamored of the game of ice hockey. The popularity of the sport, it seems, is due to the many Northerners who have relocated to Florida. Tampa is also home to the spring training camp

for baseball team the New York Yankees, and exhibition games are always sellouts. Tickets for all of Tampa's sports events are available by calling **Ticketmaster** on 813/287-8844.

Ice Hockey

The plush Ice Palace is home to the Tampa Bay Lightning, and the arena is equipped with every amenity the modern-day sports fan might desire, including a full restaurant and bar. The ever-improving Lightning won the coveted Stanley Cup in the 2003/04 season.

➕ **224 B2** ⌧ **The Ice Palace, 401 Channelside Drive, Tampa** ☎ **813/ 229-8800**

Football

The Tampa Bay Buccaneers, who won Super Bowl XXXVII in January 2003, will be a force to reckon with in the future. Tampa residents are always fiercely loyal and games are always lively. The faithful fill the Raymond James Stadium for every home game.

➕ **224 B2** ⌧ **Raymond James Stadium, Tampa** ☎ **813/879-BUCS; www.buccaneers.com**

Baseball

Home to the legendary New York Yankees during their mid-February to March preseason, Legends Field is the largest of all the spring training facilities in Florida. The facility is actually a miniature replica of Yankee Stadium in New York. During the real baseball season, from April to September, the Yankees' minor league team, the Tampa Yankees, plays at Legends Field, providing spectators with a good opportunity to see some big talent before players get scooped up by the majors.

➕ **224 A2** ⌧ **1 Steinbrenner Drive, Tampa** ☎ **813/875-7753; tickets 727/287-8844**

The newest team in baseball, the Devil Rays, earned quite a following after their impressive initial seasons. The indoor Tropicana Field stadium is a great place to see a game.

➕ **224 A2** ⌧ **Tropicana Field, 1 Stadium Drive, St. Petersburg** ☎ **727/825-3137; www.devilrays.com**

Golf

About a 90-minute drive from Tampa is the **World Woods Pine Barrens Golf Course** (17590 Ponce de León Boulevard, Brooksville, tel: 352/796-5500; www.worldwoods.com), rated in 1998 by Florida Golf Magazine readers as the best course in the state.

Pine Barrens' sister course, **Rolling Oaks**, closer to the city and with lower green fees, isn't bad either. You can drive and putt your way along several municipal courses, including **Babe Zaharias Municipal Course** (11412 Forest Hills Drive, tel: 813/631-4374) and the **Rogers Park Municipal Golf Course** (7910 N. 30th Street, tel: 813/673-4396). Or sign up for some lessons at the **Arnold Palmer Golf Academy World Headquarters**, at Saddlebrook Resort (5700 Saddlebrook Way, Wesley Chapel, tel: 813/973-1111).

The Panhandle and the North

Getting Your Bearings

It's roughly a third of the entire state (and to many its most beautiful region), yet few tourists take time to explore Florida's Panhandle, the northern section stretching from Jacksonville on the Atlantic Ocean to Pensacola at the border with Alabama. For most, it's simply a matter of being unaware that anything exists north of Orlando, and it's easier to fly to the center of the state, see Walt Disney World®, rent a car, drive to the beach and go home.

What they're missing, however, is Florida in its close-to-natural state. In the Panhandle, there are wonderful back roads such as Highways 20 and 90 and coastal road 98. There are small antebellum towns like Quincy, Havana, Monticello and DeFuniak Springs. There are hundreds of square miles of forests as well as hundreds of miles of Gulf of Mexico shoreline. Crystal-clear natural springs and the famous Suwannee River are here, as is Tallahassee, the state's capital, St. Augustine (America's oldest city) and Daytona Beach.

If you have time, see this region. What you will discover is how Florida used to live, look and work. Back then, hospitality wasn't an industry – it was actually the fabled Southern hospitality that residents shared with their guests. What's more, the Panhandle places you within a short drive of Georgia and Alabama, and you'll seldom be more than an hour's drive from a great beach.

More akin to America's Deep South than the cosmopolitan pace of Miami, the Panhandle is less populated and more rural. It runs at a slower pace that, once you get accustomed to it, means you can take your time and still enjoy a great vacation.

The roots of tall oak trees laden with Spanish moss dip into the Florida bayou

If your vision of Florida is defined simply by theme parks and beaches, here's a chance to expand your horizons. Florida's Panhandle has enough diverse destinations to make you think that you're actually visiting two distinct states.

The Panhandle and the North in Five Days

Day One

Morning Wake up in ❶ **St. Augustine** (► 184), settled by the Spanish in 1563. Walk along the promenade to the **Castillo de San Marcos** (left), the never-defeated fortress on Matanzas Bay. Step inside and, from the parapets, imagine what it was like here 400 years ago awaiting the arrival of the dreaded French fleets.

Afternoon Step aboard a trolley tour for a guided ride through the **Historic District**. Long after the Spanish left, wealthy tycoon Henry M. Flagler made this one of his way stations on an East Coast railroad en route to Miami. The grand hotels and churches he built are still here. Stop for lunch at the 95 Cordova, a restaurant in one of these hotels – the 1883 Casa Monica (► 196).

Evening A casual and romantic cruise on the bay would be the perfect way to wrap up the evening.

Day Two

Morning The choice is yours: An hour's drive down the coast to ❹ **Daytona Beach** (► 191) or an hour's drive up the coast to ❸ **Amelia Island** (► 191). Or, better yet, skip both for now and head west via I-95 and I-10 to the state capital: ❷ **Tallahassee** (► 186).

Afternoon Head straight to the city's **Museum of Florida History** (► 186). This is the best place in the state to learn what shaped Florida. Afterward, head across the street to the 22-story **Capitol** building and its observation deck.

Evening Tallahassee is a college town. Find a bar near the university and drop in.

Day Three

Morning/Afternoon Head out for
⑧ **Pensacola** (left, ➤ 188) via Highway
90, a quiet back road that takes you
through a handful of charming small
towns: Quincy, ⑥ **Marianna** (➤ 192),
DeFuniak Springs, and Crestview.

Evening Get settled at your Pensacola
hotel. If you have the stamina, go out for
the evening at the **Seville Historic District**.

Day Four

Morning Start the day at the
Seville Historic District, touring
some of the old homes – many
of which were part of a settlement built in the late 1500s.

Afternoon Drive a few miles
to see the restored flyers and
IMAX film at the **National
Museum of Naval Aviation** (right,
➤ 188–189) at the home of
the Blue Angels, the Pensacola
Naval Air Station.

Evening If you're not too exhausted, a visit to the **Seville Square Historic
District** or a ride out to the beaches for a sunset meal will be fun.

Day Five

Morning Give yourself a break. Head straight to one of the many beaches
on **Perdido Key** and **Santa Rosa Island** and laze on the powder-soft sands.

Afternoon If you can pick
yourself up and dust yourself
off, start all over again by
heading east along Highway 98
and choosing the end of the tour
in Destin, Seaside, ⑩ **Panama
City Beach** (right, ➤ 190) or
Apalachicola (➤ 193).

Evening Spend a real Old
Florida evening in at your
favorite Gulf Coast community,
dining on fresh seafood, watching the sunset, and figuring out
how to extend your stay.

St. Augustine

Nearly half a millennium after it was settled, you might assume that America's oldest city had settled into a routine. On the contrary, St. Augustine's multiple personalities are displayed throughout this quiet town of hidden courtyards, antiques shops, cobblestone streets, and horse-drawn carriages.

Located just two hours from Orlando, it was popularized as a turn-of-the-19th century oceanfront resort and was once known as the Newport of Florida. Now history is repeating itself as elegant and seductive inns rise beside rustic attractions. You can be lured into a refined restaurant or a rowdy bar; reside in an opulent grand hotel or clean motel; enjoy a family vacation on touristed shores or find solitude along a quiet, flower-draped alley.

Anchored on the north by the sturdy **Castillo de San Marcos**, and on the south by a fleet of yachts moored at the small and lovely marina, the historic district is where most travelers begin their voyage into the past – and most start at the *castillo*. Built by the Spanish between 1672 and 1695, the never-defeated fort and its 24-foot-thick (7-m) walls are steeped in history. You can tag along on a free guided tour. Outside the fort, sightseeing trains and trolleys circle the town in about an hour and you can hop on and off along the way. Too far to reach by foot, the **Fountain of Youth** suggests that it's the landing site of Ponce de León (it's not) and that the fountain here was the subject of his journey (it wasn't). Still, beyond the fountain, the grounds are covered with soft grass and shady oaks and a cemetery built for Spanish settlers and Timucua Native Americans. Just south of the fountain is the tranquil **Mission de Nombre de Dios**, highlighted by the 208-foot (85-m) tall Cross of Christianity, which marks the site of the first Mass celebrated in America.

The grand facade of the Lightner Museum – once a luxury Flagler hotel

Leading back to the historic district, **San Marco Avenue** has several blocks of antiques shops, gift shops, clothing consigners, collectibles stores, and a superb antiquarian bookseller, **Wolf's Head Books** (48 San Marco Avenue, tel: 904/824-9357).

Back on the waterfront, to the west of the bridge and marina, lies the **Plaza de la Constitución**. If you arrive on a Thursday evening in summer, spread out a blanket and enjoy a free concert.

From here, walk two blocks west on Cathedral Place to Cordova Street and before you is the old **Ponce de León Hotel**. As part of his plan to build an empire of railroads and resorts along Florida's East Coast, Henry M. Flagler created this castle in 1888. Today the hotel is **Flagler College**,

arguably the most elaborate campus in America and open to visitors who join a tour.

Across the street, Flagler's second effort was the stunning Hotel Alcazar, which now houses **City Hall** and the well-stocked **Lightner Museum**. Whether you visit the museum or not, you shouldn't leave town without entering this building.

Across the street at the corner of Cordova and King is the **Casa Monica Hotel** (► 196). Built by YMCA founder Franklyn Smith, it was bought by Flagler three

Nearly 500 years after his visit, Ponce de León still drops by St. Augustine

months after its grand opening in 1888. Recycled as the county courthouse in the 1960s, in 1997 it was restored as a hotel with an eclectic mix of Moorish and Victorian accents. Turn and walk north past the Casa Monica, through the campus of Flagler College, and then east through the historic district. Stop at patio bars like **Scarlett O'Hara's** (► 194, 70 Hypolita Street, tel: 904/824-6535) and then walk over to **St. George Street**, a buzzing pedestrian mall during the day, but a quiet promenade for couples each evening.

A few blocks away beside the bay, carriages await, their lanterns casting a soft glow on the smooth coats of the horses. Step aboard and retrace the first leg of the Old Spanish Trail, which begins a few blocks north and tapers to a close 3,000 miles (4,800km) away in San Diego. As you roll over the old brick streets and listen as the driver shares centuries of secrets, you'll realize that Ponce de León was on the right track. You can recapture your youth in St. Augustine.

Castillo de San Marcos ✚ 223 F2 ✉ One S. Castillo Drive ☎ 904/829-6506; www.nps.gov/casa ⏰ Daily 8:45–5:15; grounds closed midnight–5:30 am 💵 Inexpensive
Fountain of Youth ✉ 11 Magnolia Avenue ⏰ Daily 9–5; tours every 15–20 mins ☎ 904/829-3168 or 800/356-8222; www.fountainofyouthflorida.com 💵 Inexpensive
Flagler College ✉ 74 King Street ☎ 904/829-6481 ⏰ Tours 10–3 pm every hour
Lightner Museum ✉ 75 King Street ☎ 904/824-2874; www.lightnermuseum.org ⏰ Daily 9–5 💵 Inexpensive

---

ST. AUGUSTINE: INSIDE INFO

For pre-trip planning, consult the **St. Johns Visitors and Convention Bureau** (88 Riberia Street, tel: 800/653-2489; www.visitoldcity.com), which has travel-planning guides and brochures. The **St. Augustine/St. Johns County Visitor Information Center** (10 Castillo Drive, tel: 904/825-1000; www.oldcity.com; daily 8:30 am–6:30 pm) is located across from the fort. Tours, lodging, dining and watersports reservations can be made here. They also have restrooms, snacks, film and cold drinks.

5 Tallahassee

Not only is Tallahassee the state's capital (it received that honor in 1824, as the midway point between the prime cities of Pensacola and St. Augustine), it's also the one and only Southern capital spared in the Civil War.

Today, Tallahassee still seems to live in a slower, easier time that makes it a pleasure to visit. It is a cityscape of canopy roads and shady lanes surrounded by country stores, Southern plantations, and gracious hospitality. A great starting point is the **Old Capitol**, located at the intersection of US 27 and Monroe Street (tel: 850/487-1902). Built in 1842, it houses a museum of Florida's political history as well as the old Supreme Court chambers and Senate Gallery.

Behind the Old Capitol is the city's focal point, the new 22-story **Capitol** (tel: 850/488-6167). The governor's office is on the first floor, and House and Senate chambers on the fifth floor provide viewer galleries for the legislative sessions (March through May). The top-floor observatory has outstanding views of Florida State University, City Hall, the León County Courthouse and other landmarks. The Florida Artist Hall of Fame is here as well, honoring citizens such as Ray Charles, Burt Reynolds, Marjorie Kinan Rawlings and Zora Neale Hurston.

A few blocks away, the must-see **Museum of Florida History** is free and informative and covers 12,000 years of history. Exhibits include the remains of a giant mastodon found in nearby Wakulla Springs and a dugout canoe that once carried Native Americans into Florida's backwaters. One floor up is the **Florida State Archives and Library** (tel: 850/487-2073), where documents and photographs form a treasure trove of government records, manuscripts, genealogical records and other research materials.

Museum of Florida History ✚ 221 F3 ✉ 500 South Bronough Street ☎ 850/245-6400; www.flheritage.com ⏰ Mon–Fri 9–4:30, Sat 10–4:30, Sun noon–4:30 ✋ Free

Mission San Luís Archeological and Historic Site ✚ 221 F3 ✉ 2020 W. Mission Rd. ☎ 850/487-3711 ⏰ Mon–Fri 9–4:30, Sat 10–4:30, Sun noon–4:30 ✋ Free

Tallahassee Museum of History and Natural Science ✚ 221 F3 ✉ 3945 Museum Drive ☎ 850/576-1636; www.tallahasseemuseum.org ⏰ Mon–Sat 9–5, Sun 12:30–5 pm ✋ Inexpensive

Even more Panhandle pastimes

Antiques buffs make it a point to check out three communities. **Havana**, about 20 miles (32km) north of Tallahassee on Highway 27, has the greatest amount of antiques and adds a few sidewalk cafés and tea rooms. **Monticello**, 20 miles (32km) east on Highway 90, is centered on a town square. Although the shops are not as plentiful, the preserved Victorian homes give this ride a pleasing payoff. The most intriguing community is **Quincy**, about 10 miles (16km) west of Tallahassee on Highway 90. Although it may look rough, it's claimed that there are more millionaires here per capita than any area in the nation. Why? About 100 years ago, a local banker suggested that his customers invest in a little-known soft drink. Coca Cola.

Opposite:
The imposing
portico of the
neoclassical
Old Capitol

After visiting the historic district, head for the **Tallahassee Museum of History and Natural Science**. Actually a combination museum and zoo, it's a little difficult to find, but worth the effort. Animals, many of which have been injured or orphaned, are given relatively free rein within an expansive 52-acre (21-ha) natural habitat. You can see the endangered Florida panther from the safety of an elevated walkway. There's also the Big Bend Farm, an 1880s-era homestead with a yard full of mules, chickens, roosters, turkeys and ducks.

To see how important football is to America, on a Saturday in autumn, try to get a ticket for the **Florida State University Seminoles** (tel: 850/644-3246), who play at the Doak Campbell Stadium.

One of the most enjoyable aspects of Tallahassee is that it's surrounded by well-preserved examples of Florida's past. Within a 30-mile (50-km) radius are intriguing and pleasurable sites such as the **Mission San Luís Archeological and Historic Site**, where explorer Hernando de Soto celebrated the New World's first Christmas.

In a half hour, you can be sunbathing on Gulf beaches; a little farther and you can order a platter of oysters in Apalachicola or watch dolphins leap off 9 miles (15km) of undeveloped shores at the **St. George Island State Park** (tel: 850/927-2111). Other sites within an hour's drive of the capital city include **Wakulla Springs State Park** (tel: 850/922-3633), a natural retreat highlighted by a 1920s Spanish-Mediterranean lodge which may not be four-star, but the grounds are quiet and restful, and walking among the oaks is a completely peaceful experience. With a population of 125,000, somehow this metropolitan city has managed to preserve the gentility of the Old South. It's Florida – with a Southern accent.

TALLAHASSEE: INSIDE INFO

For additional information on events, accommodations, attractions and a walking tour and canopy lane guidebook, call the **Tallahassee Area Convention and Visitors Bureau** at 800/628-2866 or 850/413-9200, or www.seetallahassee.com. You can also call the selected attractions directly.

8 Pensacola

Far removed from the crowded tourist corridor of Orlando and the high-density cities of South Florida, residents of the state's westernmost city have the time and the space to appreciate their beautiful rivers, quiet lagoons, sparkling beaches, well-preserved historic district and thriving cultural calendar. In Pensacola, each worthwhile district abuts the next, so exploring can be done fairly easily by car or on foot.

One logical place to begin a tour is near downtown at the beautiful bayside setting of the **Seville Square Historic District** (tel: 850/595-5985; www.historicpensacola.org) that actually was downtown when it was first settled in 1559. Avenues with names like Barracks, Government and Church reveal the original purpose of the area, and guided tours are offered in this park-like setting, where rows of historic houses are lined up amidst oak trees and gazebos.

A few blocks from Seville is the **Palafox Historic District**, a surprisingly active cultural conglomeration of music stores, theaters, stores and museums – including the **T.T. Wentworth Museum** (330 S. Jefferson Street, tel: 850/595-5585), which is filled with artwork, artifacts, antique photographs and a discovery center for kids. If you're fascinated by the city's rich

history, the **Pensacola Historical Museum** rotates exhibits on geology, maritime history, Native Americans and the city's multicultural heritage. A few blocks away, the restored Spanish baroque architecture of the 1925 **Saenger Theatre** (118 S. Palafox, tel: 850/444-7686; www.pensacolasaenger.com) provides a historic setting for performances by the local symphony orchestra and opera.

If you don't have time to see the beaches now (about a 15-minute drive away), invest an afternoon at the **Pensacola Naval Air Station,** which is the home base for the US Navy's aerobatic team, the Blue Angels. A must-see on the base is the 300,000-square-foot (28,000sq-m) **National Museum of**

A vintage fire truck looks right at home in the Seville Historic District

A mansion typical of those in Pensacola's preserved Seville Historic District

Naval Aviation, one of the three largest aviation museums in the world.

In the community of Gulf Breeze, halfway between Fort Walton and Pensacola, is **The ZOO**, a 30-acre (12-ha) zoo where around 700 animals roam (relatively) free in their (artificially) natural habitats. The African wild dogs here make this one of only 18 zoos in the country to have them. You can see them up close and also ride the Safari Line train that travels around the perimeter. There are also botanical gardens.

When it is time for the beach, the sugar-white sands cover 52 miles (84km) of the shoreline, and much of the seaside activities are found on a pleasing barrier island south of the city. Santa Rosa Island's Pensacola Beach is part of the **Gulf Islands National Seashore** (tel: 850/934-2600) and is also home to **Fort Pickens** (tel: 850/934-2600), a pre-Civil War brick fortress held by Union forces during the conflict.

Quieter and less populated are the top-rated beaches of **Perdido Key** (tel: 850/492-4660 or 800/328-0107; www.perdidochamber.com) located about 15 miles (24km) southwest of Pensacola. For privacy as well as services, try the **Perdido Key State Recreation** Area (tel: 850/492-1595), a 247-acre (100-ha) recreation area with plenty of beach access.

PENSACOLA: INSIDE INFO

For additional information on events, accommodations, attractions, beaches, and a walking tour and canopy lane guidebook, contact the **Pensacola Area Convention and Visitors Bureau** (1401 E. Gregory Street, tel: 800/874-1234 or 850/434-1234; www.visitpensacola.com). For information on the quartz-sand beaches of the Perdido Key State Recreation Area, Santa Rosa, Casino, Langdon, Opal and Quietwater, contact the **Pensacola Beach Visitor Center** (tel: 850/932-1500 or 800/635-4803; www.visitpensacolabeach.com).

Pensacola Historical Museum ➕ 220 A3 ✉ 115 E. Zaragoza Street ☎ 850/433-1559; www.pensacolahistory.org ⏰ Mon–Sat 10–4:30
National Museum of Naval Aviation ➕ 220 A3 ✉ 1750 Radford Boulevard ☎ 850/453-2389 or 800/327-5002; www.naval-air.org ⏰ Daily 9–5
The ZOO ➕ 220 A3 ✉ 5701 Gulf Breeze Parkway ☎ 850/932-2229; www.the-zoo.com ⏰ Daily 9–6 (last entry 5 pm) 💵 Inexpensive

10 Panama City Beach

Be sure to set your compass for the seaside community of Panama City Beach. As in Pensacola, wide white beaches and cloud-soft sands make it an extremely popular resort area. So popular, in fact, that the natural setting is rapidly being overshadowed by growth that peaks each spring and between June and August, when college students on break and families on vacation descend en masse from the neighboring states of Georgia, Alabama and Mississippi.

They – and you – are here because Panama City Beach still has a natural beauty that showcases the incredible white sands, navigable waterways and popular watersports. You can rent cabanas, umbrellas, sailboats, wave runners and floats from the vendors along the beach or, for a thrilling aerial view of the coast, you can strap yourself beneath a parachute and go parasailing behind a speedboat a few hundred yards offshore. Snorkeling and scuba diving are extremely popular in the clear waters here. You can also dive among dozens of ships sunk by the city to create artificial reefs.

Another option is staying on dry land at the **Gulf World Marine Park** (15412 Front Beach Road, tel: 850/234-5271; www.gulfworldmarinepark.com). Although it pales in comparison to Orlando's SeaWorld, the park features sea lions, parrots, tropical gardens and a dolphin show. Interactive programs such as Trainer for a Day allow you to tag along with handlers to see how the animals are cared for.

Located at the eastern tip of Panama City Beach, the **St. Andrews State Recreation Area** (4607 State Park Lane, tel: 850/233-5140; inexpensive)

includes 1,260 acres (510ha) of beaches, pinewoods and marshes as well as campgrounds, swimming areas, fishing piers and hiking along nature trails. From here you can board a ferry to **Shell Island**, a 700-acre (280ha) barrier island in the Gulf of Mexico.

There's plenty of fun to be had at the Shipwreck Island Water Park, on the beach

PANAMA CITY BEACH: INSIDE INFO

For additional information on events, accommodations, attractions and beaches, call the **Panama City Beach Convention and Visitors Bureau** (✚ 221 D3; 17001 Panama City Beach Parkway, tel: 850/233-6503 or 800/722-3224; www.800pcbeach.com).

At Your Leisure

2 Jacksonville

Among the downtown areas that may be worth visiting in this large city, the Avondale, San Marco and Riverside districts offer a special mix of cafés, antiques shops and trendy boutiques. The **1927 Florida Theatre** (128 E. Forsyth Street, tel: 904/355-2787; www.floridatheatre.com) is a stunning example of a Mediterranean Revival concert hall. They still hold concerts here, but few can top the day in 1956 when Elvis Presley played here. For party central, **Jacksonville Landing** (tel: 904/353-1188; www.jacksonvillelanding.com), on the St. Johns River's Riverwalk, is a large entertainment/shopping complex. If you have time, the **Jacksonville Jaguars** (tel: 904/633-2000; www.jaguars.com), the city's NFL football team, play their Sunday home games between August and December at Alltel Stadium.

> **Jacksonville Visitors Bureau**
> ✚ 223 E3 ✉ 550 Water Street, Suite 10,000 ☎ 904/798-9111; www.jaxcvb.com

3 Amelia Island/Fernandina Beach

Sitting right at Florida's northern border across the river from Georgia, Amelia is the barrier island and Fernandina its only city. Recognized as the shrimp capital of Florida, it is also the only place in America to have been ruled under eight flags of domination during the past five centuries. In addition to beaches on the Atlantic coast, there's a 50-block historic district dotted with various styles of homes, plus gift shops, pubs, antiques malls and restaurants found along **Centre Street**. The **Palace Saloon** (117 Centre Street, tel: 904/261-6320) is said to be the oldest in the state, just as the **Amelia Island Museum of History** (233 S. Third Street, tel: 904/261-7378) is one of the best local museums in Florida.

Skyscrapers tower over the St. John's River

Lastly, visit **Fort Clinch State Park** (tel: 904/277-7274), a Civil War-era fortress that was occupied by Union troops. Docents in costume portray the engineers stationed here in 1864 and offer tours of the fort. There are also nature trails, bird watching and saltwater fishing from the 1,500-foot (460-m) fishing pier.

> **Amelia Island Chamber of Commerce**
> ✚ 223 F3 ✉ 961687 Gateway Boulevard, Suite 101G ☎ 904/261-3248; www.islandchamber.com 🕓 Mon–Fri 9–5

4 Daytona Beach

Claiming to be the "World's Most Famous Beach," this city on the Atlantic is notorious for the annual party known as Spring Break, when college students from across America descend upon it. They're just following in the footsteps of **Bike Week**, February's motorcycle meet-up, which attracts about half a million riders from around the world. While the beach, with its miles of wide white sands, is the place that attracts most tourists, a few miles inland is the **Daytona International Speedway** (tel: 386/253-7223; www.daytonaspeedway.com), which offers year-round tours of the track and racing museum and also hosts the legendary Daytona 500.

> **Daytona Beach Chamber of Commerce**
> ✚ 225 D5 ✉ 126 East Orange Avenue ☎ 386/255-0981

At Marianna, cave formations have an orange-yellow tint from iron oxide in the soil

6 Marianna/Florida Caverns State Park

Thanks to the water-filled aquifer that sits just below the surface, few homes in Florida have basements. To see why Floridians face this construction challenge, stop here and join a ranger-led spelunking tour: You'll travel below ground to see limestone caverns that reveal an impressive array of stalactites, stalagmites, soda straws, columns, rimstones and draperies. **Marianna**, the closest town to the park, is quite picturesque and makes a great introduction to the park, where you'll also find quiet hiking trails, campgrounds, and areas for fishing, swimming and canoeing on the Chipola River.

➕ 221 E4 ✉ 3345 Caverns Road (off, Highway 90 on Route 166), Marianna
☎ 850/482-1228 🕐 Tours daily 9:30–4
🎟 Inexpensive (not covered by parks pass)

7 Ponce de León Springs State Recreation Area

Spanning two sparsely populated counties in the Panhandle (Holmes and Walton), this 443-acre (180-ha) park rests atop the site where two subterranean rivers meet and release 14 million gal (53 million L) of crystal-clear spring water each day. Ignore the neighborhood around the park (it's rather derelict) and enjoy splashing in the 68°F (20°C) waters.

To see Florida in its natural state, wander across the rolling hills and floodplain forests and beside swamps leading into small creeks that flow into the Choctawhatchee River. Incidentally, there's no evidence that the Spanish explorer ever assumed this really was the Fountain of Youth.

➕ 220 C4 ✉ Off Highway 90 on SR 181A, Ponce de León ☎ 850/836-4281
🕐 Daily 8–dusk 🎟 Inexpensive

8 Grayton Beach

Off Highway 98 and tucked into the piney woods is this 100-year-old community of narrow streets, crushed gravel paths and weather-worn clapboard cypress shacks – many of which can be rented. A small market and a few restaurants have added some modernity to this rustic village, but the most popular destination here is 1,133-acre (460-ha) **Grayton Beach State Recreation Area**. Amazingly untouched, the park showcases a natural side of Florida with salt marshes, soft sand dunes covered with sea oats, and crystal-white sands meeting the blue-green waters of the Gulf. Stay awhile to enjoy swimming, fishing, snorkeling and camping.

Grayton Beach State Recreation Area ➕ 220 C3 ✉ 357 Main Park Road (off 30A) ☎ 850/231-4210
🕐 Daily 8–dusk 🎟 Inexpensive

State Park Update

Florida's state parks are open from 8 am–dusk. For $43.40 per person (or $85.80 for a family), travelers can buy an annual pass that will get them (and/or their families) into most Florida state parks for a year. Check out the latest information at www.floridastateparks.org. If you want to camp out in a state park, go to www.reserveamerica.com. The **Florida State Parks Information Center** is at 850/245-2157.

⑪ Apalachicola and the Barrier Islands

The surprisingly artsy **Apalachicola** has several claims to fame. First, it became popular as the southern terminus for Florida steamboat travel in the mid-1800s. Second, the oysters harvested in the muddy waters offshore are known across America. A third highlights a local hero: In 1851, as physician John Gorrie was working to invent a machine that would lower the body temperature of patients with yellow fever, he accidentally invented the ice machine – a story told at the **John Gorrie State Museum** (tel: 850/653-9347; closed Tue–Wed).

Off the coast is **St. George Island**, a 28-mile (45-km) barrier island with secluded beaches, and clear waters for swimming and fishing. On the far eastern end of the island **St. George Island State Park** has nine miles of pristine shoreline, dunes, and hiking trails for bird-watching.

West of St. George Island is the **St. Vincent National Wildlife Refuge** (tel: 850/653-8808). This untouched barrier island, just offshore from the mouth of the Apalachicola River, boasts a preserved mix of habitats: wetlands, scrub oaks, cabbage palms and slash pines. There are also Sambar deer, bald eagles, loggerhead sea turtles and peregrine falcons.

St. George Island State Park
➕ 221 E2 ✉ 1900 E. Gulf Beach Drive
☎ 850/927-2111 ⏰ Daily 8 am–dusk
💲 Inexpensive

⑫ Suwannee River State Park

Stephen Foster's classic song "Old Folks at Home" popularized the Suwannee River, and this 1,800-acre (730-ha) park will put you right on its banks and on its waters. Outfitters can provide you with canoes and kayaks, and several two-bedroom vacation cabins can accommodate overnight guests. The natural setting of the park, where the **Withlacoochee River** joins the historic **Suwannee**, showcases a panoramic view of the rivers as well as the surrounding wooded uplands. Admission is on the honor system, with camping available for $15 per night.

➕ 222 C3 ✉ 20185 County Road 132,
13 miles (21km) west of Live Oak, off
US 90 ☎ 386/362-2746 ⏰ Daily
8 am–dusk 💲 Inexpensive

⑬ Cedar Key

It's about 25 miles (40km) off the main highway (Highway 19) and 4 miles (6km) out in the Gulf of Mexico, but the remote setting of **Cedar Key** off Florida's central west coast appeals to a surprising number of travelers seeking a quiet hideaway. One of the state's oldest ports, it was a vital part of Florida history when the railroad came to town and gave the tiny island a means to ship seafood and lumber north. Nowadays, Cedar Key is a haven for artists and writers who crave the peaceful, unspoiled environment. In the center of the village are stores and galleries, while bayous and side streets lead to hidden restaurants with seafood fresh from local waters. If you like solitude, nature and history, Cedar Key may be well worth a visit.

Cedar Key Chamber of Commerce
➕ 222 C1 ✉ P.O. Box 610, Cedar Key
☎ 352/543-5600; www.cedarkey.org

A great, and popular, way to see the Suwannee River

Where to...
Eat and Drink

Prices Expect to pay per person for a meal, excluding drink
$ under $25 $$ $25–50 $$$ over $50

ST. AUGUSTINE

☕☕ Gypsy Cab Company $

This independent restaurant across the Bridge of Lions near the northern end of Anastasia Island, does everything right. You can find it by looking for a line outside the door. It's worth the wait. The Gypsy style is called "Urban Cuisine," and the menu of fish, steak, veal and chicken dishes changes almost daily. It's always good. Especially the cajun shrimp.

✚ 223 F2 ⊠ 828 Anastasia Boulevard ☎ 904/824-8244

Scarlett O'Hara's $–$$

In the historic district, this old wooden house is great for a lunch break or a place to wind down. The menu is basic, but sometimes eating something as simple as a hamburger or red beans and rice while sitting on the front porch is perfect. Service is good, prices are fair, and the patio bar is a shady hideout.

✚ 223 F2 ⊠ 70 Hypolita Street ☎ 904/824-6535

☕☕ A1A Aleworks $

A very popular spot, this combination microbrewery and restaurant will satisfy you whether you want regular food (with a Jamaican/Caribbean twist) or are on a liquid diet. Usually crowded with young locals, it's also a great place to grab a balcony table and enjoy yourself with a view of the bridge and the bay.

✚ 223 F2 ⊠ 1 King Street ☎ 904/829-2977

AMELIA ISLAND

☕☕☕ Beech Street Grill $–$$

In a cozy converted two-story 1889 home, well-trained waiters serve fresh seafood seasoned with freshly cut herbs, homemade sauces and chutneys. The atmosphere is quaint, the meals creative but not ostentatious, and the wine list is extremely extensive.

✚ 223 F3 ⊠ Beech Street, Fernandina Beach ☎ 904/277-3662

Palace Saloon $–$$

Since 1903, barkeeps here have been priming the pumps and delivering frosted mugs of beer to sailors, locals, shrimpers and tourists. The menu now includes shrimp, burgers, sandwiches and wings, but there's also apple-glazed broiled salmon, sea-salt crusted NY steak, and rosemary-glazed broiled rack of lamb, plus frequent live blues or rock 'n' roll.

✚ 223 F3 ⊠ 117 Centre Street, Fernandina Beach ☎ 904/491-3332

APALACHICOLA

Boss Oyster $

A rustic waterfront diner next door to Apalachicola's River Inn, where they've created 1,001 ways to spice up oysters (Greek, Mexican, English, fried, with garlic, with shrimp, with crab, with asparagus or hot peppers or sherry, etc.). If you can't stand oysters, don't worry – they also serve jumbo Gulf shrimp, blue crabs, bay scallops, fresh Gulf grouper, steaks and hot pizza.

✚ 221 E2 ⊠ 123 Water Street ☎ 850/653-9364

Nola's Grill (Gibson Inn) $

Housed in the historic Gibson Inn, Nola's serves breakfast, lunch and dinner Wednesday through Sunday. Staples are fresh Apalachicola shrimp, oysters and other seafood entrées, such as grouper Florentine, chicken portabella or a filet mignon topped with crabmeat, complemented by hot baked breads and a dessert of Key lime pie. The setting is old-fashioned and orderly, with crisp, pressed linen tablecloths and fresh-cut flowers on the tables.

🚪 221 E2 ⊠ 51 Avenue C
☎ 850/653-2191

PANAMA CITY BEACH

Capt. Anderson's $-$$

You know you're on to something good when you arrive early and a hundred people are already waiting to get in for some of the freshest seafood in Florida. And that's off-season. The restaurant is massive, with a main dining room and several smaller dining areas, most of which offer a view of the fishing boats bringing in the catch of the day. Dishes include grilled grouper, amberjack and yellowfin tuna, crab-stuffed jumbo shrimp, and generous portions on the seafood platter. Servers are efficient and friendly. Be warned: They take no reservations, so the wait can be long.

🚪 221 D3 ⊠ 5551 N. Lagoon Drive
☎ 850/234-2225

Picolo Restaurant & Red Bar $

Located in secluded Grayton Beach, Picolo is a favorite with locals and tourists, in large part due to the toy chest-style items that dangle from the walls and ceilings. Old album covers, posters, dolls, shoes… it's all here, as well as smoked salmon salads, fish with citrus beurre blanc, and assorted shrimp, crawfish and baked eggplant (aubergine). Check out the Red Bar, where there is live jazz. Bring cash – they don't accept credit cards.

🚪 220 C3 ⊠ 70 Hotz Avenue,
Grayton Beach ☎ 850/231-1008

PENSACOLA

Marina Oyster Barn $

Located at the marina, this is a slice of Old Florida – the state that existed before Disney came along. You can order freshly shucked oysters – down-home and a long-time local favorite, whether raw, steamed, fried or Rockefeller – but don't forget to save room for the fish, shrimp and oysters breaded with cornmeal. This is a true Southern-style experience – and at a fair price.

🚪 220 A3 ⊠ 505 Bayou Boulevard
☎ 850/433-0511

☞ Mesquite Charlie's $-$$

When you've had enough of Gulf Coast fish dishes, mosey over to this popular Western-style saloon for cuts of charbroiled meat as small as a filet to the 32-oz (0.9-kg) porterhouse (share it with friends).

🚪 220 A3 ⊠ 5901 N. W. Street
☎ 850/434-0498

TALLAHASSEE

Nicholson Farmhouse $-$$

If you're searching for a true American dining experience, this is one of the best. Built in 1828, this 45-acre (18-ha) spread covers a 650-seat complex of dining, banquet and party rooms. Each meal starts with boiled peanuts on the table and leads to hand-cut steaks and chops, broiled chicken, fish, pork loin, grouper and shrimp.

🚪 221 F3 ⊠ State Road 12, Havana
☎ 850/539/5531

Wakulla Springs Lodge $

Inside the lodge at the Wakulla Springs State Park (▶ 187) is a wide, sunny dining room that overlooks a broad lawn and clear springs. The menu here is, naturally, Southern, with bean soup, home-baked muffins, fried seafood, Southern fried shrimp and oysters, and pecan-crusted chicken.

🚪 221 F3 ⊠ 550 Wakulla Park Drive,
Wakulla Springs ☎ 850/224-5950

Where to... Stay

Prices Expect to pay per room per night
$ under $125 $$ $125–250 $$$ over $250

ST. AUGUSTINE

☞☞ Casa Monica Hotel $$

In the heart of downtown, this is a grand 1888 hotel. The original Moorish-Revival accents are visible throughout, from its 137 rooms and suites (including three-story suites in the towers) to the themed dining room, pool, cafés and shops.

➕ 223 F2 ✉ 95 Cordova Street,
☎ 904/827-1888; www.casamonica.com

AMELIA ISLAND

☞☞ Elizabeth Pointe Lodge $$

You may think you're in New England when you check in to this sprawling Nantucket-style oceanfront

bed-and-breakfast. If you're not swimming or sunbathing, the historic district and Fort Clinch are close by. Wide porches are perfect for reading and resting. Complimentary breakfast.

➕ 223 F3 ✉ 98 South Fletcher Avenue ☎ 904/277-4851;
www.elizabethpointelodge.com

APALACHICOLA

☞☞ Gibson Inn $-$$

On the National Register of Historic Places, this inn is easily identified by its wraparound porches, fretwork and captain's watch. Rooms have four-poster beds, antique armoires, and pedestal lavatories that have wide basins and porcelain fixtures.

➕ 221 E2 ✉ 51 Avenue C ☎ 850/653-2191; www.gibsoninn.com

PANAMA CITY BEACH

Flamingo Motel $-$$

One of the rare family-owned beach properties. A tropical garden surrounds a heated swimming pool, a sundeck overlooks the Gulf, and clean rooms have a full kitchen or refrigerators and microwaves. Next to the motel are suites that have living rooms, dining tables and kitchens.

➕ 221 D3 ✉ 15525 Front Beach Road ☎ 850/234-2232;
www.flamingomotel.com

PENSACOLA

New World Inn $$

Sitting between the scenic bay and the historic district, this boutique hotel (only 15 rooms) has a colonial theme. Rooms are spacious and artfully decorated with antiques that reflect Pensacola's history and influences. It's warm, cozy and

perfectly situated. A complimentary continental breakfast is served.

➕ 220 A3 ✉ 600 S. Palafox Street

TALLAHASSEE

☞☞ Calhoun Street Inn Bed & Breakfast $

The only bed-and-breakfast in downtown Tallahassee, this historic district inn is in walking distance of all major sights. Large, sunny, uncluttered rooms (four have private baths) have antiques, hand-made quilts and fresh flowers.

➕ 221 F3 ✉ 525 N. Calhoun Street
☎ 850/425-5095

☞☞ Governors Inn $$

This restored historic warehouse is popular with politicians, press and lobbyists. After visiting nearby attractions (a short walk away), come home to a cozy retreat with soft beds, warm mahogany and classic prints.

➕ 221 F3 ✉ 209 S. Adams Street
☎ 850/681-6855

Where to...
Shop

AMELIA ISLAND

Centre Street in Fernadina Beach is the island's main shopping district, where you'll find the greatest concentration of bookstores, antiques shops, gift galleries, candy stores and boutiques. Art galleries feature unique nautical items, and the owner-operated shops along Centre Street feature one-of-a-kind items.

APALACHICOLA

You'll likely walk away with a nautical souvenir from this waterfront town, and at **William Trotter Lighthouse Maritime Studio** (257 Highway 98, tel: 850/653-1042) there are hundreds of lighthouse prints and figurines as well as

historic Apalachicola paintings, prints and books. Have a rummage through the **Apalachicola Antiques Mall** (117 Market Street, tel: 850/653-3894). A former ship's chandlery is now the **Grady Market** (76 Water Street, tel: 850/653-4099), home to more than a dozen antiques shops, boutiques and restaurants.

PANAMA CITY BEACH

You don't come to a gorgeous beach to shop, but you may just want to take a break at the **Panama City Mall** (2150 Martin Luther King Jr. Boulevard, tel: 850/785-9587). With more than 100 stores, it's a good place to find travel and gift items.

PENSACOLA

The Palafox District in the heart of old Pensacola may be your best bet for browsing. Art lovers will find galleries displaying art glass, wood, metal, paintings and jewelry. The

Quayside Art Gallery (15–17 E. Zarragossa Street, tel: 850/438-2363) is the largest co-op art gallery in the Southeast. There are numerous other stores in this area, while about 10 miles (16km) north is the **Cordova Mall** (5100 N. Ninth Avenue, tel: 850/477-5563), the area's largest with three department stores, 140 specialty stores and nearly a dozen restaurants.

ST. AUGUSTINE

The best concentration of stores is along **St. George Street**, in the historic district. The popular pedestrian mall is active day and night, and here small restaurants sit beside gift shops and beachwear and candy stores. A few blocks away, in the back of the grand hotel that is now the **Lightner Museum** (75 King Street, tel: 904/824-2874), is a collection of antiques shops that have old maps, books, silver, crystal and many other fine, beautiful and quirky items. Several blocks north,

San Marco Avenue has a string of antiques and collectibles shops, gift shops, clothing consigners, and a superb antiquarian bookseller, **Wolf's Head Books** (tel: 904/824-9357), one of the best in the state.

TALLAHASSEE

There are some interesting items to be found in the gift shops of the **Old Capitol** building and the **Museum of Florida History**. Aside from the plentiful stores of the **Governors Square Mall** (1500 Apalachee Parkway, tel: 850/671-4636), the most shopping fun you'll have is 20 miles (32km) outside town in the old farming community of **Havana**. Old canning plants and tractor showrooms have been converted to antiques malls where an eclectic collection of Americana is sold. Also outside of town is **Bradley's Country Store** (10655 Centerville Road, tel: 850/893-1647), which is known for its freshly made country sausage, grits and cane syrup.

Where to...
Be Entertained

AMELIA ISLAND

In addition to the **Palace Saloon** (▶ 194), at the end of Centre Street in Fernandina Beach, **Brett's Waterway Café** (1897 Island Walk Way, tel: 904/261-2660) has an outdoor bar that's right on the Amelia River overlooking Georgia. On the north end of the island, **Sandy Bottoms** (2910 Atlantic Avenue, tel: 904/277-0814) is a beach bar that's actually right on the beach.

APALACHICOLA

The best bars here are attached to restaurants (▶ 194–195), but for a more highbrow outing, consider an evening at the **Dixie Theatre** (21 Avenue E, tel: 850/653-3200).

Opened in 1913, it was a theater for years, and after nearly disintegrating and being rebuilt, today it's a regional theater that offers a summer repertory between June and September, and other plays, musicals and music fests throughout the year.

PANAMA CITY BEACH

The **Martin Theatre** (409 Harrison Avenue, tel: 850/763-8080) hosts traditional plays and concerts throughout the year. Definitely not a family spot is the **Club LaVela** (8813 Thomas Drive, tel: 850/234-3866), which claims to be the largest nightclub in America. They feature 15 clubs, a pool, beach and a hedonistic feel that reaches its climax during Spring Break.

PENSACOLA

The long-reigning king of Pensacola nightlife is the **Seville Square Historic District** (130 E. Government Street, tel: 850/434-6211). With seven different rooms, nine bars and two courtyards, it appeals to different crowds. **Rosie O'Grady's Goodtime Emporium** is a 1920s jazz club with a live band, sing-alongs and saloon girls; **Phineas Phoggs** is the disco, **Apple Annie's Courtyard** features easy listening folk music, and **Fast Eddie's Billiard Parlor** is just that. More soothing is the **Pensacola Opera** (75 S. Tarragona Street, tel: 850/433-6737), which showcases traditional selections, and the **Pensacola Symphony Orchestra** (205 E. Zaragoza Street, tel: 850/435-2533).

ST. AUGUSTINE

The **A1A Aleworks** (▶ 194) is a popular microbrewery/restaurant and, along with the small pubs and bars found along **St. George Street** (▶ 185), it is worth a visit. Also in the historic district is the **Tradewinds Lounge** (124 Charlotte Street, tel: 904/829-9336). A local icon, it's been here since 1964 and is a popular watering hole (with a house band) for locals, tourists, students and beach bums. A few blocks south is **O. C. White's** (118 Avenida Menendez, tel: 904/824-0808), a restaurant with a nice outdoor patio.

TALLAHASSEE

As well as being the state capital, Tallahassee's also a college town, so you could maybe get an invite to a frat party on the campus of **Florida State University**. Easier is phoning the university's school of music (tel: 850/644-4774) for a schedule of the free concerts and performances the students offer each year. The theater department (tel: 850/644-7234) has one of America's leading drama programs and also hosts performances on campus.

Walks & Tours

1 WINTER PARK

Walk

Red-brick streets, the sound of the Sunset Limited rolling into the train station, a cool and pleasing park, great shops... when you're in Greater Orlando, why walk anywhere other than Winter Park? The avenue is filled with sidewalk cafés, ice-cream parlors, antiques and craft emporiums, art and gift galleries, fashion boutiques, perfumeries and jewelers.

To reach Park Avenue from the attractions area, take I-4 east to Exit 87 (Fairbanks Avenue) and head east 1.5 miles (2.5km) to Park Avenue. Turn left (north) and travel two blocks to park on the avenue or a nearby side street.

DISTANCE 1 mile (1.6km) **TIME** 2 hours (4 if you shop. And you should)
START POINT North end of Park Avenue ✚ 228 E6
END POINT South end of Park Avenue ✚ 228 E6

Leafy Park Avenue – reminiscent of European style

1–2

Begin your walk at the corner of Park and Comstock avenues, and stop by the intriguing **Restoration Hardware** chain store (400 S. Park Avenue, tel: 407/622-1050), which sells art deco-era reproductions. Head north on the right side of Park Avenue, crossing New England Avenue, then Welbourne Avenue. You're cruising through the shopping district. Just after Welbourne, duck into **Greeneda Court**, a cozy courtyard featuring interior design stores and **Brandywine Books**, a great little used-book store (114 S. Park Avenue, Suite E, tel: 407/644-1711, Mon–Sat 10–5:30). Back on Park Avenue, head north again to Morse Boulevard and turn right (east).

2–3

Morse Boulevard ends at Lake Osceola, the departure point for the popular **Winter Park Scenic Boat Tour** (312 E. Morse Boulevard, tel: 407/644-4056; inexpensive). The casual one-hour cruise skirts past luxurious lakefront mansions, parks and along narrow interconnecting canals on Winter Park's famed chain of lakes.

3–4

Return to Park Avenue and turn right. Stop for lunch at the **Briar Patch Restaurant** (252 N. Park Avenue, tel: 407/628-8651). Back on the street, you'll notice chain stores such as Talbot's, Ann Taylor and Victoria's Secret. **The Garden Shops** (324 Park Avenue) includes small gift shops and decorator boutiques. A narrow garden path to your right leads to a group of delightful, interesting stores.

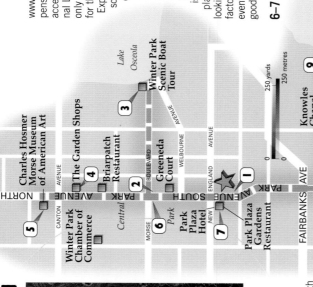

www.morsemuseum.org; open Tue–Sun; inexpensive. For a nominal charge, you will gain access to the world's largest collection of original Louis C. Tiffany stained glass, including the only surviving Tiffany interior, a chapel designed for the 1893 Chicago World's Columbian Exposition. Also on display are paintings, sculptures, and arts and crafts created by other artists between 1850 and 1930.

5–6

Now head south on Park Avenue on the west side of the street. On your right between Canton and New England avenues is **Central Park**. The lush park is a gathering place for young lovers, families and squirrels looking for handouts. It's also Winter Park's de facto town square where concerts, special events and art festivals are presented and is a good place to stop for a while and do nothing.

6–7

On the corner of Park and New England avenues, the **Park Plaza Hotel** (307 S. Park Avenue, tel: 407/647-1072; www.parkplazahotel.com) is a charming boutique hotel. A genteel ambiance is provided by

Exquisite Tiffany glass at the Charles Hosmer Morse Museum of American Art

4–5

Return to Park Avenue and continue north until you reach Canton Avenue. Cross to the west side of the street, walk north to the **Charles Hosmer Morse Museum of American Art** (445 N. Park Avenue, tel: 407/645-5311;

Charles Hosmer Museum of American Art

Winter Park Chamber of Commerce

The Garden Shops

Briarpatch Restaurant

Greeneda Court

Winter Park Scenic Boat Tour

Park Plaza Hotel

Park Plaza Gardens Restaurant

Knowles Chapel

Cornell Fine Arts Museum

Rollins College Campus

Lake Osceola

Lake Virginia

Central Park

NORTH

CANTON AVENUE

PARK AVENUE

BOULEVARD

WELBOURNE AVENUE

MORSE

NEW ENGLAND AVENUE

SOUTH PARK AVENUE

FAIRBANKS AVE

HOLT AVENUE

250 yards

250 metres

campus of **Rollins College** (tel: 407/646-2000). Founded in 1885, it has consistently been a popular college for the offspring of wealthy Northern families. It also has some of the most beautiful Mediterranean-themed architecture in America. At the end of Park Avenue, you'll reach Holt Avenue. Turn left and walk down the red-brick road to **Knowles Chapel**, the favored venue for the springtime Bach Festival and visiting speakers such as former President Jimmy Carter and author John Berendt.

8–9

Remain on Holt, passing the Knowles Chapel. At the end of Holt is the **Cornell Fine Arts Museum** (tel: 407/646-2526; www.rollins.edu/cfam), one of Florida's hidden treasures, and well worth a visit (undergoing renovation until fall 2005). Exhibits range from Old Masters to contemporary sculptures to historically significant photographs. Behind the Cornell Museum is Lake Virginia, another soothing setting where you can lie on the grass and watch the beautiful wildlife.

9–start

After you've had your fill of serenity, return up Holt, turn right onto Park Avenue, find your car and drive back to the hustle and bustle of the theme-park attractions.

rich woodwork, a cozy fireplace and gift shops. In an intimate courtyard, the **Park Plaza Gardens Restaurant** (319 S. Park Avenue, tel: 407/645-2475) is a pleasant place for a drink and a superb meal.

The campus of Rollins College

7–8

Keep heading south on Park Avenue, passing your car and crossing Fairbanks to enter the

2 SPACE COAST
Tour

Only 50 miles (80km) from Orlando, you can wring the most out of Florida's Space Coast with a full-day visit. The obvious starting point is Kennedy Space Center (9–dusk, tel: 321/452-2121 or 800/KSC-INFO; www.KennedySpaceCenter.com).

To reach Kennedy Space Center from downtown Orlando, travel east on Highway 50 and at the first light past I-95, turn right onto Highway 405/Columbia Drive. Follow Columbia past US 1 and the Kennedy Space Center is about 7 miles (11km) down on your right. From Disney or International Drive, take the Beeline Expressway (Highway 528, a toll road) east to Highway 407, which leads to Highway 405. Turn right and follow the signs.

1–5
The Kennedy Space Center **Visitor Complex** (▶ 96) has the largest collection of space arti-facts in the world, as well as presentations that are thoughtful, intriguing and entertaining. After

DISTANCE Round trip from Orlando, approximately 130 miles (210km)
TIME Full day for space-related attractions **START POINT** Kennedy Space Center ✚ 225 E3
END POINT U.S. Astronaut Hall of Fame (or Atlantic Ocean) ✚ 225 E3

paying one admission price, you'll enter the complex where you should turn to your right to reach the bus loading dock. The tour takes you past the **Vehicle Assembly Building** and to the 60-foot-tall (18-m) Launch Complex 39 Observation Gantry.

The next stop, the **Apollo/Saturn V Center**, begins at the Firing Room Theater, which re-creates the lunar mission of Apollo 8. With a great pre-show

Add fuel and this Saturn V rocket could fly again

and actual consoles from the 1968 mission, you'll feel like you're witnessing the real thing.

The simulated launch of Apollo 8 leads to the main concourse where, believe it or not, there's an actual 363-foot-long (111-m) **Saturn V** rocket built for a moon mission that never took place. It lies on its side and stretches the entire length of the building. As you walk from one end of the rocket to the command module at the tip, check out other interesting displays such as the van that ferried astronauts to the launch pad, as well as an actual moon rock you can touch.

The next show is one of the best in Central Florida. At the **Lunar Surface Theater**

you'll revisit the amazing story of the Apollo 11 landing. A pre-show film clip plays scenes of circa 1969 mission control officers trying to re-establish communication with the command module Columbia as several television screens broadcast the chilling phrase 'Loss of Signal' – an eerie reminder of the loss of the Columbia shuttle in February 2003. In a brilliant re-creation of the events of July 20, 1969, you'll be reminded that Neil Armstrong and Buzz Aldrin's onboard computers failed during their descent and, with less than 30 seconds of fuel to spare, Armstrong had to land the lunar module himself.

If you're feeling a little hungry now, the Moon Rock Café serves standard attraction foods.

5–6

After taking the bus back to the main entrance area, invest time in one of three IMAX films: Tom Hanks' "Apollo 13", "The Dream Is Alive", or "Space Station 3-D".

Map labels: Cape Canaveral; Launch Pad 39A; Launch Complex 39; Observation Gantry; Vehicle Assembly Building; Apollo/Saturn V Center; Kennedy Space Center; NASA PARKWAY; Kennedy Space Center Visitor Complex; US Astronaut Hall of Fame; Indian River; St Johns River; Merritt Island; Banana River; Port Canaveral; Cape Canaveral; Cocoa Beach Pier; Ron Jon Surf Shop; Cocoa Beach; CAUSEWAY; BENNETT CAUSEWAY; Merritt Island; Cocoa; Lake Poinsett; Lone Cabbage Fish Camp; BEE LINE EXPRESSWAY; Walt Disney World® Resort; Orlando; 0 4 miles; 0 4 km

The Space Station film is an amazing example of cinematography. Shot by astronauts and cosmonauts, the super-crisp images place the nearly life-size International Space Station within your grasp – it may be the most realistic vision you'll ever have of space travel.

6–7

Outside the theatre, KSC has planted the **Rocket Garden**, which is a collection of spare rockets and equipment from the early Atlas rockets of the late 1950s to the Saturn 1 from 1967. Leading to an Apollo capsule is the actual service arm that led to the Apollo 11. Although Armstrong, Aldrin and Collins did it first and 30 stories above the ground, it's still a privilege to follow in their footsteps.

7–8

A few feet away, a **museum of Early Space Exploration** focuses on the highlights of the fledgling days of rocketry, and features an actual-size mock-up of the first liquid-fuel rocket. There are additional exhibits on the glory days of the Mercury and Gemini space programs.

8–9

Time your schedule to catch the **"Astronaut Encounter"** in a pavilion near the entrance. Every day an astronaut answers questions, helping to explain space travel in down-to-earth terms. For an even closer encounter, "Lunch with an Astronaut" (about $60, including KSC admission) adds a meal and more time to chat.

9–10

Before leaving, stop at the **Astronaut Memorial**. Sadly, the names of the crew of Columbia etched into the 60-ton marble mirror join 17 other astronauts who also gave their lives to help advance space exploration.

10–11

Leave the Hall of Fame for a trip to **Cocoa Beach**. Take Highway 405 east to State Road 3 and go south to Highway 528 east, which then turns into A1A at Port Canaveral. Drive another few miles to reach the intersection of Highway 520 and A1A.

11–12

You're at the most popular section of Cocoa Beach, the intersection highlighted by **Ron Jon Surf Shop** (4151 N. Atlantic Avenue, tel: 321/799-8820; www.ronjons.com). This huge surf shop has become legendary. Tourists from far and wide head here not for surfboards but for T-shirts and Ron Jon paraphernalia.

One block east of A1A is Ridgewood Avenue. For miles south or north, there are entrances to some of Florida's finest beaches. A few blocks north of Ron Jon's, the **Cocoa Beach Pier** (401 Meade Avenue, tel: 321/783-7549) contains a collection of stores, bars and restaurants.

12–13

When you're done at the beach, return to Orlando by taking Highway 520 east. About 6 miles (10km) past I-95, stop at the rustic **Lone Cabbage Fish Camp** (tel: 321/632-4199) for an airboat ride or a platter of gator tail and frogs' legs.

13–14

At the Beeline Expressway (Highway 528), head east to return to **International Drive** or **Walt Disney World® Resort**.

Space Coast Office of Tourism
8810 Astronaut Boulevard, Suite 102, Cape Canaveral, FL 32920 ☎ 321/868-1126; 800/872-1969; 800/93-0CEAN; www.space-coast.com

Kennedy Space Center ☎ 321/449-4400; www.kennedyspacecenter.com; Nasa Launch Hotline; 800/572-4636

3 Art Deco District/ South Beach

Walk

DISTANCE 1.5 miles (2.5km) **TIME** 4 hours
START POINT Lincoln Road and Collins Avenue, Miami ⊞ 230 C3
END POINT Delano Hotel ⊞ 230 C3

The streets and the beaches of the Art Deco District (▶114–116) are so gorgeous that the area deserves a closer look. While it's easy to be dazzled by the bronzed bodies, white sands, blue waters and the bright pastel colors of art deco hotels, look a little closer and you'll find cool shops, quiet bookstores and small cafés that provide oases of respite within this high-energy area.

There are dozens of places that can kick your adrenaline into overdrive after dark, so here's an easy daytime walking tour that will introduce you to some comforting and peaceful zones.

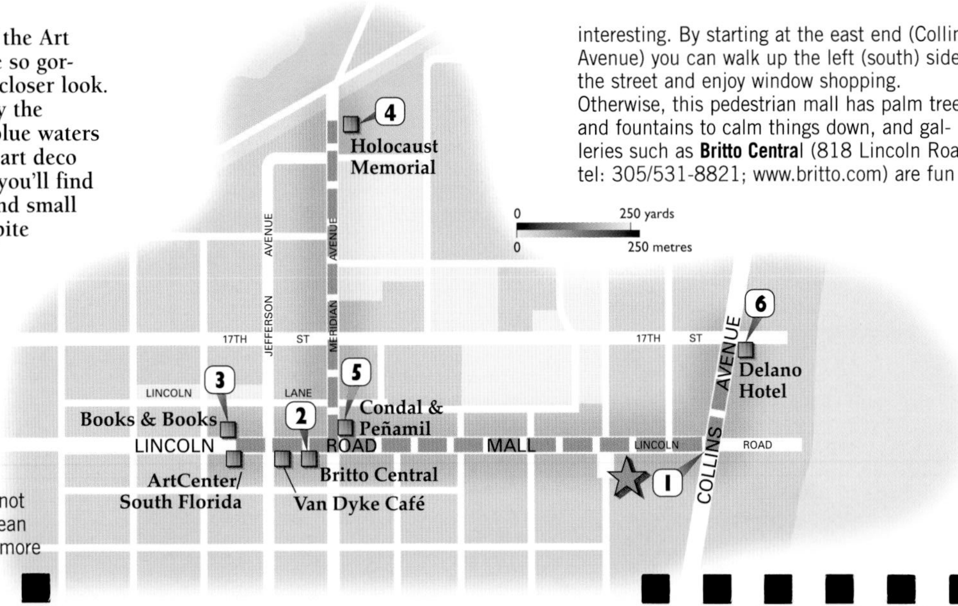

1–2

While the Lincoln Road Mall may not be any more or less lively than Ocean Drive or Collins Avenue, it can be more

interesting. By starting at the east end (Collins Avenue) you can walk up the left (south) side of the street and enjoy window shopping. Otherwise, this pedestrian mall has palm trees and fountains to calm things down, and galleries such as **Britto Central** (818 Lincoln Road, tel: 305/531-8821; www.britto.com) are fun to

Map labels:
Holocaust Memorial — 4
Condal & Peñamil — 5
Britto Central
Van Dyke Café
Books & Books — 3
ArtCenter/ South Florida
Delano Hotel — 6

17TH ST
MERIDIAN AVENUE
JEFFERSON AVENUE
LINCOLN ROAD MALL
COLLINS
LINCOLN ROAD
LINCOLN AVENUE

0   250 yards
0   250 metres

Miami's café society actually does meet at cafés. The Van Dyke on Lincoln Road Mall is a prime spot

Taking a Break

Van Dyke Café is the most active sidewalk (pavement) café on Lincoln Road Mall. If the weather's nice (and it usually is), get your day off to a slow start with a meal at an outdoor table. No need for recommendations – everything tastes great and the service is as good as the food.

☒ **846 Lincoln Road** ☎ **305/534-3600**

visit. Romero Britto's bright pop art images have found a perfect backdrop in SoBe.

2–3

Keep walking west and at the corner of Lincoln Road and Jefferson Avenue, the enormously

popular **Van Dyke Café** (➤ box above) is a great place to stop.

Work off your meal by heading west, dropping into any of the eclectic shops that pique your interest.

Miami inspires artists the way the Mississippi Delta inspires the blues. At the **ArtCenter/South Florida** (924 Lincoln Road, tel: 305/674-8278; www.artcentersf.org) more than 40 "yet-to-be-discovered" artists have their goods on display. The gallery is located at nearby 800 Lincoln Road.

Books & Books (933 Lincoln Road, tel: 305/532-3222), just across the road from the Art Center/South Florida, has books and magazines on nearly every topic and is definitely worth a stop. It's a quiet yet active little store that serves snacks, coffees and espressos. Inside the door to your right is a table filled with discounted books – most of which deal with Miami art, architecture and history. Reading a good book in a cool city can be one of the best ways to enjoy a vacation.

3–4

Before you reach your next stop, take a detour. As you head east, look for Meridian Avenue and turn left. Walk three blocks to the end of the street and the **Holocaust Memorial** (1933–1945 Meridian Avenue, tel: 305/538-1663). It's worth spending some time at the memorial, so don't limit yourself to a quick glance from across the street. Pay a modest donation, walk down a hall with a timeline of the Holocaust, then turn left toward a monumental, 42-foot-high (13-m) arm, the "Sculpture of Love and Anguish," on which Jewish victims are depicted climbing to escape. The absence of all sounds, save spiritual music, makes this a chilling experience.

Miami's celebrated art-deco architecture

4–5

Backtrack to Lincoln Road, turn left and drop in at **Tropical Cigars** (741 Lincoln Road, tel: 305/673-3194). Miami is known for cigars and this place doesn't disappoint. Soft terra-cotta and earth tones enhance the setting here, that of an Italian villa. Smokers will be in ecstasy over the selection of ashtrays, cutters, humidors and a "cigar cave" where they can complement their smoke with a coffee or cocktail.

5–6

It's been a casual day. You've enjoyed a drink, a meal, a book and a cigar. Now you have only to walk to Collins Avenue, turn left and head to the corner of 17th Street and into the **Delano Hotel**, instantly recognizable by its fin-like towers (▶ 142). This, more than any place in Miami, epitomizes the creativity and undiluted weirdness that descended upon the city. Savor the moment with a drink by the poolside bar, where furniture sits in the pool and mirrors rest on the lawn. After a moment you'll start to feel as if you are in a Salvador Dalí painting!

Saved from Demolition

In the 1980s, many deemed the colorful facades of the Art Deco District passé and the developers began to move in. Activist Barbara Baer Capitman spearheaded a movement to preserve the area, and as more people realized the value and beauty of the architecture, the district was saved.

Hot tip

The **ELECTROWAVE** (tel: 305/843-9283, ▶ 40) is the best thing to arrive in Miami Beach since sand. The electric trolleys run throughout SoBe and cost only 25 cents.

For an interesting historical perspective of the Art Deco District, take one of the excellent guided or audio walking tours that depart from the **Art Deco District Welcome Center** (1001 Ocean Drive, tel: 305/531-3484; www.mdpl.org; open daily 11–6). Audio tours (90-minutes long) are available in English, German, Spanish and French. Guided tours are offered on Thursdays at 6.30 pm and Saturdays at 10:30 am (inexpensive). No reservations are necessary.

4 THE FLORIDA KEYS

Tour

DISTANCE 254 miles (408km)
TIME at least 2 days
START/END POINT Miami ⊞ 227 F3

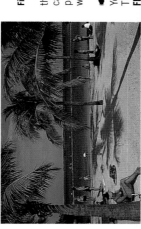

The Florida Keys evoke images of an island paradise – azure blue waters, white sandy beaches and some of the best snorkeling, scuba diving and fishing in the world. It's all this – plus crowded roads, broken-down old trailers and tacky tourist shops on the 110-mile (177-km) journey from Key Largo to Key West. On a casual drive to the southernmost point in mainland America, you'll find parks, dive centers and restaurants to keep you entertained. Addresses along the way are clearly marked by small green and white mile markers, which start with MM 127 south of Florida City and end at MM 0 in Key West.

1–2

To reach **Florida City**, the start for the Florida Keys, you can take one of two southern routes out of Miami. US 1 is the main road, but it has thick city traffic for several miles. The

Florida's Turnpike is a less trafficked and faster road, although it's a little west of Miami, and you'll pay a small toll to take it. The choice is yours.

2–3

Once you reach Florida City, a 19-mile (31-km) stretch between MM 127 and 108 serves as a buffer zone between Miami and the more laid-back mood that begins in **Key Largo**, the longest of the Keys. Be cautious, because even though

Fine tune your Florida vacation with time on the beach

the speed limit is 55mph (88kph), some drivers can be reckless (they frequently pass in no-passing lanes). For safety's sake, always drive with your main beams on.

🐦

Your first stop will be on your right at MM 106. The **Key Largo Chamber of Commerce and Florida Keys Visitor Center** (tel: 305/451-1414; www.keylargochamber.org; daily 9–6) is well stocked with brochures, pamphlets and discount coupons for Keys attractions, and the staff can help you make lodging reservations if needed. They also carry brochures for nearly 30 nearby dive stations. Most offer similar snorkeling trips and scuba-diving excursions (moderate for a half-day of snorkeling to expensive for a scuba-diving trip; certification required, equipment rental extra). Spencer Slate at the **Atlantis Dive Center** (51 Garden Cove Drive, MM 106.5, tel: 305/451-3020 or 800/331-3483) has earned a reputation for his knowledge of the waters, the underwater weddings he organizes, and the fact that he feeds moray eels fresh fish held in his mouth.

Drive farther south to MM 102.5 and look to your left for the entrance to the **John Pennekamp Coral Reef State Park** (tel: 305/451-1202; www.pennekamppark.com), arguably the most popular spot between Miami and Key West. Starting on the shoreline, the underwater preserve stretches 3 miles (5km) into the Florida Straits and runs 21 miles (34km) along the southern coast of the Keys. It is a refuge for a variety of corals and fish. After paying admission (inexpensive), you will drive along a trail to the visitor center (daily 8–5), where there's a small exhibit about Florida wildlife, as well as John Pennekamp, the newspaper editor who helped establish the preserve.

Chances are you'll be more interested in hit-ting the water. Next to the visitor center, there's a gift shop, snack shop and a ticket counter where you can book various water excursions. Snorkeling, diving, glass-bottom-boat tours, and canoe and kayak rentals are arranged here, and they rent out swim fins, snorkels and masks. There are lots of submerged wrecks to

explore, and the popular bronze statue, "Christ of the Deep." And if you don't have time for a dive trip, there are small, shallow swimming areas, lavatories and changing facilities.

Head south and consider a stop at the **Dolphin Cove Research Education Center** (tel: 305/451-4060; www.dolphinscove.com), on your right at MM 101.9. Swimming with dolphins is one of the more popular (and expensive) recreational activities in the Keys, so you have to pay and book well in advance. During a boat ride and training session you learn how to interact with the dolphins before getting in the water with them. Your actual time in the water is only about 15 minutes, making this an expensive, but unforgettable, experience.

Head south to MM 100 and take a look at the boat Bogart and Hepburn made famous. The *African Queen*. It's docked on a canal next to a Holiday Inn and is free to look at, as is *Thayer IV*, the boat Hepburn used in "On Golden Pond." When you've seen these, you've seen most of Key Largo.

Still following in the wake of Jacques Cousteau, **World Watersports** (MM 99, tel: 305/451-0118; www.diversdirect.com) claims to be America's largest dive store. It has every-thing you need for a day in the water. The staff can also answer your questions about local dives.

3–4
Continue south past shopping plazas and fishing charters until you reach Windley Key and the entrance to **Islamorada**. When the Spanish arrived, they saw the violet shells of the Janthina sea

there's less entertainment and a lot more drinking. The likes of Barbara Bush and General Norman Schwarzkopf have occasionally dropped in. Don't expect a resort – it looks more like a beach movie from the 1960s.

A half-mile (0.8km) south at MM 81.5, the **Green Turtle Inn** (tel: 305/664-9031; www.green turtleinn.com, Tue–Sun, noon–9) has been serving seafood since 1947. Try the Key lime pie.

Farther south at MM 81.1, **Tarpon Flats** is where former president George Bush Snr. goes fishing when he's down in the Keys. Professional anglers claim this is one of the best fishing spots in the world.

4–5

From here, the attractions of nature hold sway. Vaulting from key to key, US 1 follows the old seagoing railroad that passes emerald-green lagoons, deep-blue seas, nodding palms and an abundance of white herons, roseate spoonbills, pelicans, seagulls and ospreys. The islands become increasingly narrow and, in a loose sense, you are driving across the Atlantic Ocean

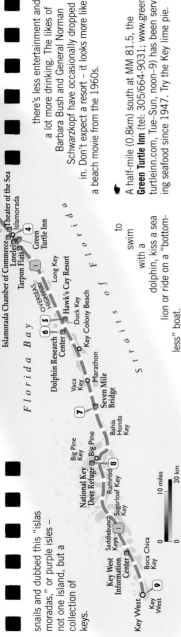

snails and dubbed this "islas moradas," or purple isles – not one island, but a collection of keys.

There are only a few things here worth seeing, but if you like fishing, then there are plenty of things to do.

At MM 86.7 on your left you'll see a huge lobster statue. There's a collection of a dozen stores here, but the lobster is the real draw.

Halfway down the Keys at MM 84.5, **Theater of the Sea** (tel: 305/664-2431) is an old aquatic attraction where shows feature dolphins and other sea creatures. Not that impressive if you've seen SeaWorld, but worth it if you want

to swim with a dolphin, kiss a sea lion or ride on a "bottomless" boat.

A few miles down at MM 82.5 is an old train car housing the **Islamorada Chamber of Commerce** (tel: 305/664-4503, Mon–Fri 9–5, Sat 9–4, Sun 9–2), a good place to stop for local information on the area's biggest draw: Sportsfishing.

At MM 82, look for the huge mermaid on your right, and you will have stumbled across the restaurant/bar **Lorelei** (tel: 305/664-4656; www.loreleirestaurant.com, daily 7 am–1 pm). If you arrive here at sunset, the celebration is a precursor to the one in Key West, but here

– enjoy the view. At MM 61, you'll see the entrance to a large resort, **Hawk's Cay** (tel: 305/743-7000). It has watersports rentals including power boats, wave-runners and parasailing (rates vary). They also promote a "dolphin connection," but since you don't actually get to swim with them (you stand next to them in the water) pass this one by.

5–6

Just past Duck Key, you'll arrive at MM 59, Grassy Key, and the **Dolphin Research Center** (tel: 305/289-0002 or 289-1121; www. dolphins.org, daily 9–4). If you had to pick just one dolphin swim based on celebrity endorsements, you may have the best luck here. Jimmy Carter, Sandra Bullock, Jimmy Buffett and Arnold Schwarzenegger have latched onto the dorsal fins of these dolphins to be pulled and

The Keys

The Keys are a string of islands that, until 1912, were only accessible by boat. Then Henry M. Flagler built a railroad that spanned 29 islands all the way from Homestead, just south of Miami, to Key West. A road followed, US 1, the only way in and out of the Keys.

pushed around the lagoon. You have to book well in advance if you plan to do this, and make sure you bring an extra $115 for the privilege.

If you'd rather not swim, you can take a tour ($17.50 adults, $11.50 children) and watch sea lions and dolphins, who stare back at you with equal curiosity. The tour lasts about 30 minutes and can drag in places, and the Florida heat can wear you down quickly. Be prepared to seek refuge in the air-conditioned gift shop.

Taking a Break

After a day diving in Key Largo, if you are too worn out to drive afterward, the **Largo Lodge** (MM 101.7, tel: 305/451-0424; www.largolodge.com; inexpensive) epitomizes the Keys of the 1940s. This low-key collection of cottages is surprisingly inexpensive for what it offers: $95–125 affords an in season evening in a secluded, house-size unit complete with exposed beam ceilings, kitchenettes, a large living room, bedroom and screened porch. If you're stressed out, you can calm down in the soothing setting of your room or in the grassy bayfront area out back.

6–7

After this, the road continues south past Marathon. This is a crowded island, dense with traffic, and holds little of interest for travelers. At MM 47, the main attraction is the famous **Seven Mile Bridge**, an impressive span leading to Bahia Honda Key. There's not much to see except the Florida Straits, which stretch forever on your left.

7–8

Once the bridge has been crossed, the scenery begins to suffer. The grass is sunburnt and there are numerous abandoned cars by the roadside. The only section worth observing is at MM 36.5, when you leave Bahia Key and arrive in Key deer territory. About 300 Key deer (a subspecies of the Virginia white-tailed deer) live here and are threatened by little else but speeding cars. Slow down and keep your eyes open and you may see one.

8–9

At MM 10, you can stop at the **Key West Information Center** (tel: 888/245-5397; www.keywestinfo.com) and stock up on brochures. Otherwise, keep on heading south and into the liveliest and most popular of all the Keys, Key West (▶ 134).

GETTING ADVANCE INFORMATION

Websites
- Visit Florida:
www.flausa.com
- Orlando Tourist
Information Center:
www.go2orlando.com

- Greater Miami C&VB:
www.miamiandbeaches.com
- Kissimmee/St Cloud
C&VB:
www.floridakiss.com

- Tampa Visitor Information
Center:
www.gotampa.com
- Key West Welcome Center:
www.fla-keys.com

BEFORE YOU GO

WHAT YOU NEED

	● Required ○ Suggested ▲ Not required	Entry requirements differ depending on your nationality and are also subject to change without notice. Check prior to a visit and follow news events that may affect your situation.	U.K.	Germany	U.S.A.	Canada	Australia	Ireland	Netherlands	Spain
Passport/National Identity Card			●	●	▲	○	●	●	●	●
Visa (waiver form to be completed)			▲	▲	▲	▲	▲	▲	▲	▲
Onward or Return Ticket			●	●	▲	▲	●	●	●	●
Health Inoculations (tetanus and polio)			▲	▲	▲	▲	▲	▲	▲	▲
Health Documentation (▶ 218, Health)			▲	▲	▲	▲	▲	▲	▲	▲
Travel Insurance			●	●	▲	○	●	●	●	●
Driver's License (national)			●	●	●	●	●	●	●	●
Car Insurance Certificate			n/a	n/a	●	●	n/a	n/a	n/a	n/a
Car Registration Document			n/a	n/a	●	●	n/a	n/a	n/a	n/a

WHEN TO GO

Central Florida/Orlando

▭ Peak season   ▭ Off season

JAN	FEB	MAR	APR	MAY	JUN	JUL	AUG	SEP	OCT	NOV	DEC
22°C	23°C	25°C	27°C	27°C	30°C	32°C	32°C	30°C	28°C	25°C	22°C
72°F	73°F	77°F	81°F	81°F	86°F	90°F	90°F	86°F	82°F	77°F	72°F

☀ Sun   ☁ Cloud   🌧 Wet   ⛅ Sun/Showers

Temperatures are the **average daily maximum** for each month. At night temperatures fall to 70–75°F (21–24°C).

Florida has a subtropical climate: It is warm in the winter and extremely hot and humid in the summer. Cooling sea breezes help to dissipate the summer heat of Miami and Tampa (77–86°F/25–30°C). Winter temperatures in Central Florida are a little cooler than in the southern part of the state.

In **Orlando** the summer heat is more stifling and the humidity can become unbearable. During summer (Jun–Sep), most mornings are sunny, but expect afternoon thunderstorms which cool temperatures a little. Few days in February and March are cloudy all day. Best times to visit Orlando are October and early May.

In the U.S.A.
Visit Florida
P.O. Box 1100
Tallahassee
FL 32302-1100
☎ 888/735-2872

In the U.K.
Visit Florida
Roebuck House
Palace Street
London SW1E 5BA
☎ 0891 600 555

In Canada
Consular Affairs Bureau
☎ (1800) 267-6788;
www.dfait–maeci.gc.ca
In Australia
U.S. Consulate
☎ (02) 9373 9200

GETTING THERE

By Air Many airlines serve Florida from all over the world. International flights land in Miami, Tampa, Orlando, Sanford (charter flights for Orlando), Daytona Beach, Jacksonville and Tallahassee. There are also some charter flights to Fort Lauderdale and Fort Myers. The easiest destination to reach is Orlando; in addition to its proximity to the parks, it makes a great hub to visit both coasts, South Florida, Daytona and St. Augustine. U.S. domestic airlines serve numerous local airports.

Ticket prices tend to be highest in summer and at Easter and Christmas. Check with the airlines, travel agents, flight brokers, travel sections in newspapers, and the Internet for the best deals and special offers. Airlines operating **non-direct** flights may offer substantial savings on standard fares. Tickets for short stays are generally expensive unless a Saturday night is included.

Fly-drive packages are popular: These include flights and car rental, accommodations (optional) and sightseeing discounts. **Charter flights** are a good option but can be more crowded and cramped than scheduled flights.

Approximate **flying times** to Florida: Sydney (via Los Angeles) 19 hours, New Zealand 17 hours, Berlin 10 hours, London and Dublin 8 hours, Vancouver 8 hours, Montréal 2½ hours, Toronto 3 hours.

All **airport taxes** are usually included in the price of the ticket.

By Rail and Bus Alternative options for travelers from Canada or elsewhere in the U.S. are **Amtrak** trains (tel: 800/872-7245; www.amtrak.com). Long-distance **Greyhound buses** (tel: 800/231-2222; www.greyhound.com) serve all major cities in the United States.

TIME

Florida is on Eastern Standard Time (GMT -5), apart from the Panhandle region, west of the Apalachicola River, which is on Central Standard Time (GMT -6). Daylight Saving Time (GMT -4) applies from early April to late October.

CURRENCY AND FOREIGN EXCHANGE

Currency The basic unit of currency in the United States is the dollar ($). One dollar is 100 cents. **Bills** come in denominations of $1, $5, $10, $20, $50 and $100. All bills are green and are the same size, so look carefully at the dollar amount on them. **Coins** are: 1 cent (penny), 5 cents (nickel), 10 cents (dime), 25 cents (quarter) and 50 cents (half-dollar). There are also one-dollar coins but these are comparatively rare.

An unlimited amount of U.S. dollars can be imported or exported.

U.S. dollar **travelers' checks** are the best way to carry money and they are accepted as cash in most places (not taxis), as are **credit cards** (Amex, VISA, MasterCard, Diners Card).

Exchange The best place to exchange non-U.S. currency in Florida is at a bank. There are also currency exchange offices at airports. Automated teller cards can be used to withdraw money from your bank account in U.S. currency. Your bank will provide you with details of where your cards will be accepted in Florida. Avoid check-cashing stands – these are high-interest money-lending operations.

TIME DIFFERENCES

GMT	Most of Florida	The Panhandle	USA West Coast	Spain	Australia
12 noon	→ 7 am	← 6 am	← 4 am	→ 1 pm	→ 10 pm

WHEN YOU ARE THERE

CLOTHING SIZES

U.K.	U.S.A.	
36	36	
38	38	
40	40	
42	42	**Suits**
44	44	
46	46	
7	8	
7.5	8.5	
8.5	9.5	
9.5	10.5	**Shoes**
10.5	11.5	
11	12	
14.5	14.5	
15	15	
15.5	15.5	
16	16	**Shirts**
16.5	16.5	
17	17	
8	6	
10	8	
12	10	
14	12	**Dresses**
16	14	
18	16	
4.5	6	
5	6.5	
5.5	7	
6	7.5	**Shoes**
6.5	8	
7	8.5	

NATIONAL HOLIDAYS

Jan 1	New Year's Day
Third Mon Jan	Martin Luther King Day
Third Mon Feb	Presidents' Day
Mar/Apr	Easter
Last Mon May	Memorial Day
Jul 4	Independence Day
First Mon Sep	Labor Day
Second Mon Oct	Columbus Day
Nov 11	Veterans' Day
Fourth Thu Nov	Thanksgiving
Dec 25	Christmas Day

Boxing Day (Dec 26) is not a public holiday in the U.S. Some stores open on national holidays. Some attractions may be closed on national holidays.

OPENING HOURS

- ○ Stores
- ● Offices
- ● Banks
- ● Post Offices
- ● Museums/Monuments
- ● Pharmacies

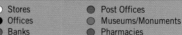

8 am 9 am 10 am noon 1 pm 2 pm 4 pm 5 pm 7 pm

☐ Day   ▨ Midday   ☐ Evening

Stores Most open Mon–Sat. Malls usually open Mon–Sat 10–9 and Sun noon–5.
Banks Some larger branches have a drive-through service on Sat 8–noon. All theme parks have ATMs (cashpoints) for cash withdrawals.
Post Offices Some open Sat 9–noon.
Museums and Parks Theme park hours vary seasonally. Many museums are closed on Mondays, but stay open late one night a week.
Pharmacies Some open 24 hours in major towns.

POLICE 911

FIRE 911

AMBULANCE 911

HIGHWAY PATROL (from cell phone) *FHP

PERSONAL SAFETY

Florida is not generally a dangerous place but to help prevent crime and accidents:
- Never open your hotel room door unless you know who is there. If in doubt call hotel security.
- Always lock your front door and/or patio doors when sleeping in the room or going out. Use the safety chain/lock for security.
- When driving keep all car doors locked.
- If lost, stop in a well-lit gas station or ask for directions in a hotel, restaurant or store.
- Never approach alligators; they can outrun a human.

Police assistance:
☎ **911** from any phone

TELEPHONES

Public telephones are found in hotel lobbies, pharmacies, restaurants, gas stations and at the roadside. Use AT&T (dial (1-800-225-5288 before dialing your main number) for inexpensive long-distance calls. Prepaid phone cards are available from drugstores and visitor centers; calls cost around 30 cents a minute from any phone. From public phones dial 0 for the operator. Dial 1 plus the area code for numbers within the U.S. and Canada. Dial 411 to find U.S. and Canadian numbers.

**International Dialing Codes
Dial 011 followed by**

U.K.:	**44**
Ireland:	**353**
Australia:	**61**
Germany:	**49**
Netherlands:	**31**
Spain:	**34**

MAIL

Vending machines sell stamps but at a 25 percent premium (keep small change for these). Post offices usually open Mon–Fri 9–5; hotels and major attractions often provide full postal services, including shipping.

ELECTRICITY

The power supply is 110/120 volts AC (60 cycles).
Sockets take two-prong, flat-pin plugs. An adaptor is needed for appliances with two-round-pin and three-pin plugs.
European appliances also need a voltage transformer.

TIPS/GRATUITIES

Tipping is expected for all services. As a general guide:
Yes ✓   No ✗

Restaurants (service not included)	✓	15–20%
Bar service	✓	15%
Tour guides	✓	discretion
Hairdressers	✓	15%
Taxis	✓	15%
Chambermaids	✓	$2 per day
Bellmen	✓	$1 per bag

CONSULATES

 U.K.
305/374-1522;
407/426-7855

 Ireland
(Washington D.C.)
202/462-3939

 Canada
(Miami)
305/579-1600

 Australia
(Miami)
305/858-7633

 New Zealand
(Washington)
202/328-4800

HEALTH

 Insurance Medical insurance coverage of at least $1 million is strongly recommended; medical fees in the United States are unregulated. If you are involved in an accident, you will be cared for by medical services and charged later.

 Dental Services Your medical insurance coverage should include dental treatment, which is readily available but expensive. Some dentists will accept credit cards, but most prefer cash or travelers' checks.

 Weather By far the most common source of ill health in Florida is too much sun. Orlando in the summer is very hot and humid, and the sun is strong throughout the state all year. Use a good sunscreen, cover up and drink plenty of fluids.

 Drugs Medication can be bought at drugstores, but certain drugs generally available elsewhere require a prescription in the U.S. Acetaminophen is the U.S. equivalent of paracetamol. Use an insect repellent containing DEET, and cover up after dark to avoid being bitten by mosquitoes. Ask-a-Nurse (tel: 407/897-1700) is a free 24-hour helpline for information on symptoms and services.

 Safe Water Tap water is drinkable throughout Florida, though not very palatable. Mineral water is inexpensive and readily available.

CONCESSIONS

Students Holders of an International Student Identity Card are entitled to discounts on many attractions. Children under three are generally allowed into attractions free; children's tickets are usually available up to age 12. Teenagers often have to pay the full adult rate. Most concessions at major theme parks apply to children under 17. (At Walt Disney World® Resort, children over 9 pay the full adult price.)

Senior Citizens Discounts on many services and attractions, and reductions on hotel room rates during the low season, are available to senior citizens (seniors). Qualifying age varies from 55 to 65.

TRAVELING WITH A DISABILITY

The Americans with Disabilities Act (1990) has required hotels, public transportation and attractions to make special provision for travelers with disabilities, although some theme park rides are not accessible. If you have a disability, request a specially adapted hotel room.

CHILDREN

In Orlando the larger hotels provide special children's programs. In Miami attractions are geared toward adults so you will need to be selective. Tampa's beaches and Busch Gardens are child friendly. Most theme parks provide baby-changing and nursing facilities. Many restaurants offer "Earlybird" children's meals.

RESTROOMS

Cleanest and safest lavatories are in hotels, convenience stores, shopping malls and highway rest stops.

LOST PROPERTY

If you lose an item in a theme park, report it to the Lost and Found office.
If something is stolen from your hotel or car, contact the police (tel: 911) and get a copy of the paperwork for your insurance company.

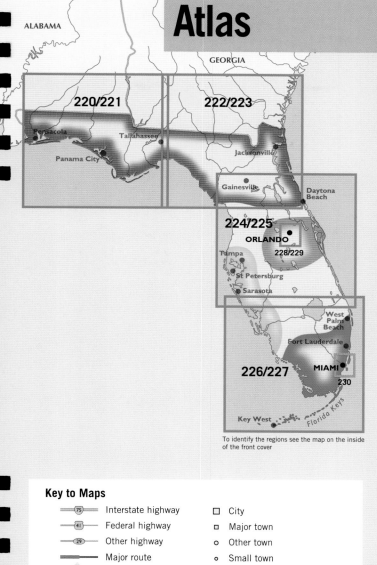

Atlas

ALABAMA

GEORGIA

220/221

222/223

Pensacola
Tallahassee
Panama City
Jacksonville

Gainesville
Daytona Beach

224/225

ORLANDO
228/229

Tampa
St Petersburg
Sarasota

West Palm Beach

Fort Lauderdale

226/227

MIAMI
230

Key West
Florida Keys

To identify the regions see the map on the inside of the front cover

Key to Maps

⌁75⌁ Interstate highway	□	City
⌁41⌁ Federal highway	▫	Major town
⌁29⌁ Other highway	○	Other town
Major route	°	Small town
Built-up area	▣	Featured place of interest
✈ Airport	▪	Other place of interest

220/227 0   10   20   30 miles
0   10   20   30   40   50 km

228/229 0   1   2   3 miles
0   1   2   3   4   5 km

230 0   1   2   3 miles
0   1   2   3   4   5 km

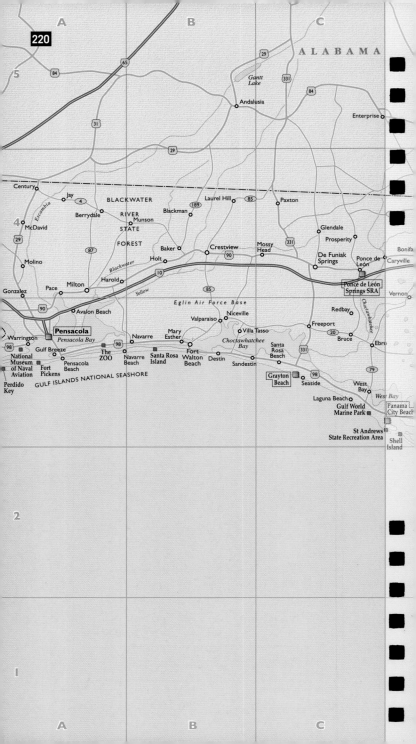

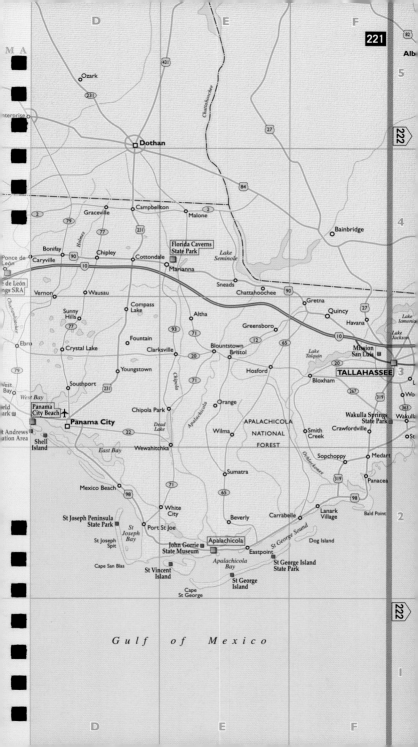

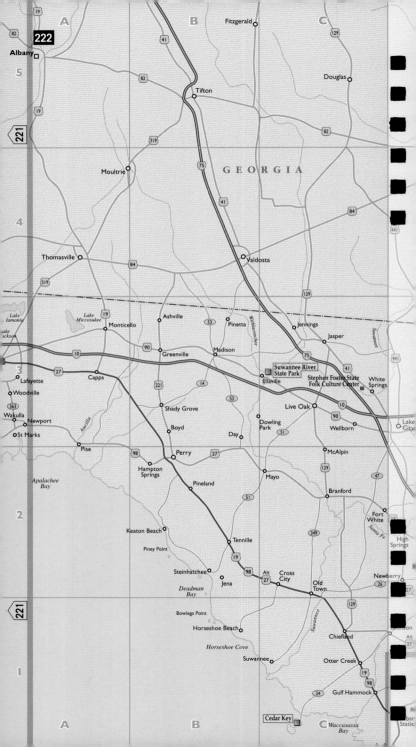

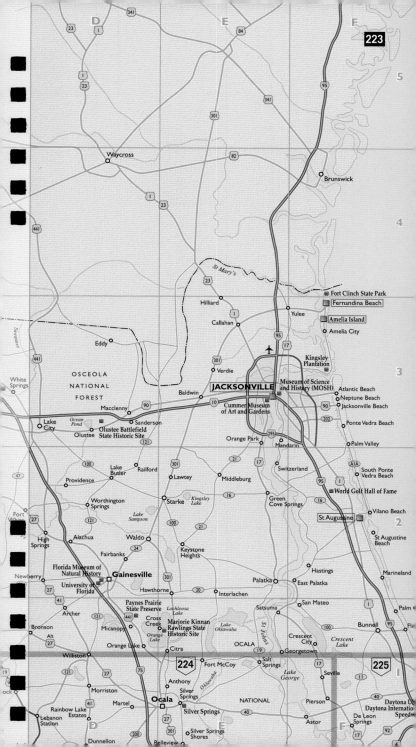

D E F

5

23
1
341
84

1
23
223

Waycross

1
23
341

Brunswick

441
82

St Mary's

23

Hilliard
441
Eddy
Callahan
1
Yulee
Fort Clinch State Park
Fernandina Beach
Amelia Island
Amelia City
95

OSCEOLA
NATIONAL
FOREST
White Springs
441

301
Verdie
JACKSONVILLE
Museum of Science and History (MOSH)
Kingsley Plantation
17

Macclenny
90
Baldwin
10
Cummer Museum of Art and Gardens
Atlantic Beach
Neptune Beach
Jacksonville Beach
90
Lake City
Ocean Pond
Olustee Battlefield State Historic Site
Sanderson
202
Ponte Vedra Beach
47
Olustee
121
Orange Park
Mandarin
295
Palm Valley

100
Lake Butler
Railford
301
21
17
Switzerland
A1A
South Ponte Vedra Beach
Providence
Lawtey
Middleburg
95
World Golf Hall of Fame
1
Worthington Springs
Starke
Kingsley Lake
16
Green Cove Springs
16
Vilano Beach
Fort White
27
Lake Sampson
100
21
St Augustine
St Augustine Beach

High Springs
Alachua
Waldo
24
Keystone Heights
Hastings
Marineland
Fairbanks
Florida Museum of Natural History
GAINESVILLE
University of Florida
301
Palatka
East Palatka
27
Newberry
Hawthorne
20
Interlachen
San Mateo
Palm
41
Archer
121
Paynes Prairie State Preserve
Lochloosa Lake
Satsuma
1
Bronson
Micanopy
441
Cross Creek
Marjorie Kinnan Rawlings State Historic Site
Lake Oklawaha
St Johns
Crescent City
Bunnell
95
Alt
27
Orange Lake
OCALA
19
Georgetown
Crescent Lake
Williston
121
Citra
Lake George
17
Seville
11
19
27
75
224
Fort McCoy
Salt Springs
225
Morriston
Anthony
Pierson
40
Daytona U
Daytona Internatio
Speedw
Rainbow Lake Estates
41
Martel
Ocala
Silver Springs
NATIONAL
De Leon Springs
Lebanon Station
27
301
Silver Springs
Astor
92
Dunnellon
200
Belleview
Silver Springs Shores
40
17
D E F

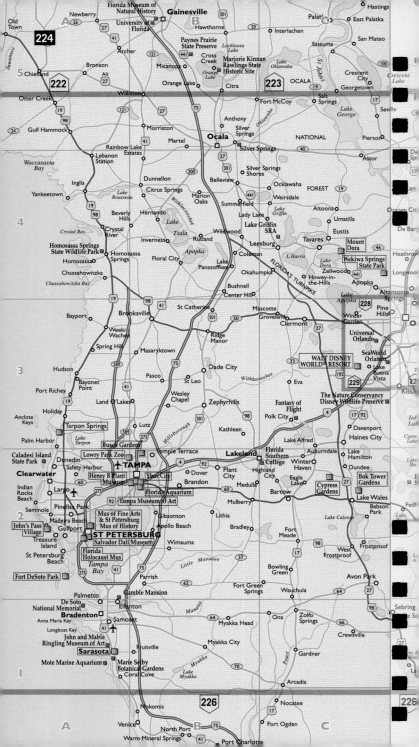

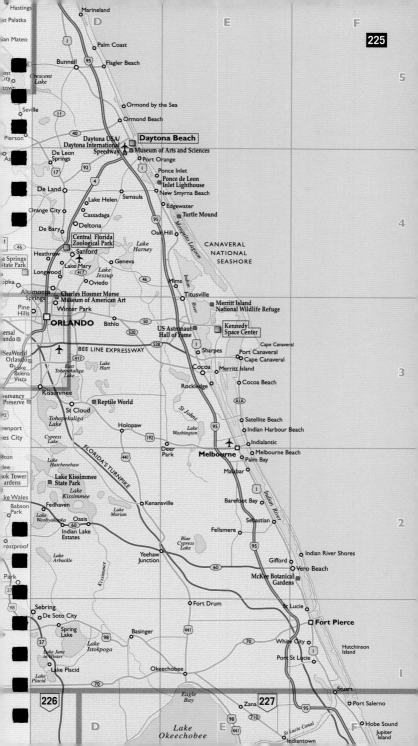

Hastings
st Palatka
San Mateo

D
E
F

Marineland
Palm Coast
Bunnell
Flagler Beach

Crescent
Lake

Seville

Pierson

Ormond by the Sea
Ormond Beach

De Leon
Springs

Daytona USA/
Daytona International
Speedway
Daytona Beach
Museum of Arts and Sciences
Port Orange
Ponce Inlet
Ponce de Leon
Inlet Lighthouse
New Smyrna Beach

De Land

Lake Helen
Samsula
Edgewater
Turtle Mound

Orange City
Cassadaga
Deltona
De Bary
Oak Hill

Central Florida
Zoological Park
Sanford

Lake
Harney

CANAVERAL
NATIONAL
SEASHORE

Heathrow
Lake Mary
Geneva
Longwood
Oviedo

Lake
Jessup

Mims
Titusville

Altamonte
Springs
Charles Hosmer Morse
Museum of American Art
Winter Park

Pine
Hills

ORLANDO
Bithlo

Merritt Island
National Wildlife Refuge

US Astronaut
Hall of Fame

Kennedy
Space Center

BEE LINE EXPRESSWAY

SeaWorld
Orlando

Lake
Buena
Vista

Sharpes
Cape Canaveral
Port Canaveral
Cape Canaveral
Cocoa
Merritt Island
Rockledge
Cocoa Beach

Kissimmee

Reptile World

St Cloud

Tohopekaliga
Lake

Holopaw

Lake
Washington

St. Johns

Satellite Beach
Indian Harbour Beach
Indialantic
Melbourne
Melbourne Beach
Palm Bay

Cypress
Lake

Deer
Park

Malabar

Lake
Hatchenehaw

FLORIDA'S TURNPIKE

Lake Kissimmee
State Park

Lake
Kissimmee

Kenansville

Barefoot Bay

Sebastian

Fedhaven

Lake
Weohyakapka
Oasis
Indian Lake
Estates

Lake
Marian

Fellsmere

Indian River Shores

Lake
Arbuckle

Blue
Cypress
Lake

Yeehaw
Junction

Gifford
Vero Beach

McKee Botanical
Gardens

Sebring
De Soto City
Spring
Lake

Fort Drum

St Lucie
Fort Pierce

Lake June
in Winter

Lake
Istokpoga

Basinger

White City
Port St Lucie

Hutchinson
Island

Lake Placid
Lake
Placid

Okeechobee

Stuart

Port Salerno

226
Eagle
Bay
Zana
227

*Lake
Okeechobee*
Indiantown

St Lucie Canal

Hobe Sound
Jupiter
Island

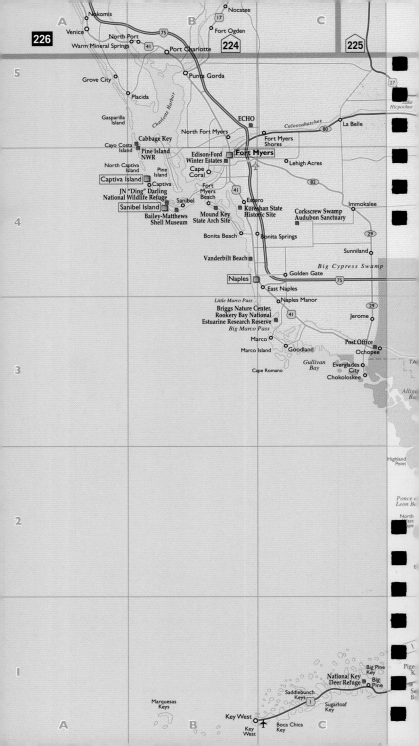

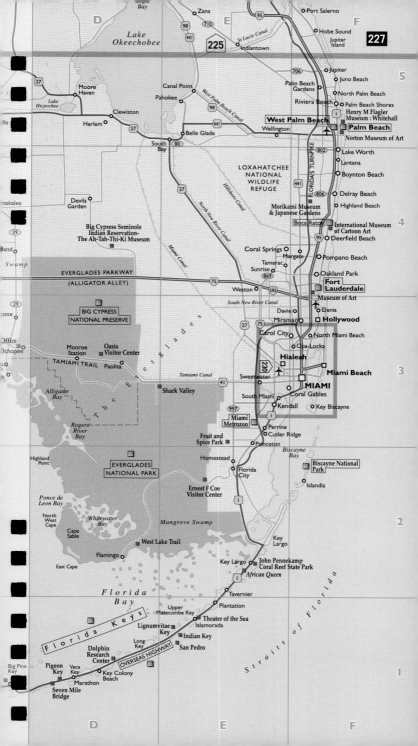

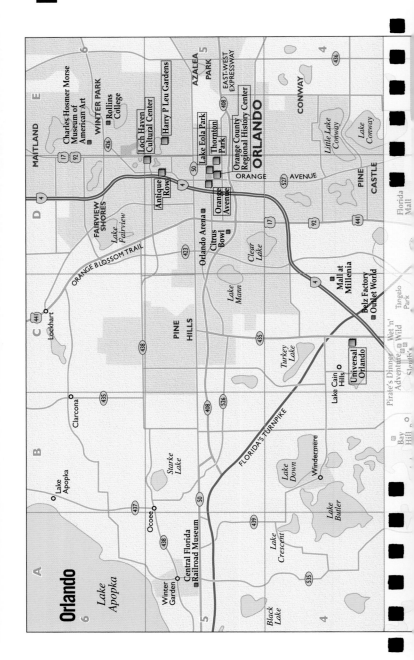

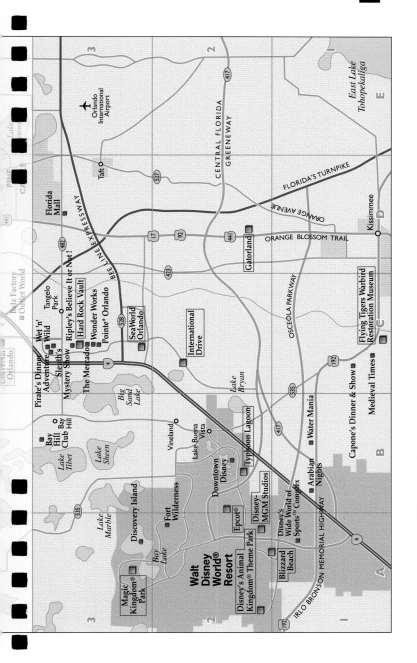

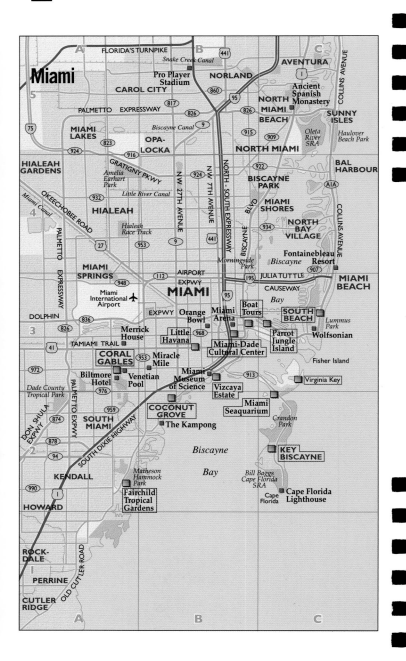

Miami

Picture credits

Abbreviations for terms appearing below: (t) top; (b) bottom; (l) left; (r) right; (c) center. The Automobile Association wishes to thank the following photographers, libraries and associations for their assistance in the preparation of this book.

Front and back cover (t) AA World Travel Library/Jon Davison, (ct) AA World Travel Library/Jon Davison, (cb) AA World Travel Library/Tony Souter, (b) AA World Travel Library/Jon Davison, Spine AA World Travel Library/Tony Souter.

Aquarius Picture Library 35t; **Bruce Coleman Collection** 34b; **Busch Entertainment Corporation** 152c, 154/155, 156; **Charles Hosmer Morse Museum** 201; **The Conch Republic, Used with Permission, Office of the Secretary General** 27t, 27b, 28t, 28c, 28b, 29; **Corbis** 30 (John Henley), 31 (Les Stone), 167 (Lee Snider); **DACS 1999** 153 Salvador Dalí-Foundation Gala-Salvador Dalí; **James Davis Worldwide** 160; **Disney Enterprises, Inc** 7, 52t, 56, 58, 60, 62, 64, 66/67, 69, 71, 72/73, 74/75, 76; **Eye Ubiquitous** 14/15, 16t; **Florida Aquarium, Tampa** 163t (Tim Riber), 163b (Jeff Greenberg); **Florida International Museum** 165c; **Flying Tigers Warbird Museum** (K Budde Jones) 94t; **Genesis Space Photo Library** 9, 10, 11, 12/13; **Ronald Grant Archive** 35c, 35b, 36; **Robert Harding Picture Library** 138, 158; **Robin Hill** 2b, 109, 114/115/116, 123; **Hulton Getty** 34t; **Images Colour Library** 10/11; **Kennedy Space Center** 13, 203; **Harry P Leu Gardens** 90; **Museum of Fine Arts, St. Petersburg** 169; **Orlando/Orange County CVB** 89, 200; **National Park Service, America** 120c; **Peter Newark's American Pictures** 20c, 20b, 22, 23; **Pictor International, London** 26; **Pictures Colour Library** 92t, 113t, 169; **Rex Features Ltd** 6, 8, 21; **Ripley's Believe it or Not** 93; **Salvador Dalí Museum, St. Petersburg** 166; **Frank Spooner Pictures** 32; **Tampa Bay Holocaust Museum** 165t; **Tampa Museum of Art** 161; **Tony Stone Images** 2t, 2cb, 5, 17, 19b, 49, 130/1; **Universal Studios, Florida** 53t, 77, 78, 79, 80, 81, 83, 84; **Visit Florida** 117, 120b, 121, 133b, 134, 135, 185, 186, 192; **World Pictures** 162t.

The remaining photographs are held in the Association's own library (AA WORLD TRAVEL LIBRARY) and were taken by the following:
P Bennett 3c, 14, 19t, 24b, 25, 33b, 94c, 95, 97, 112b, 118, 124, 125, 126, 152b, 168, 170, 179, 182c, 182b, 183t, 183b, 184, 188, 189, 191, 207, 208; **J Davison** 112t, 122, 127, 128t, 128b, 137t, 181, 190; **D Lyons** 16b, 18t, 119, 153; **P Murphy** 24t; **L Provo** 3c, 18c, 113b, 114b, 129, 131, 133t, 199, 209; **T Souter** 2ct, 33t, 37, 52b, 53b, 86/87, 87, 88, 91, 92b, 96, 193, 202; **J A Tims** 3t, 3b, 132, 136, 137b, 149, 151, 159, 162b, 171, 172, 183c, 213, 217t, 217l, 217r.

Questionnaire

Dear Traveller

Your comments, opinions and recommendations
are very important to us. So please help us to improve
our travel guides by taking a few minutes to complete
this simple questionnaire.

You do not need a stamp (unless posted outside the UK). If you do not
want to remove this page from your guide, then photocopy it or write your
answers on a plain sheet of paper.

Send to: The Editor, Spiral Guides, AA World Travel Guides,
FREEPOST SCE 4598, Basingstoke RG21 4GY.

Your recommendations...

We always encourage readers' recommendations for restaurants, night-life or shopping
– if your recommendation is used in the next edition of the guide, we will send you a
FREE AA Spiral Guide of your choice. Please state below the establishment name,
location and your reasons for recommending it.

_____

_____

_____

_____

_____

Please send me AA Spiral _____
(see list of titles inside the back cover)

About this guide...

Which title did you buy?

_____ **AA Spiral**

Where did you buy it? _____

When? m̲m̲/ y̲ y̲

Why did you choose an AA Spiral Guide? _____

_____

_____

_____

Did this guide meet your expectations?

Exceeded ☐   Met all ☐   Met most ☐   Fell below ☐

Please give your reasons _____

_____

_____

_____

_____

continued on next page...

Were there any aspects of this guide that you particularly liked?

Is there anything we could have done better?

About you...

Name (Mr/Mrs/Ms) ______________________

Address ______________________

____

______________________ **Postcode** ______________________

Daytime tel no ______________________ **email** ______________________

Please *only* give us your email address and mobile phone number if you wish to hear from us about other products and services from the AA and partners by email or text or mms.

Which age group are you in?

Under 25 ☐ **25–34** ☐ **35–44** ☐ **45–54** ☐ **55–64** ☐ **65+** ☐

How many trips do you make a year?

Less than one ☐ **One** ☐ **Two** ☐ **Three or more** ☐

Are you an AA member? Yes ☐ **No** ☐

About your trip...

When did you book? mm/ y y **When did you travel?** mm/ y y

How long did you stay? ______________________

Was it for business or leisure? ______________________

Did you buy any other travel guides for your trip? ☐ **Yes** ☐ **No**

If yes, which ones? ______________________

____

Thank you for taking the time to complete this questionnaire. Please send it to us as soon as possible, and remember, you do not need a stamp (unless posted outside the UK).

The information we hold about you will be used to provide the products and services requested and for identification, account administration, analysis, and fraud/loss prevention purposes. More details about how that information is used is in our privacy statement, which you'll find under the heading "Personal Information" in our terms and conditions and on our website: www.theAA.com. Copies are also available from us by post, by contacting the Data Protection Manager at AA, Southwood East, Apollo Rise, Farnborough, Hampshire GU14 OJW

We may want to contact you about other products and services provided by us, or our partners (by mail, telephone) but please tick the box if you DO NOT wish to hear about such products and services from us by mail or telephone. ☐